THE
MANAGER'S MOTIVATION
DESK BOOK

THE
MANAGER'S MOTIVATION
DESK BOOK

THOMAS L. QUICK

A Ronald Press Publication

JOHN WILEY & SONS

New York   Chichester   Brisbane   Toronto   Singapore

Library of Congress Cataloging in Publication Data:

Quick, Thomas L.
   The manager's motivation desk book.

   "A Ronald Press publication."
   Includes index.
   1. Employee motivation.   2. Personnel management.
I.   Title.

HF5549.5.M63Q48   1985   658.3'14   84-19587
ISBN 0-471-88377-8

Printed in the United States of America

10 9 8 7 6 5 4 3 2 1

To Nicholas, Robert, and Thomas

PREFACE

If you agree that the effective performance of your employees is your highest priority as a manager, this book has been written with you in mind. It doesn't matter at what level you manage, or in what size or type of organization. Ultimately your success as a leader is measured by how well you enable your employees to achieve your and the organization's goals, to work up to their potential, to become even more valuable assets to the organization, and to identify and promote the well-being of the operation of which they are a part.

The key to that effective performance is their motivation. Strictly speaking, you cannot motivate them. Only they can do that, since motivation comes from within. But you can make it possible for them to want to do a good job. You can help them to acquire the skills as well as the self-confidence in their ability to do that job. You can create a work environment in which people feel valued and rewarded when they turn in the kind of performance you want.

This book is designed to help you to accomplish all those ends, in short, to enhance the motivating forces in the people who report to you.

The format of this book has been determined by three considerations.

The first derives from my own experience as a manager as well as my involvement in the field of management development for nearly 25 years. Looking for reliable techniques to help me in the everyday practice of management and to counsel other managers, I was continually frustrated by the fact that many of the books and articles on motivation were written by professionals for other professionals—psychologists, academicians, consultants, and so on. They were often highly theoretical, sometimes speculative, and usually difficult to translate into application. Thus I felt a need to write a book that, while based on sound theory, emphasizes the pragmatic.

Second, this book views the management of motivation as a system. Unfortunately, many managers have learned about motivation in bits and pieces. It's not surprising therefore that when managers set goals with employees, criticize or give positive feedback, appraise, or allocate merit increases, they may tend to see themselves performing separate functions or acts. But, in fact, those seemingly discrete acts are or should be related. Criticism, for example, may correct an immediate work problem, but it may also have an impact on how the employee views the work in general and his or her relationship with the manager. That one act of criticism could affect the employee's motivation, positively or negatively. Any book on motivation should stress the relationship of one managerial act to another and to the performance of subordinates.

Finally, most managers, it seems to me, prefer the ready access to answers that a reference book offers more than the logical structure of a textbook. When they have a problem, they want a management tool that they can consult quickly and that will direct them to a solution. The principles of good management are relatively few and apply across-the-board, but the practice of management is one-to-one, presenting as many challenges as there are people working for you. Consequently this book guides you to practical recommendations that cover various contingencies. It provides fast how-to, hands-on help.

Those recommendations are the distillation of years of first-hand management experience, of consulting with other successful managers, of thousands of hours of participation in programs, conferences, courses, and workshops all over the country, of collaborating with many other specialists in training and development, and of adapting the theories and techniques from countless books and articles written by our leading management experts. Much of this work was done while I was a Managing, then Directing, Editor at the Research Institute of America, where I was responsible for the preparation of management and supervisory development programs, in which tens of thousands of managers from the government, corporate, and not-for-profit sectors were enrolled.

THOMAS L. QUICK

New York, New York
January 1985

CONTENTS

THE
MANAGER'S MOTIVATION
DESK BOOK

INTRODUCTION

There is an urgency to the American manager's concern for the motivation of employees that is relatively recent. No doubt the severe recessions of the past 10 years have elevated the priority of individual worker productivity. Certainly the economy has become far less forgiving than it was formerly, when even uncontrolled costs and sloppy management practices could not impede the making of a profit. The increased costs of doing business today demand greater and more effective productivity.

The situation has been severely aggravated by the growing intensity of foreign competition. Other countries are quite capable of outselling the United States in the world market with goods of comparable or even of better quality at prices that can be substantially below what has to be charged for the products of American industry.

An important key to greater productivity and increased effectiveness of the American worker lies in the motivation of that worker. People who are committed to achieving organizational objectives, it is safe to say, generally outperform those who are not. That distinction is hardly news to any manager, but that it has become a matter of concern to him or her does count as news to those of us who have been working in the management development field for many years. In the postwar expansion of the economy, although admittedly cyclical, it was possible to hear executives

1

echo the statement of one man who said to me in the 1960s, "We've made money regardless of what we've done."

People who are making money regardless of what they do may be less than open to the notion that employee motivation could be a critical factor in whether they continue to do so. This resistance was amply evident to those who were instrumental in the emergence of what came to be called Organization Development in the early 1970s. Organization Development, or OD, has many definitions, but its distinctive character is owed to its purpose: to help employees in an organization to work more effectively in the achievement of the organization's goals. But to those managers who even knew of OD a decade ago, it represented an interesting experiment and a vaguely promising shift in orientation. With few exceptions, management saw little that was compelling about it.

There is no question that OD's emphasis on increasing the effectiveness of people at work is no longer on the periphery of management's interests. The management today that does not concern itself with employees' commitment and effectiveness is courting disaster.

HAWTHORNE—THE BEGINNING

Probably the first major intervention by behavioral scientists into the human systems of a large organization took place at the Hawthorne Works of the Western Electric Company in Chicago in the late 1920s and early 1930s. The so-called Hawthorne studies were prompted by the desire to establish some relationship between the conditions of work and the incidence of fatigue and monotony among employees. In broad terms, there were experiments that consisted of altering various factors involved in the work situation and measuring what effects, if any, these changes had on the workers involved.

For example, an initial experiment, which involved changing the lighting in three departments, was inconclusive. The intensity of the lighting was varied, and production varied as well, but not always in relation to the changes in the illumination. Therefore another experiment was set up. It involved test groups working under different illumination intensities and a control group that had a relatively constant intensity of light. Production increased in both test and control groups. Further research led to two conclusions: (1) The production variances were not directly related to the level of intensity of the lighting, and (2) there were apparently human factors involved that needed to be studied.

This need for further study led to observations and tests conducted over a period of time: Rest periods were introduced; the method of payment was changed; the workers were allowed to talk freely. The rest periods and working hours were adjusted periodically. Output increased and remained high.

Employees in the tests were asked to explain the higher production. Their answers indicated that the contributing factors were greater freedom over their work, increased attention, decreased direct supervision, and the chance to set one's own pace. Another factor contributing to the production rate was probably the employees' revised attitudes about their work: Absenteeism in the work groups dropped off sharply.

Two other experiments were arranged to determine the role of wage incentives in increased production, one in the Relay Assembly Test Room and the other in the Mica Splitting Room. But the relationship between more money and higher output was not firmly established. Some increased production could be assumed to follow from increased pay, but it was becoming clear to the experimenters that other factors such as supervision were involved. Employees sometimes rated as poor supervisors whom management regarded as effective. That was important information, since the employees were the producers. A mass interviewing program was designed to gather from employees data that would guide supervisors in doing a better job as leaders.

Another factor that could temporarily affect production was discovered and labeled the Hawthorne effect. This phenomenon has to do with the attention given a work group. During the illumination experiment, production in the control group, where the lighting had remained constant, went up. Similarly, during the data gathering, many of the employees interviewed enjoyed the mere fact of the interview and experienced increased morale. Subsequent researchers have had to take this phenomenon into account in measuring how much temporary change in morale and productivity has taken place as a result of the attention and how much substantial, permanent modification has occurred as a result of successful efforts to change conditions and relationships.

A HIATUS

The Hawthorne studies were terminated by the Depression, although the interviewing–counseling program was later reinstated. Possibly because the studies were incomplete, their significance was long ignored or misunderstood. Certainly there were misinterpretations. For example, it was assumed by some that there is a direct relationship between morale and productivity. This presumed relationship has not been established by hard evidence. You can, however, see vestiges of this presumption in what has become known as the human relations school of management: If you make employees happy, they produce more. In truth, all we know of happy employees is that they are happy. Employees who are unhappy or suffer from low morale paradoxically produce greatly under some conditions. Employees who are content sometimes produce poorly.

The Hawthorne studies discovered or pointed to certain factors and relationships that have heavily influenced the direction of research to this day. Had they continued, they would undoubtedly have refined our knowledge of people's behavior in work groups and of those factors that encourage greater individual productivity in those groups. But Hawthorne was a significant beginning. The next major impetus came in the 1950s.

MASLOW

Abraham H. Maslow, professor of psychology at Brandeis University and president of the American Psychological Association, became known for his hierarchy of needs, as defined in his book *Motivation and Personality*, published in 1954. People are motivated, according to Maslow, to satisfy certain needs, ranging from the very basic and bodily to the very complex and psychological. Here are the needs in ascending order of complexity:

☐ *Physiological.* These are bodily needs: food, sex, drink, and sleep.

☐ *Safety.* People have a desire to be safe and secure; they crave stability and protection. They want to be free from fear. They have a need for structure and order.

☐ *Belongingness and Love.* At this level, the need is for friends, family, and intimacy.

☐ *Esteem.* People want the esteem of others as well as self-esteem. They want to be regarded as useful, competent, and important.

☐ *Self-actualization.* At this highest level of motivation, people strive to actualize their potential, to become more of what they are capable of being.

Maslow held that a person seeks a higher need only when the needs lower in the hierarchy are predominantly satisfied. The corollary is that the need that has been largely satisfied does not motivate. Thus, a person has little drive for esteem when the stomach is crying for food. In Maslow's view, there are comparatively few people who are motivated by the need to actualize themselves, since they are still trying to satisfy the needs lower in the hierarchy.

Some people have interpreted the hierarchy literally and rigidly, much more so than Maslow did. For example, he pointed out that one may make love or seek physical intimacy not only for sexual release but also to achieve feelings of power over others. Furthermore, Maslow suggested that a need may have been satisfied for such a long time that it has become undervalued and its motivational force reduced. As an illustration, one may enjoy such wide esteem of others for so long that it doesn't seem as important as the love of one person, which is a lower level need.

This hierarchy has raised all sorts of questions. When, for example, is a need predominantly satisfied? Indeed, are the lower level needs ever really satisfied? Probably not. Thus, whether the lower needs are satisfied or not may play little part in a person's search for the satisfaction of the higher needs. And there are times when the higher needs take priority over the lower ones. Obviously the gratification some politicians feel from shaking hands and making speeches is more powerful than what they would derive from stopping to eat and sleep. Esteem in the case of people seeking political office usually takes precedence over both physiological and safety needs. It is also possible that people can be self-actualizing while still working to satisfy lower needs.

What Maslow did in the 1950s and 1960s was to show that individuals have needs they strive to fulfill, that those needs are complex, and that the needs a person is trying to satisfy today may be quite different from those motivating him or her next month. Needs in people vary from day to day, task to task, and situation to situation. The implications for anyone who supervises the work of others are clear. People are motivated by a variety of factors, and the manager may not always know what they are.

Interestingly, Maslow's approach, in the era of the "organization man," became rather popular, especially in the late 1960s. His humanism and his ability to relate to people undoubtedly had much to do with that popularity. Probably the most attractive aspect of the hierarchy is a need different from the other needs: self-actualization. The other needs are considered deficits. People lack sufficient food, or esteem, or love and, thus, work to acquire them. They don't really have a choice. But Maslow sees people seeking to actualize themselves not out of a deficiency but to complete their growth. Some people may never reach this stage and, hence, they are never impelled to begin the process of actualizing themselves.

Self-actualizing people, according to Maslow, accept themselves. They don't become defensive about their shortcomings, and they don't allow themselves to be self-satisfied about their virtues. They are spontaneous, natural, and concerned with basic issues, not trivia. Undoubtedly their naturalness and high self-acceptance help them to relate to others well.

People at the self-actualizing level of development are independent and able to govern themselves. They work not only for material rewards but for many other kinds of rewards as well: satisfaction in doing a good job, a sense of accomplishment, pride, a desire to grow, and the development of their skills and talents. They are creative and problem-centered rather than self-centered.

In defining the self-actualizer, Maslow emphasizes that such a person is highly motivated by internal rewards. This is a significant piece of information for the manager. That is not to say that such an employee does not appreciate the external rewards that a manager can provide, but a more important key to how this person performs on the job lies with the number of opportunities to achieve, grow, and feel pride and self-esteem. Managers tend to pay far too little attention to the internal rewards structure in high or potentially high performers. It is a powerful motivator.

The humanism of Abraham Maslow began to break barriers and molds. In the better-educated, newly affluent working population of the 1950s and 1960s, there was a growing perception that people were more than economic animals, working largely for material gain. The notion that people had other kinds of needs that they worked to satisfy, needs that were within them and could be satisfied by working, was appealing.

McGREGOR

Maslow popularized the idea that people have needs, and social psychologist Douglas McGregor said those needs were satisfied at work. McGregor, who was heavily influenced by Maslow, published a famous book in 1960 called *The Human Side of Enterprise*, in which he set forth his Theory X – Theory Y. McGregor, a professor at Massachusetts Institute of Technology and a former president of Antioch College, described two sets of assumptions about people. Theory X is traditional and familiar:

☐ People don't really like to work and will avoid it when they can.

☐ If you want most people to work for you, you must coerce, control, and threaten with punishment, to persuade them to put forth even adequate effort.

☐ Actually most people want to be directed. They don't want responsibility. They have little ambition and are far more interested in security.

In his Theory X, McGregor was not saying necessarily that this is the way people are, or that a manager is totally wrong to think that people are as Theory X describes them. He was simply saying that this has been a traditional way of looking at people at work. In short, it is generally assumed that they don't want to be there. Rather than work, most people would probably play or do nothing.

In contrast, Theory Y represents work as very natural to people, just as much as play or rest. Furthermore:

☐ Most people will direct themselves to achieve objectives to which they are committed. The commitment has much to do with the rewards that are associated with the achievement of those objectives.

☐ Most people can learn to seek responsibility, not only to accept it.

☐ Most people are creative on the job. However, in most organizations, the intellectual potentialities of most people are only partially utilized.

Theory Y sees people as having to work not because someone is making them, but because it is built into them as human beings. It is natural. People work not to avoid punishment but to achieve something that is valuable to them. As Theory Y views people, they don't seek to be dependent on and controlled by other people in all that they do; rather, they actually seek responsibility so as to have some control over their own efforts (a theme that is becoming increasingly important in behavioral science research relating to work). The effective organization is not so much one that creates control and penalties as it is one that tries to remove the obstacles to better performance.

McGregor's Theory Y had appeal. The needs Maslow saw in people were relevant on the job because those needs could be satisfied, at least in part, by working in an organization. Now managers were beginning to think they had a new handle on "motivating" subordinates.

Thus, during the 1960s and early 1970s it became commonplace, though erroneous, for managers to speak of Theory X or Theory Y management. If managers tended to be autocratic, tough, task-oriented; if they declined to trust employees to work on their own without constant, skeptical supervision; if they took it for granted that people would cheat, lie, take shortcuts rather than put out a fair day's work, they were labeled Theory X managers. Their style was termed Theory X management.

Theory Y management in contrast was open and trusting, democratic as opposed to autocratic, concerned with people, extending authority and responsibility further down in the organization, involving employees in decisions that affect them and their work. Human relations became a familiar, honored term.

Some of the interpretations given to Theory X—Theory Y distressed McGregor who, it should be pointed out, had enormous impact on the thinking of both managers and management scholars. He had attempted to formulate two particular views of people, views that reflected assumptions that were held about human beings. These two views were not at opposite ends of the spectrum but were two points on a continuum extending through all perspectives on people. McGregor was not attempting to give a definitive description of people, their motivations and attitudes toward work. Nor was he under any illusion that he was producing the ultimate management manual (which many assumed would be based on Theory Y).

The mistake that produced these erroneous interpretations of McGregor's theories has always been with us in industrial society: People are often seen as members of groups, not as individuals. Labels tend to be applied indiscriminately. Exchanging one set of assumptions about humanity for another doesn't necessarily result in going from an ineffective management style to an effective one. Such a move perpetuates a hit-or-miss tradition of managing people. In any organization there are some people who want more direction and some who want less. There are employees who take pleasure in being creative and innovative. There are others who feel no inclination to be so. Some people derive their greatest satisfaction from activities off the job; they regard work as the way to subsidize those outside interests. Many jobs are boring; they have to be tolerated, but not enjoyed. There are people who are psychologically dependent upon others, and there are those who are autonomous and prefer to direct themselves.

In short, some people in the work force justify Theory X assumptions about them, just as there are those who make Theory Y assumptions legitimate. And there are many people at various other points along the continuum.

The importance of Theory X—Theory Y is twofold. First, stating the theory gave form to certain perspectives that had long been in existence but had never before been articulated in a scientific manner. Second, McGregor made it respectable to think of people as achieving personal objectives through their efforts to help organizations achieve theirs. The work itself, therefore, could be a powerful motivator.

HERZBERG

No one has done more to emphasize work itself as a potential motivator than Frederick Herzberg. Maslow defined those common needs in us that we strive to satisfy. McGregor suggested that at least some of those needs could be satisfied on the job through attainment of organizational objectives. Herzberg believes that people can be motivated by the work itself, that accomplishing organizational tasks and objectives fulfills a human need and that job content can be varied to provide a greater or lesser motivating force, depending in part on its degree of challenge.

Professor Herzberg, formerly at Carnegie Institute of Technology, then at Case—Western Reserve, and for many years now at the University of Utah, based his concept of "job enrichment" on what is called the two-factor theory, the components of which are job satisfiers and dissatisfiers. First advanced in the 1959 book, *The Motivation to Work,* and fleshed out in *Work and the Nature of Man,* published in 1966, the theory equates job satisfiers with motivators. These motivators are:

□ *Achievement.* The successful completion of a job or task; a solution; the results of one's work.

☐ *Recognition of Achievement.* An act of praise or some other notice of the achievement.

☐ *Work Itself.* Tasks as sources of good feelings about work; extent of duties.

☐ *Responsibility.* For one's own work or that of others; new tasks and assignments.

☐ *Advancement.* An actual improvement in status or position.

☐ *Possibility for Growth.* Potential to rise in the organization.

According to Herzberg, these are the factors that motivate and satisfy people, that encourage them to want to work—and to work well. The presence of any of these factors will satisfy or motivate. Their absence will not necessarily demotivate or cause dissatisfaction.

In the two-factor theory, there is another set of influences on how an employee views the job: dissatisfiers (also called hygiene or maintenance factors). They don't motivate. Their presence won't cause job satisfaction. Their absence, however, will cause dissatisfaction:

extrinsic

☐ *Supervision.* The willingness to teach or delegate responsibility.

☐ *Company Policy and Administration.* Company or personnel policies, structure, communications authority.

☐ *Positive Working Conditions.* Environmental and physical conditions.

☐ *Interpersonal Relations with Peers, Subordinates, and Superiors.* Social and working transactions.

☐ *Status.* How one's standing or position is seen by others; perquisites of rank.

☐ *Job Security.* Stability, tenure.

☐ *Salary.* Compensation.

☐ *Personal Life.* How aspects of the work, such as long hours, required transfer, or relocation, affect the employee's life.

Good supervision doesn't motivate, Herzberg says. However, bad supervision or the lack of supervision will create dissatisfaction. Unpleasant working conditions can make people unhappy, though they probably won't affect motivation. Some of the dissatisfiers, however, can constitute recognition of achievement, which is a motivator; for example, increased status, better working conditions, peer approval (interpersonal relations). Contrary to a long prevailing view, most people are not strongly motivated to attain job security.

Herzberg's ideas, like those of Maslow and McGregor, found early and enthusiastic acceptance. Some cynics claim that management was delighted to see that salary was not a motivator, especially if they weren't willing to pay any more than they had to. However, what employees were expressing to Herzberg was that they don't work for the dollars as such. Presumably everyone likes money and, if there isn't enough of it, people get unhappy. But an employee isn't necessarily motivated to achieve greater work output by being given a raise in earnings.

Salary, however, can play an important role as a symbol of recognition of achievement, a motivator. Salary may be a measure of growth and advancement, which are also motivators. Thus it may be difficult to overlook the indirect part that salary plays in motivation. Dollars probably have a short-term rather than a long-term influence on motivation: The person who is led to believe that special effort will result in a large raise could conceivably be motivated to work hard to get the extra money. However once the raise has been granted, the money is no longer a motivator. Herzberg would say its hygiene value has dropped to zero: no satisfaction, no dissatisfaction.

As already pointed out, supervision may not in Herzberg's terms be a motivator, but good supervision based on providing growth opportunities, increased responsibilities, and regular recognition can play a big role in motivation.

There are two serious problems in connection with Herzberg's research. First, it presumes a clear relationship between motivation and job satisfaction. In other words, what satisfies, motivates. There is a connection in all probability. But what is lacking is solid evidence that when people enjoy those conditions that they say satisfy them, the result is increased motivation and productivity. Second, Herzberg's research had too narrow a data base, that is, too few people were studied. However, for many of us, the research has generally been validated strongly by experience. And subsequent work by researchers and consultants has lent much credibility to the original research.

In addition, the two-factor theory confirmed the trend in motivation thinking: People can satisfy needs through work and by helping organizations achieve their goals. From this trend has come an effort in enlightened organizations to make work more satisfying and more rewarding for employees, for example through job enrichment, an approach in which the nature and responsibilities of a job are changed to provide greater growth and challenge.

In an affluent society such as we had in the 1960s, with a work force composed of people who knew there were job and career options and who enjoyed mobility because of a nearly full employment, people knew they did not have to settle for a job. Instead they sought pleasing, satisfying work. Smart organizations supplied that kind of work. Maslow, McGregor, and Herzberg became widely quoted. Some cynics irreverently referred to them as the Holy Trinity!

Their contributions were innovative, seminal, and timely. There was a need for a new way of looking at people at work, and many people identified with the theories and the motivating forces that were defined.

But in truth and fairness, it was very difficult for a manager to apply the theories. How does a manager know with any assurance what need in the hierarchy of needs an employee is satisfying at a given time? Maslow said that when one need was predominantly satisfied we move on to the next higher one. It's hard for a manager to get in someone else's head to know that. And it's probably true that most people are trying to satisfy more than one need at a time.

Some managers did try to practice what they called a Theory Y management style. But no one style is effective in all situations with all people.

Herzberg's theories had better luck. People such as Robert Ford of AT&T and Roy Walters, also of AT&T and later a well-known consultant, became famous for their efforts to introduce the concept and practice of job enrichment, of providing high performers with more responsibility.

But for the most part, managers didn't quite know what to do with the broadly defined needs that these theorists had described. They sounded good and read well, but more pragmatic and specific help was needed.

SKINNER

Perhaps no psychologist has been more specific and pragmatic than B.F. Skinner, known for his work in operant conditioning or behavior modification. Talking about modifying human behavior makes people very nervous. There are suggestions of personality molding and brainwashing. But behavioral scientists such as Skinner, who for many years was a professor at Harvard, are not referring to anything so sinister and dehumanizing when they talk about behavior modification. The way a person acts can be shaped in part by the foreseeable consequences of his or her actions. To use a not uncommon example, let us say that a person drinks too much at a party. There are unpleasant consequences. For one thing, the partygoer feels that his or her body is being punished for excessive drinking when the results are headaches, nausea, nervousness, and the like. Also, the excessive drinker learns that some friends at the party have expressed disapproval of the way the drinker downed the martinis and subsequently behaved.

Thus the person recognizes that the consequences of such actions are painful. At the next social outing, the realization of those consequences may encourage more moderate consumption. Behavior in a small way has been shaped.

There is positive influence on behavior: Behavior that is rewarded tends to be reinforced and therefore is likely to be repeated.

There is much talk of reinforcement these days (and in this book). People do things that have value to them and that produce the results they want. If they are successful, the chances are that they will repeat the action when they want the same or similar results. Positive reinforcement is seen as a reward, and if the reward is of value to the person performing the act or behavior, the person will repeat the behavior. That is a concept in psychology that is very important to the manager. People have needs, as has been shown. People will work in such a way as to satisfy those needs. If they are successful, and experience those needs again, they will act in a similar way. As a manager, you can try to supply those rewards. You reward or reinforce the behavior you want and, when you do so, you will find you can be effective in modifying behavior. Obviously you reward only the behavior that is important to you. You do not reward behavior that you don't find useful. Eventually you will have people acting in ways that will enable them to be rewarded by you.

Rewarded behavior is what this book deals with.

VROOM AND ROTTER

It may not be possible for today's managers to have all the answers to what motivates the people who report to them. But those managers should at least know the right questions to ask. And some very helpful questions have been developed in the research and writings of two psychologists who teach in Connecticut: Victor Vroom of Yale University and Julian Rotter of the University of Connecticut. Both have relied on experimental methods to develop their models of behavior, and both have published their theories and the results of their empirical research.

Vroom has become identified with what is sometimes referred to as the expectancy model. Rotter is a proponent of social learning theory. Their conclusions, which parallel each other, provide the opportunity for this book to talk about the technology as well as the theory of motivation. The specific recommendations in this book have to a large extent been built on the theoretical and empirical work advanced by Vroom and Rotter.

The work of Vroom and Rotter can be briefly described in these terms: People will usually consider two questions in choosing a course of action. The first has to do with the value of the action: How important is *this* goal to me as opposed to *that* one? Such decision making extends from the minor and immediate choices to the major and long term. The young college graduate ponders whether to get an advanced degree in business administration or to accept a job offer. The manager looks at the in-box and wonders whether to go through its contents or whether to start work on a long-delayed plan to reorganize some of the work units. Which course of action looks more rewarding at this time? Which course holds the greater reward or gratification at this moment? In each case, the value of the reward to the person doing the choosing will play a large part in whether he or she prefers outcome A to outcome B.

Vroom defines this preference for an outcome as *valence*. He makes the point that the individual's preference for a particular outcome may extend beyond the immediate consequence of an action to that which happens later. For example, an employee may postpone a vacation for a couple of days to have dinner with the boss. The dinner invitation itself is not preferable, nor is the conversation with the boss. But possible advancement may eventually result from the dinner as a consequence of the impression that the employee makes. This is the ulterior outcome that *is* preferred.

But the value of the reward is only part of the decision-making process. The other critical question concerns the person's expectation of actually achieving the outcome: Will I be able to have the reward I prefer? Sheila may not take the attractive job offer from another company because she fears she has certain inadequacies in technical knowledge that the company expects her to have. The pay is much better than she has at present, the promotion opportunities greater, and the position more prestigious than the one she holds now. But the risk of failure is higher than if she stays at her current job.

A manager may try to enhance the value of an assignment for an employee by saying, "If you take this on and do it successfully, I'll promote you to supervisor." The boss may have made the work more valuable, true. But the employee may not believe that the manager has the authority to promote, or may not trust the manager to keep his or her word. Therefore, in the subordinate's eyes, the probability of being successful in reaching the goal of promotion is vastly reduced.

There are many factors that influence a person's expectation of a successful outcome. Obviously there must be a cause-and-effect relationship in the person's mind. The perceived ability of the person to influence the outcome is paramount: If I do this, that will occur. People often feel that their ability to affect conditions is impaired because of inadequate training or education: I want to do this, but I'm not sure I know how. Or they may feel a lack of control because of external factors such as interference by others, unpredictable equipment, and so on.

In addition, Rotter points out, the *situation*, or the conditions surrounding the doing, can affect how a person views the value of the choice and its outcome. A young ambitious salesman looks forward to his promotion to field manager, but the opening is in the Mountain West. He knows his business, and he is quite sure of his ability to hire, train, and manage a sales force. But what disturbs him is that, because of the tremendous distances involved, he will have to fly everywhere. He has an inordinate fear of flying, especially in mountains. Thus the value of the work is vastly reduced.

Another employee may be delighted to learn that she has been transferred to a promising new department, a ground floor opportunity. But then she learns that her new boss is a manager who has the reputation of being exceedingly difficult to work for, who requires more than is reasonable from subordinates. Although she is competent and wants the opportunity, she worries about her ability to perform successfully under this demanding person.

Vroom's expectancy model and Rotter's social learning theory offer substantial guidelines for the manager involved in the motivation of people. The guidelines continue in the tradition that human behavior is goal-oriented. People do things to achieve something. Those who supervise the work of others and who are concerned about their motivation can take steps to enhance the value of a task, function, or assignment. They can also facilitate the success of other people's efforts.

The manager needs to ask questions and to observe the behavior of subordinates in the context of those questions. For example, is this the kind of work the employee likes, feels gratified in doing, and is rewarded for? Are there obstacles in the way of achievement? Does the employee anticipate problems that could be roadblocks to successful performance or to success in more generalized or long-term ways? Does the employee seem to lack confidence in his or her ability to perform the work and to gain the rewards that will come as a consequence of successful completion? Are there factors in the environment—people, location, or physical features of the work—that make it less valuable or that increase the employee's fear of failing?

Knowing the right questions to consider can point the manager in the right and effective direction in managing the motivation of employees. The value of a job can be enhanced in many ways, with money, prestige, and advancement, as well as with any number of other rewards. Many resources are available—training, equipment, professional expertise, the availability and coaching of the manager—to increase the employee's confidence that he or she can do the job.

Of course, approaching the matter of motivation in this way means a great deal of work for the manager. Each employee, after all, has his or her own values. Each has differing abilities. The manager has to get involved on a personal, individual level. That increases the complexity of the managerial job. And it requires the manager's continuing attention because people, work, values, and conditions change.

The chief point—and it is an encouraging one for managers—is that the expectancy model and social learning theory offer more than just explanations. They also offer ways managers can affect those around them for the better. You are not restricted to passively understanding what goes into motivation. You can now actively influence the motivating forces in people.

Techniques for accomplishing the successful management of employees' motivation are discussed in the following chapters.

1

THE MANAGEMENT
OF MOTIVATION

Managers manage the motivation of employees. It is a complex task. If you have 20 people reporting to you, you'll find 20 different sets of motivating factors. Identifying and enhancing those motivating factors is unquestionably one of your most challenging responsibilities. There is no way you can afford to ignore employees' motivations, because those motivating factors are the key to productivity and help to determine the following:

- ☐ How efficiently subordinates work to help you achieve the results you want.
- ☐ How much time and energy subordinates spend on the tasks you assign them and on the usual functions of their positions.

☐ Whether the performance of those tasks and functions meets your standards and the needs of the organization.

☐ The degree of enthusiasm employees feel about their work and the commitment they make to achieving those goals that are important to you.

In short, how effectively employees perform, that is, how often and well they produce the results you desire, depends in very large part on their motivation. It's almost an understatement to say that employees who want to do a good job usually produce more and better work than employees who don't much care.

WHAT MOTIVATION IS

This book is based on certain principles. Every recommendation it contains is in some way rooted in those principles. To apply the techniques of managing motivation that you find herein, you must understand the following:

1. *People have reasons for everything they do.* All human behavior, as the psychologists put it, is directed to some goal. People choose among goals. People do not act blindly. Of course, while it is true that people have reasons for what they do, that does not necessarily mean that other people find their behavior reasonable. When you don't understand or sympathize with another's act, you must still believe that the person has chosen to behave in that manner to achieve a goal.

This book will deal with voluntary behavior, which is what motivation is. Motivated behavior is behavior over which a person has some control. Involuntary behavior such as behavior rooted in addiction, severe neurosis, and psychosis is not discussed in this book. If you are unfortunate enough to have an employee who is addicted or disturbed, you probably won't have much influence over that person's behavior.

However, voluntary behavior is not always conscious. Your mind sets are a good example. Everyone develops certain patterns and habits to such an extent that he or she performs actions without thinking about them. If you drive to work regularly, you have probably had the experience of becoming aware that you took your usual route without making a conscious choice. You may have been thinking about something else when you selected the streets or roads unconsciously. The conscious selection was actually made some time ago.

But sets and habits can be changed. New choices can establish new patterns of behavior. That is an essential point for you to remember as a manager: New choices based on new goals can result in a change of behavior. That fact gives you a certain amount of power in dealing with your subordinates.

Another related point that you should keep in mind is that as the selected goals are achieved, they act as reinforcers. As the psychologist puts it, the behavior that led to the achievement of the goal is reinforced. It will probably be repeated. Reinforcement of desired behavior in subordinates is a powerful managerial tool.

2. *Whatever people choose as a goal is something they believe is good for them.* It has value in the mind of the *doer*. You may observe someone else doing something for reasons you don't understand, but you can be sure that the goal the other person is pursuing has value to that person. Sometimes that behavior can be very mystifying. For example, the employee who always ties up meetings by challenging a boss's thinking would seem to be self-destructive. Not only does the boss get upset but so does everyone else. Suppose Jay is an employee who makes meetings dull and interminable. But he has a "good" reason. It's probably his self-image that he is acting out; he sees himself as the questioner, the gadfly, the deep thinker, the department intellectual. Each time he acts in this way, he feels reinforced. Because it is *good* for him, he is rewarded. Psychologically the terms mean the same: goal, reinforcement, reward. They can therefore be used interchangeably and will be in this book.

When people ask such questions as, "Why does she act that way?" or "What makes him behave like that?" the answer is, "Because they feel rewarded for doing it." Thus the key to behavior that is mystifying, self-destructive, and counterproductive is in understanding the reward that the person perceives. If you want to change that person's behavior, or more accurately, if you encourage him or her to act in a different manner, you must substitute a more valuable reward for the one the person is enjoying now.

That point leads to another important consideration for the manager: When choosing one course of action over another, people tend to choose the goal, reward, or reinforcer that appears to be most valuable, *all other things being equal*. This fact is pervasive. It determines your choices, small and large. From what you wear to what you decide to order for lunch to what jobs or tasks you tackle first in your career, all are subject to this reality.

The question you ask yourself when you are confronted with a decision is, "What's in this for me?" Some managers seem to object when they detect that self-interest in employees, especially in the younger employees in today's work force. But in one way or another people have always asked that question and determined the answer before they chose.

3. *The goal people choose must be seen as attainable.* This will explain the phrase that appeared earlier, "all other things being equal." People do not choose a course of action solely because of the value of the reward. They have to feel also that they have a reasonable chance of gaining it. No matter how valuable the reward may be, people generally will not make the effort to achieve it if they believe the chances of reaching it are slim or the effort required is more than they want to expend. The production supervisor may fantasize about being corporate president. The reward is certainly valuable enough. But the path to the presidency will require several years of night school. She can't afford to go to school full-time. Going to classes for three or four nights each week for several years is more of an investment of time and energy than she believes she can make. She will settle for something less.

There is a prominent exception to this rule: the so-called gambler's fallacy. A gambler will pursue a reward that may have much value but is remotely attainable. Occasionally you will see this behavior duplicated by others, such as the dark horse who runs for president. Such a person is motivated by the big payoff and not demotivated by the small probability. Most people, in most situations, however, measure the value *and* the probability of enjoying it.

If these two principles involving the value of the reward and its relative attainability are nearly universal, it might reasonably be asked whether a manager ought to be able to predict how an employee will perform on a task or job so long as the manager has an idea of how the employee values the reward and how much confidence he or she has in being able to gain it. The answer is "probably," if you could be sure that you knew how the employee perceived the reward. But employees don't always reveal their values and personal goals. (Sometimes they are not clear about them in their own minds.) In the absence of certainty, the manager may assume that he or she knows how employees feel. Or the manager projects his or her own perceptions onto employees and then wonders why they don't perform predictably.

4. *The conditions under which the work is done can affect its value to the employee and his or her perceptions of attainability or success.* The situation surrounding the doing can add to or detract from the value of the reward or the employee's perception of the chances for gaining it. For example, you are a salesperson who has always wanted to be a sales manager. Finally, you are offered the job. But the company offering it is rumored to be in financial trouble. Or the vice-president to whom you will be reporting impresses you as being incompetent or untrustworthy. In either case the value or the probability of success is affected by the situation.

Thus, in assigning tasks, you must take into consideration all three factors—the value, the employee's perception of success, and the situation.

THE MANAGER'S POWER

Now that you understand the principles of motivation, what can you do about or with them? A great deal. You can increase the value of a goal or reward for an employee. You can increase the employee's confidence in his or her ability to do the work, thereby increasing the chances for gaining the reward that comes with achievement. And you can enhance the situation surrounding the doing of the work to add to the value of the reward and the probability of success. At least you can take steps to avoid having the situation detract from the value or the probability. For the manager, it isn't sufficient to know what the motivation is—how people behave and why. You need to know how you can influence people's choices, how you can provide them with the means that will inspire them to want to do a good job. With that knowledge, you become the key to the deeper commitment of employees to your own—and the organization's—goals.

Every successful manager has to recognize that a large part of that success is due to the performance of subordinates. The quality of that performance is related largely to the success of the manager's motivation management techniques. A manager can leave subordinates to work disappointingly or help them to perform outstandingly.

WHAT MOTIVATION IS NOT

It might surprise many managers to learn that most workers say their employers have little knowledge of how to motivate them. That was a finding of a study conducted and published by the nonprofit Public Agenda Foundation of New York in 1983. Worse, the study, "Putting the Work Ethic to Work: A Public Agenda Report on Restoring America's Competitive Vitality," concludes that most Americans want to do quality work, but their desire to do so is seriously undermined by their managers' practices. Much of the managerial deficiency stems from a lack of understanding of what motivation really is. The knowledge many managers have about what makes people go is seriously tainted with myths and half-truths about motivation. Here are some examples.

Some People Are Just Unmotivated

The answer to the question, "What do you do with unmotivated employees?" is, you bury them. The only unmotivated people are dead ones. When a manager complains that subordinates are not motivated, he or she is really saying that the employees don't seem to do what the manager wants them to do. They are motivated, but perhaps in quite different directions. But the trap for the manager is more than semantic. Managers who see employees as unmotivated may convince themselves that such employees are beyond influencing.

Good Managers Know How to Motivate People

Good managers may know how to motivate themselves. They don't motivate others. Motivation comes from within the individual. It is not something that one person does to another. What a manager must do is to find ways to enhance and reinforce the motivating forces within the employees. Employees who hear their bosses talking about motivating them may worry about being manipulated rather than motivated.

It Takes Charisma to Inspire and Motivate People

If you don't have charisma, you're out of luck. And most people don't. No one seems to know how you get it. Actually most managers are made, not born. The most comfortable aspect of that truth is that nearly anyone can become an effective manager. Charisma is nice to have, especially in crises when people must be inspired to put forth tremendous effort. But even a charismatic leader may not be very effective in handling everyday, mundane tasks.

Most People, Given the Choice Between Working and Not Working, Would Choose Not to Work

You'll recall that psychologist Douglas McGregor defined this perception of people as Theory X. A manager who makes such an assumption about his or her employees is saying that, without the manager's constant vigilance and efforts, employees would do nothing. There is no scientific evidence to support the contention that most people would prefer to avoid work. There is, however, much evidence pointing to people's wanting to avoid a certain kind of work—or the conditions under which they have to perform that work. Managers can do much to lessen that desire for avoidance.

Fear Is the Best Motivator

Fear is a too widely used substitute for management of motivation. What's the payoff for doing a good job? "We let you keep it," replies the fear-inspiring manager. Everyone laughs, as indeed they should. Fear is a poor motivator. True, the employee may see value in avoiding punishment, pain, and loss, but avoidance as a motivating force operates strongly for only a short time and with relatively few people. Even in an economy that is cyclical, many employees would not hesitate to tell this vestige of the Great Depression where he could stow his job. Of course, they might choose to respond covertly by doing just what they have to do to keep the job.

The Way You Get People to Work Hard for You Is to Be Nice to Them

This theory flows from the so-called human relations school. The basic tenet of this approach to motivation: If you are nice to employees, they will be happy and work better. Experience and science have not established this as a workable premise. Generally employees are there to achieve certain things they want—money, status, and many other rewards and reinforcements that will be detailed later in the book. If you help them achieve these objectives, the probabilities are that they will work better. Being patient, nice, considerate, a careful listener, maintaining an open door policy, expressing interest in their personal problems, and putting their welfare above all other considerations may add a pleasant frosting to conditions on the job. These things will not, however, take the place of effective management that gets results for everyone.

There are no convincing data to support the be-nice-to-people approach. All that is known about happy employees is that they are happy employees. Happy employees do not necessarily produce more than unhappy employees, although it is undoubtedly true that most people would prefer to work in an environment that is pleasant and warmly human.

Paternalism, similar to but actually predating the human relations school, is an old and familiar approach to hooking employees. The paternalistic manager emphasizes loyalty to management and the organization. Management is a benevolent master, giving lots of benefits, being considerate of the employee as a whole person up to a point. But no one is ever permitted to forget the master part. Paternalism is not very effective with employees who can read the purpose of the niceness. It is a means by which management gets what it wants, without genuine concern for the objectives of the employees. Paternalism, as one employee of a large corporation said, "is how they buy us."

A concern for morale is often indicative of the people-should-be-happy approach. Morale is frequently referred to in the same context as motivation. But research has established no clear relationship between morale and motivation. There are any number of instances of departments or organizations in which morale among employees was quite low and yet productivity was surprisingly high. You'll also find work places in which morale is high but because of poor management productivity is low. It is probably true that over a prolonged period, high productivity and motivation require high morale. But that is an assumption unproved by data.

High Job Satisfaction Is Necessary for Motivation

The role of job satisfaction continues to be the subject of an intense and interesting debate. Asking employees how they feel about what they are doing can produce a wealth of data, but how to interpret the data is open to question. Frederick Herzberg equates "satisfiers" with motivators. The relationship between the two terms is not settled.

HOW YOU SEE SUBORDINATES

While the emphasis in this book is on the behavior of others, something needs to be said about attitude—yours. There isn't much point in discussing the attitudes of others. You can't see attitudes, and they're difficult to measure. Also you can never be quite sure if you've influenced the attitudes of others.

But you do know about your own attitudes, and there are times when they influence your behavior. Certainly other people will observe your behavior and try to guess what attitudes are behind it.

An important consideration in the management of the motivation of others is how you regard the people who report to you. A
number of years ago, transactional analysis, then very popular,
described the healthy interaction as "I'm OK, you're OK." According to TA, the person who operates from this position is mentally
quite healthy. He or she is realistic in expectations about self and
others (those expectations are not too high or too low). The OK
person accepts others without great difficulty. One reason for this
relatively easy acceptance is that the expectations one has about
oneself apply to others. Just as you have goals toward which you
are working and which are important to you, you assume that the
same is true of others. You accept others as having aspirations and
standards of behavior as you do. You do not insist that those
aspirations and standards be the same as yours in all cases (although you may, as a manager, impose your standards on their
job performance). You may not always agree with others' perceptions of what is good and valuable. But you accept the fact that
they have them.

According to transactional analysis, everyone wants to win.
You want to be what you are capable of being without depriving
others of the same chance. You want to do what you are capable of
doing without getting in the way of others who want the same
thing. Winning, then, is when you can *be* and can *do*. But as a
manager, you are in a position to do much more for your subordinates. The I'm-OK-you're-OK manager says, in effect, "I want to
win. I know you want to win. And we can both help each other to
do just that."

When you convey such a positive, accepting message, your
chance of influencing employees' behavior and performance is
better than if you show suspicion and doubt their goodwill, or if
you suggest that in some way they are lacking in trustworthiness.
(Occasionally you will meet someone who justifies your suspicion
and is indeed not trustworthy. In such a case, prompt action, as
described later in the book, is necessary.) The manager who conveys his or her expectation to employees so that they want to
commit themselves to a worthwhile task and they would prefer to
do a good job rather than a poor one, has a much better chance of
getting that commitment and that good job than a manager who
suggests the opposite.

Respect for the individual is essential for effective motivation management. Some managers bemoan that their subordinates are not more like themselves. In fact, those managers often project their own values onto employees: "This is what motivates me. It should motivate them as well." That projection may lead those managers into trying to control the behavior of subordinates. You have the ability to influence choices, but when you try to control them, you risk a reduction in motivated behavior. Controlled employees perform under duress.

The key words then are trust, respect, and results. Results are what you want. You should assume that results are what employees hope for, too.

You can involve employees in the achievement of your goals by following these recommendations:

1. *Tell people what you expect them to do.* Don't just assume that your subordinates, even those who have worked for you a long time, know what kind of performance you expect of them. Subordinates may not always understand the standards you expect them to observe. In some cases, they will not realize that you want them to take certain means to certain ends. How you see their role in your department, their responsibilities, and their priorities may differ from how they see them. You must close the gap by clarifying your expectations.

2. *Make the work worth doing and doable.* As you will see, you can add value to the work and increase the employee's confidence to carry out the job and assignments. The more clearly employees can see that, by working to help you to achieve your objectives, they can gain something that is important to them, the more intense their involvement and commitment will be.

3. *While employees are trying to do what you expect them to do, let them know how they are doing.* Many employees complain often that they hear when they make mistakes or don't perform according to managers' expectations but not when they do the work well. People need both positive and negative feedback. If the manager withholds positive feedback, his or her people may be discouraged and say, "What's the use of working hard. We can't seem to do it right." The manager who, for whatever reason, is reluctant to criticize disappointing performance or mistakes is also cheating

employees. Most people don't want to fumble. They want to be successful. They want to take pride in what they do. Painful as negative feedback is, they know it's necessary.

4. *When employees have done what you expected them to do, reward them.*   Establish in the minds of your subordinates that there is a clear link between doing good work and having that work recognized. You want employees to say, "Around here when you do a good job, they appreciate it. You'll get rewarded." Behavior that is rewarded or reinforced is more likely to be repeated than behavior that is not.

Precisely and specifically how you put these basic recommendations into practice is detailed in the rest of this book. When you practice them, you'll find that there is a payoff for you. When your subordinates are highly motivated, the job of managing is a lot easier and more enjoyable. People are pulling in the same direction, voluntarily, without your prodding, pushing, and punishing. People arrive on time, put in a fair day's work, and leave feeling good about what they have done. When they do their work right, they leave time for you to do more of the things you like to do—things that can advance you, the department, your career—and those functions that only you can do, such as planning, coordinating, budgeting, and so on.

STYLE AND MOTIVATION

Is one style of managing more effective in enhancing the motivating forces of employees than another?

Long ago the eminent psychologist Kurt Lewin identified three basic styles of managing:

☐ *Authoritarian or Autocratic.* The boss makes the decisions, does the planning, and often specifies how the work is to be done. Employees probably have a minimum of input in how the department is to run. There is a hierarchy, a chain of command.

☐ *Democratic.* Where possible, the manager involves employees in decisions that involve them. The boss regards subordinates as important resources that can be called upon in planning and assigning work. There is a chain of command, but employees generally feel free to offer opinions, suggestions, even criticism.

☐ *Laissez-faire.* For the most part, the laissez-faire manager tends to leave much of the operation up to the employees. They make many of the decisions, do much of the planning, and decide how things are to be done.

Most authorities on management would probably agree that, given the values, education, and acculturation of today's work force, democracy is the atmosphere that in most cases is most conducive to high motivation among employees. There are at least three reasons why a democratic approach to management has a positive effect on motivating forces:

1. People are encouraged to make inputs. They are, in most cases, experts on their work. They can suggest ways in which the work can be done more effectively, permitting a sense of greater accomplishment when the increased effectiveness brings about better and more results.

2. They participate in decision making and setting objectives, a process that helps them to more closely match their own personal goals with those of the organization. They also feel more like partners in the operation. They enjoy additional status, which for some is one reason for working well. They have a sense of "ownership" of goals.

3. Two-way communications are usually best in a democratic atmosphere. Better communications mean that problems can be discussed quickly and openly, and corrected before frustration and failure set in. Obstacles to productivity can be spotted and talked about in a frank manner.

Although most employees prefer the democratic style of management, it has to be emphasized that no one style, the democratic style included, works equally well with everyone in every situation. There are subordinates who seem to need direction. They respond to orders and feel comfortable following procedures that have been set forth for them. They don't wish to participate in a democratic process. There are other employees who seem to require a firm hand. Their primary interest is not in the job. You may have to monitor their work closely, supervise them strictly, and occasionally remind them of the penalties for not turning in good work.

There are situations that call for being autocratic, for taking unilateral action, for pulling rank. For example:

- ☐ *There Is an Immediate Danger or Emergency.* An obvious situation falling into this category is the need to lay it on the line for an employee who violates a safety precaution. Or perhaps the whole department is involved in a crisis. There isn't time for consultation with employees. The well-being of the operation is threatened. Time is desperately short. You must step in, organize your resources, establish emergency procedures, and issue orders.

- ☐ *The Overall Welfare or Morale of the Group Is Being Harmed.* One person's disruptive behavior or general troublemaking can become dangerously contagious. It has to be stopped—immediately and firmly.

- ☐ *One Person's Actions Recurrently Hurt or Anger Someone Else.* He or she causes friction or creates conflict, interfering with the ability of others to function. Warnings and talking have not produced results. You have to take unpleasant action.

- ☐ *You Aren't Permitted to Explain Your Action.* Sometimes you are privy to organizational information that you can't share with subordinates. Yet you have certain actions you must take. You must require that subordinates follow your orders with no explanations or consultations.

- ☐ *All Else Has Failed.* To illustrate, an employee has been appraised, criticized, coached, and warned. Still he or she continues in the same unproductive or destructive behavior pattern.

All of the above situations may warrant autocratic managerial responses.

Other situations may justify a laissez-faire approach. You have a work force made up of well-qualified, self-starting, and achievement-oriented people who don't require—and probably don't welcome—close monitoring. However, with people who work well on their own, who can be left relatively unsupervised, you need some controls and measurements that indicate when things are not going well and when you have to step in to take corrective action. It's called *managing by exception*, the exception to a smooth running operation.

Even if many of your subordinates need closer supervision than that described in the preceding paragraph, you may still encounter individuals who can work quite well on their own, indeed, who seem to thrive on independence. With such a person you can probably benefit from a laissez-faire style.

In all probability, within one department and within a short time you will encounter different people and varying situations that call for all three styles.

Regardless of your predominant style, what is essential is that your subordinates trust and respect you. They know that you mean what you say, that you can be relied on to follow through on promises and assurances, and that you will never subvert their efforts to achieve their goals in order to gain yours. Your base of trust and credibility is therefore more important than your managing style. If that base is firm, your style is not terribly relevant to the motivation of employees.

YOUR MOTIVATION QUOTIENT

Before continuing, you may want to check your understanding of the fundamentals of motivation. The following quiz will reinforce and help you to review what has been said in this book so far. Compare your answers with the answers given following the quiz.

	Agree	Disagree	Not Sure
1. People who are motivated to work perform better on the job.	___	___	___
2. Correcting poor work attitudes in employees is an important part of the manager's job.	___	___	___
3. If people had a choice of working or not working, most people would choose not to work.	___	___	___
4. Some people are unmotivated, and there is nothing the manager can do with them.	___	___	___
5. In general, people won't work at something they don't like to do.	___	___	___
6. Motivation is an important key to effective performance.	___	___	___
7. The attitudes that a manager has toward subordinates can affect the work they do.	___	___	___
8. Low morale of employees is one of the biggest obstacles to good performance in a work group.	___	___	___

	Agree	Disagree	Not Sure
9. Most people work primarily for money.	____	____	____
10. Fear is one of the best ways to motivate people.	____	____	____
11. Motivating employees is a manager's most important task.	____	____	____
12. The style of managing plays an important role in employee motivation.	____	____	____
13. Managers who are nice to their employees get better performance.	____	____	____
14. Few people welcome criticism of their work.	____	____	____
15. People today seem to want to know what's in it for them before taking a job.	____	____	____
16. Working conditions can affect the degree of motivation in employees.	____	____	____
17. People always seem to want to be rewarded for doing a job.	____	____	____
18. The truth is that most people have to be coerced and controlled by the manager to put forth adequate work.	____	____	____
19. The average employee will not be committed to a task or a job that he or she doesn't find valuable.	____	____	____
20. Whether people in a work group are strongly motivated			

	Agree	Disagree	Not Sure
or not depends largely on the way they are managed.	____	____	____
21. When employees suspect that they will have difficulty doing a certain kind of work, they will usually avoid the work or lose motivation.	____	____	____
22. A manager can often make work more desirable to an employee.	____	____	____
23. Employees will choose not to do any kind of work that is not valuable.	____	____	____
24. Most people value job security above almost any-thing else.	____	____	____
25. Managers have the ability to increase the value of work in employees' eyes as well as their confidence in their ability to do it.	____	____	____

Answers with Comments

If you have any questions regarding the answers that follow, you may wish to refer to the Introduction or to Chapter 1 for clarification.

1. Yes, people who are motivated to work perform better on the job. People whose work is not very important to them over the long run tend to turn in mediocre or barely adequate performance. Appropriate answer: Agree.

2. Correcting poor work attitudes in employees is an important part of the manager's job. It would be a very frustrating part if it were true. You cannot really get into the heads of subordinates to identify and measure their attitudes. On the other hand, behavior is recognizable and measurable. Stick to correcting undesirable or inadequate behavior. Disagree.

3. If people had a choice of working or not working, most people would choose not to work. There's no evidence that most people dislike work. Managers who hold to this philosophy are somewhat justified, because they tend to create working conditions that subordinates dislike. It becomes a vicious circle—a self-fulfilling prophecy. Disagree.

4. Some people are unmotivated, and there is nothing the manager can do with them. All behavior is directed toward a goal. Thus, employees are working to achieve something but it may not be what the manager prefers. Such a manager is not taking steps to make the work more valuable and doable to subordinates. To say that there is nothing a manager can do when employees are not performing as they should is to abdicate responsibility or to become a martyr, a rather unfashionable and unrewarding role. Disagree.

5. Generally speaking, people won't work at something they don't like to do. However, some people will, although you can't expect them to involve themselves deeply in it or to be exceptional performers over the long run. To work for a lengthy time at a job you don't like to do takes more energy than the job is worth. Even for work that people dislike, a

manager can take steps to add value or to lessen the burden. Therefore, you can't be sure of this answer.

6. When people are motivated to commit themselves to working with you toward the achievement of your goals, they are more likely to turn in good performance than those who are not so committed. Agree.

7. The attitudes that a manager has toward subordinates can affect the work they do. Studies have shown that your expectations of employees' work can influence that work. If you convey positive expectations—for example, that people will perform well—they are more likely to do so than if you seem to doubt whether they will. It's probably true that most people react strongly to a manager who has good feelings and good-will toward them as people. Furthermore, they are more likely to accept your guidelines, standards, objectives, and feedback if they know you have respect for them and concern for whether they achieve in their work what is important to them. Agree.

8. It has never been scientifically demonstrated that there is a causal or otherwise essential relationship between morale and productivity. Low morale groups can produce highly, and high morale groups can produce poorly. It is probably true that a work group suffering low morale over a long period of time will show a decline in productivity, but that has not been substantiated by research. Disagree.

9. Most people do not work primarily for money, according to Herzberg's claims that money is not a motivator. Under certain circumstances, for periods of time, the promise of more money for good performance may have a motivational effect. But once the increase has been earned, the money ceases to be a motivator. Also, studies made of employee groups through the years show that, while they have an interest in money, it is not as important to them as interesting work and the chance to advance in their work. Money usually appears third or fourth on the list of important motivators. Disagree.

10. Fear is not a very good way to motivate people. The avoidance of pain or punishment may move people for a short time, but they will eventually come to resent the presence of

the stick. Using fear, the manager will very likely have to accept minimally acceptable performance. What enhances the working relationship between manager and employee are respect and credibility. Fear is a poor substitute. And there are subordinates who will experience no fear at all. Disagree.

11. Motivating employees is a manager's most important task. Disagree, because you as a manager can motivate no one but yourself.

12. The style of managing plays an important role in employee motivation. No one style is totally effective with every employee all the time. Good managers are situational in their approach, altering their styles to fit time, place, conditions, and person. There's no way you can be sure how much a style of managing influences motivation.

13. Managers may be nice to their subordinates, but much more is involved with motivation than niceness. Niceness may cause employees to be happy but not necessarily productive. Some managers are nice but know how to take steps to enhance the motivation of employees, while other managers may simply be nice. There are too many other variables to make this premise certain. Thus, you can't be sure.

14. *Most* people welcome criticism of their work, if that work is not getting results. No one likes to flounder or be known as a fumbler. Painful though criticism may be, if it helps people to be more effective in their work, it is more welcome than failure. Besides, your criticism of employees can show them that you are concerned about their success. Disagree on this one.

15. Surely people want to know what's in it for them before taking on a job. People will choose the kind of task, work, responsibility, even career, that has the most value and the greater rewards. Thus, before choosing a course of action or a type of behavior, people will want to make sure that the decision will lead to some reward of value. Agree.

16. You should agree that working conditions can affect the degree of motivation in employees. The situation surrounding the doing can add to the value or detract from it, and can make

the attainment seem easier or more difficult. Since value of the reward and attainability of that reward have an essential effect on motivation, the situation does play an important part.

17. People always seem to want to be rewarded for doing work, just as they want to achieve something valuable for anything they choose to do. The encouraging side of that psychological reality is that you have the means at your disposal to make the work even more rewarding, thus increasing the motivating force. Agree.

18. People do not have to be coerced and controlled by the manager to put forth adequate work. There is much evidence that people regard work as very important to their happiness and well-being that work is how they achieve many of their personal goals in life. Managers who complain that they have to coerce and control have probably created poor working conditions in which people dislike the work or the environment. Disagree.

19. It's true that the average employee will not be committed to a task or a job that he or she doesn't find valuable to do. That doesn't mean that the employee will not do the work. Rather the employee will not be highly motivated to do a good job, especially over a period of time. It's safe to agree on this one.

20. Since you are the key to the motivation of your employees, you should have no problem agreeing that your managing has a great deal to do with how strongly motivated your employees are.

21. Keeping in mind that the probability of success in doing a job or task or the attainability of the reward that comes from doing it is an essential component of motivation, you can agree that if people perceive difficulty in doing the work, they will either avoid it altogether or suffer a decrease in motivation.

22. You can often make work more desirable to an employee by adding value or making it easier to do. Agree.

23. Employees will choose not to do any kind of work that is not valuable to them. The operative word is *choose*. That doesn't mean that they will not do the work if it is necessary for them

to do it, but left to their own devices, they won't choose it. Agree.

24. Most people value job security above almost anything else. Again, studies of employees' preferences show that their interest in job security is rather far down the list. The research of Frederick Herzberg indicates that job security acts more as a dissatisfier, that is, the absence of it causes employees to be dissatisfied. The presence of it does not constitute a motivator. It would seem that the increased mobility of workers today would contradict this old bromide. Disagree.

25. Managers have the ability to increase the value of work in employees' eyes as well as their confidence in their ability to do it. The rest of this book will show you how. Agree.

2

WORKING WITHIN THE CULTURE

Every organization has its culture, reflected in its objectives and concerns, the managing style of its managers, its traditions and heroes, its relationships with employees, clients, and shareholders, even in the informal and formal dress codes. The organizational culture has to do with the organization's values, priorities, and even structure.

Generally, the most successful members of the culture are those who share its values, style, and outlook. Those members may not be the most successful in terms of financial practice, productivity, and planning for the future but, judged by the criteria developed by the organization, they will be favored. Generally the least successful, and usually temporary, members of the culture are those who do not share its values, who do not conform to its prevailing style.

They insist on applying their own philosophies, techniques, and methodology, which are at variance with "The way we do things here."

A maverick manager is often rendered less effective when co-workers move to isolate him or her. The maverick is cut off from communications, finds creating collaborative relationships difficult, and is unable to build or is seriously hampered in forming a power base of allies. In extreme cases the manager who is alien to the organizational culture is pushed into a backwater. Employees, sensing the relative powerlessness of their manager because of his or her isolation from the mainstream, will usually experience demotivation.

Ironically, an adept manager can come into a culture in which demotivation is rife, shape an effective, productive work group and, still, if he or she is not sensitive to the demands of the culture, experience isolation as well.

This is not to say that mavericks cannot survive in an alien culture. Obviously, if your values are the same as those of the organization, if the ways in which you accomplish your work fit in with the accepted modes of doing things, your work is much easier. But even if you are essentially an "outsider," you can through competence, sensitivity, and discretion build constructive working relationships with your peers and bosses.

Thus a manager's interaction with the organizational culture is of paramount importance in his or her efforts to be successful and effective. Interestingly, if you as a manager enter an organization in which employees are severely demotivated and manage to create a productive, highly motivated department, you may find yourself also being treated as an alien by other managers even though you fit into the culture.

Your very success in managing the motivation of employees has marked you as different. You constitute a challenge, perhaps even a rebuke, to those managers who have either contributed to the demotivation or have been unable to turn it around. You are, as the expression goes, between a rock and a hard place. You cannot be successful if your employees are not motivated. Nonetheless, unless you are very alert to a delicate situation and to the culture, you cannot be successful over time without the active cooperation of your peers and bosses.

This chapter explores the relationships among you, the organizational culture, and your employees. The logical place to begin to look at the interrelationships is the motivational level of the people in your department.

DEMOTIVATION AND YOUR DEPARTMENT

Are there signs of demotivation in your department? Check your situation against the symptoms in the following checklist.

	Yes	No
1. People spend a lot of time gossiping cynically about the organization.	___	___
2. Sometimes it seems to you as if each day brings widespread petty complaints and grievances.	___	___
3. People frequently make sarcastic comments about the organization and its management.	___	___
4. There has been a drop-off in employee suggestions for better operation of the department.	___	___
5. You often hear comments such as, "All you can do is hang in," or, "The name of the game is survival."	___	___
6. There is a pronounced "them vs. us" tone when employees talk about higher management.	___	___
7. There are many covert conversations among employees from which you are conspicuously excluded.	___	___
8. Employees say with disturbing frequency, "What's the point in killing yourself?"	___	___
9. There is an increase in absenteeism, especially among employees who formerly had exemplary work attendance records.	___	___

	Yes	No

10. While employees will carry out your instructions, they are noticeably reluctant to offer to take on responsibility. ____ ____

11. People who have demonstrated a high ability to work well now seem to turn in assignments that are minimally acceptable in quality or quantity. ____ ____

12. Employees regularly label management policies and decisions as unfair. ____ ____

13. There is a disturbing trend toward procrastination and missing deadlines. ____ ____

14. People seem to you to be bored and generally fatigued. ____ ____

15. Your departmental employees seem to have developed strong cliques. ____ ____

16. Employees who used to be ambitious now seem cynical about their chances to get ahead in the organization. ____ ____

17. Employees whom you always viewed as reliable now openly display resentment when asked to take on extra work. ____ ____

18. Employees seem to you to give up quickly when engaged in a demanding or complex task and seek help from you. ____ ____

19. Organizational rules are scorned and ignored. ____ ____

20. Lateness has increased generally among your employees. ____ ____

21. Employees spend organizational time doing personal tasks or making personal telephone calls. ____ ____

22. There is a frequency in unexplained absences from offices, desks, or work stations. ____ ____

	Yes	No

23. There is disproportionate complaining about wages and salaries.

24. There is widespread grumbling about working conditions.

25. Equipment is not taken care of properly.

26. Employees are reluctant to stay after hours even to finish work that could be completed in a short time.

27. People do not seem to listen carefully when you give instructions.

28. Employees spend inordinate amounts of time doing relatively simple tasks.

29. Employees make frequent references to how well off their friends and acquaintances are in other organizations.

30. Employees complain loudly and frequently that too many objectives come down from higher management for them to meet.

31. Employees complain that higher management sets conflicting priorities that make it difficult for them to work effectively.

32. You often have to follow up your assignments of tasks and responsibilities to make sure they are done correctly and on time.

33. Many employees seem unwilling to pitch in and help co-workers.

34. There is a neglect of routine chores.

35. Employees frequently rationalize sloppiness and errors.

36. There are frequent and widespread comments made about what employees consider errors by higher management.

	Yes	No

37. There are frequent, belittling comments made about the capability, of higher management. ____ ____

38. In meetings with representatives of higher management employees often sit silently but become active in after-the-meeting meetings among themselves. ____ ____

39. Some employees complain bitterly about what they regard as preferential treatment given to others. ____ ____

40. Some employees complain frequently that other employees in the department are not carrying their share of the load. ____ ____

41. You sense that one or more employees have become informal leaders in the department in covert opposition to your authority. ____ ____

42. As you make rounds of your department, you are struck by the widespread socializing you see. ____ ____

43. There are frequent comments by employees that reveal their suspicion that management is out to manipulate or take advantage of them. ____ ____

44. There is a rise in mistakes and incompleteness even in routine work that employees have always performed well. ____ ____

45. Employees seem reluctant to discuss their long-range plans with you. ____ ____

46. There is inordinate resistance to and grumbling about even minor changes. ____ ____

47. Employees appear to need frequent monitoring by you in order to apply themselves to their work. ____ ____

48. You find yourself often giving pep talks to employees to energize them to do their work. ____ ____

Yes   No

49. There has been an increase in unpredictable delays and snafus.

50. Employees who formerly seemed easygoing and relaxed now display frequent tension and irritability.

No doubt, even in the best-run operation in which most employees are highly motivated, a manager would be forced to check off some of the above symptoms. In fact, there may be a few employees who show many of the above symptoms. However, if more than 10 of the above symptoms apply to most of your employees most of the time, you are headed for trouble—or are already there. You could have a serious demotivation problem.

You may in fact be aggravating that problem in several ways. You might consider whether you are sufficiently exercising the following managerial functions.

Communicating Your Standards

Perhaps employees are no longer quite clear about what you expect of them. If so, and if it has been quite some time since you clarified your expectations and standards, now is the moment. Deprive any employee of the excuse that he or she didn't know what you wanted.

Showing Appreciation for Good Work

You may not be complimenting employees who try to perform well in a consistent and conscientious fashion. Start brushing up on your "thank yous." You may wish to refer to Chapter 6 for a list of the ways in which you can recognize good performance.

Failing to Discipline

Failure to enforce strict rules of discipline often results in unfairness to all concerned. The rule-abiding group soon feels it is being taken advantage of. The others are taking advantage of you. The net result is that your control is undermined. Firm up on enforcement and stick by organizational rules.

SYSTEMIC DEMOTIVATION

If you checked off a large number of *yeses* in the symptoms of demotivation checklist above, chances are that there is substantial demotivation throughout your organization, and as department head you suffer along with everyone else. Nevertheless, there are steps you can take to reduce the impact of the systemic demotivation on the people who report to you. These functions will be discussed at length below.

THE CARING PROTECTOR

Some managers simply transmit whatever comes down from higher management. Employees in such departments complain that they are besieged by directives and goals and that priorities are often unclear. The result is a start-and-stop chaotic operation. Your role as a protector in such an environment is vital. When there is an avalanche of such communications from higher management without clear priority, you need to do the following:

☐ Clarify with top management which objectives and directives take precedence.

☐ Explain the objectives and priorities to your people, and help them to adjust their work schedules to accommodate the communications and directives from higher up.

☐ Make sure that all communications from outside your department are filtered through you to your employees. You don't want staff or line people elsewhere contacting your employees without your knowledge and confusing them even more.

To reduce the tensions and anxious feelings that often come with any changes from above, or indeed from you, try to answer the following questions in your presentation to your employees to allay their concerns:

- ☐ What does this change mean to the organization? Are we growing or retrenching?
- ☐ How does it affect my future? Will it help me or hurt me?
- ☐ Does the change imply any criticism of me (or employees in general)?
- ☐ What can I lose as a result of the change? Money, prestige, the opportunity for advancement?
- ☐ What can I gain from it? Money, prestige, the opportunity for advancement?
- ☐ How does it affect the people around me? Will it change my work group? Will some people get ahead of me?
- ☐ Will it make me look good or bad?

No matter how much sense the change makes to you, remember that you must see it through your employees' perceptions. It isn't necessarily that they resist change, but they will resist if they fear what is being done to them.

What if you have to introduce a change that you fear will be unpopular? The change may involve more complicated procedures, a transfer of responsibility, or an increased work load. You can't avoid making the change, but you do wish to avoid as much trauma and demotivation as possible.

Convey Positive Expectations

You can be optimistic in most cases. There is some aspect of the change that you can talk about positively. You can indicate that you have weighed the pros and cons and, despite any drawbacks, some good will come out of the change. People's expectations about a change can significantly affect its success. If you can show optimism, the change will become less threatening.

However, if some people will be hurt by the change, you should, of course, level with them. Sooner or later, they will find out that you failed to be open with them. Your credibility and their motivation will be dealt a crippling blow.

Anticipate Fears

Bring the objectives you anticipate into the open. (You may want to check the list on page 51 to help you jog your memory about the aspects of the change that your employees are fearing.) Otherwise these objectives may fester and cause problems later. Ask for comments and questions about the change. If you know of objections that aren't mentioned, bring them up yourself and provide the answers.

Try to emphasize its positive aspects. Even an across-the-board pay cut or reduction in force has some virtues when compared to shutting the operation down.

Accept the Fears

There may be some emotional reactions to the change that can't be explained away or buried by rational explanations. Accept the negative reactions. The people who have dictated the change are distant. They can't provide understanding. You can. Your acceptance may go far toward calming those fears.

Don't Show Your Disagreement or Resistance

You may not endorse the change privately but, publicly, since you are a manager, you are expected to implement it. Even if you are opposed to it, keep that fact to yourself. State the change and convey your expectation that it will be accepted and carried out.

THE MANAGER AS INFORMER

Paranoia is especially prevalent in organizations in which motivation and morale are low. Employees may feel that they have become victims of management's manipulation, poor judgment, or lack of concern. These feelings are intensified during crises—

departments or projects are wiped out, there are personnel cut-backs and reductions in force, budgets are reduced, work loads are increased, people are transferred or demoted. Employees see that something unpleasant is being done to them, and "they" who are responsible are not leveling.

You are one of the "they." You may know why management is not giving out all of the information. You realize that higher management doesn't always have complete information, that things are in transition, that people at the top are working their way through problems and forget the need to tell all. Perhaps you can't close the information gap completely, but you can reduce paranoia. And by reducing paranoia, you reduce the worrying that people do and some of the forces that may demotivate them.

Tell What You Can

Although you may not know much more than the people who report to you, share what you can with them. Because of your position, your knowledge of the organization, your own grapevine, you are bound to have more information than the people who work for you.

Encourage Employees to Ask Questions

You may not know the answers. If not, let them know that you don't. Otherwise they will suspect that you are hiding the truth, and they can only conclude that what you won't talk about is bad news for them.

The questions serve other useful purposes even if you can't answer them. First, they let you know what people are talking about, and sometimes those questions will reflect very wild speculation. You'll probably be able to quash extreme rumors. Second, they give you solid evidence with which to approach higher management and say, "Here's what people are worrying themselves with." You may get answers to some of the specific questions from your bosses. You can then take the information back.

If, however, your higher management frowns on hearing anything of an unpleasant nature from below, you may not want to take the questions and anxieties up to them. You probably won't get answers, and you will get the reputation of being a manager who identifies too closely with your employees.

Increase Your Contacts

Make yourself more visible and accessible during a crisis or when employees show anxiety. Some managers, feeling anxious themselves, spend more time behind closed doors at such times. Their isolation only increases the tension in the atmosphere. Walk around. Chat. Be seen. Even though you cannot allay all of the fears, your presence is a steadying force.

Don't Try to Put on a Happy Face

If you sense that things are serious, don't try to pretend otherwise. You don't have to be and shouldn't be dour, but you can't afford to be falsely cheerful, as if nothing bad is going on. When the truth is known, you will lose respect and credibility. Furthermore, you will appear as not caring.

THE MANAGER AS LISTENER

Here is sound advice to managers: Be open to what is going on around you. Are there dissatisfaction and demotivation among your employees? Has the anxiety level been on the rise? Are the rumor mills working overtime producing distortions of fact?

The evidence will come to you, if you stay open to it. You will hear, if you listen. But you get busy, become preoccupied with your own interests and tasks. You have good intentions. You mean to listen attentively. But perhaps you don't, always.

Busyness is not the only reason why you may fail to listen. Listening:

☐ Makes you more vulnerable to the deeper concerns and problems of your employees.

☐ Opens you up to criticism.

☐ Increases the chance that you may have to change as a result of what you hear.

Listening therefore is not without its risks. But the rewards of taking those risks are substantial. They include:

☐ More accurate information.
☐ Better understanding of your employees.
☐ Easier communication.
☐ Respect of your employees for you.
☐ An indication of your concern for employees.
☐ Reduction in unpleasant surprises.
☐ More control over your operation.

It's difficult to manage effectively without listening. You can't manage well if you don't know what's going on. And you can't really know what's going on unless you keep your ears open.

To make sure you listen well, consider the facts of good listening.

You Have to Want to Listen

If you don't believe that when the people with whom you work are speaking they are trying to tell you something important, you are likely to hear with only half an ear and may miss messages and meanings that can help you manage more effectively.

You Have to Listen Actively

This means focusing your attention on the person and concentrating on what he or she is saying. Merely being silent is not necessarily listening. If you are not listening actively, you may think you are getting the whole message, but chances are that you are not.

You Have to Listen with the Third Ear

Most words have more than one meaning, and they have to be decoded. This means paying attention to the situation, the attitudes and feelings of the persons speaking, and such subjective factors as their relationship to you, their fear of offending, and so on, if you are to get the message. Worse, you may get the wrong message if you don't.

You Have to Listen Nonjudgmentally

Nothing kills a potentially meaningful communication more swiftly and effectively than premature judgment or a critical stance on your part. People simply don't like negative reactions, and will clam up fast, even before they have given you the message, if they suspect what your response is going to be.

You Have to Listen to the Speaker's Words and Not Your Own

Too often, once people get the gist of what someone is saying, their minds start formulating a response, and they pay more attention to their own words than to the speaker's. The result is that they misinterpret and, worse, sometimes wind up arguing over something not really in dispute.

You Have to Listen with a Sense of Responsibility

Even the most articulate people will sometimes have difficulty saying exactly what they mean. As a listener, it's your responsibility to understand what the other person is saying, or trying to say.

You Have to Listen Empathetically

This means putting yourself in the other person's shoes to the extent that you can. It does not mean asking a lot of probing questions, or saying "I see" or "I understand" or "I know how you feel" if you don't. What it does mean is listening in an accepting way, maintaining eye contact, nodding when you do understand, and permitting your concern to show.

You Have to Listen Without Overreacting or Letting Your Own Emotions Get Out of Hand

Even if what the speaker is saying disturbs you, venting your anger or other emotion before the person is done will stifle further communication of that particular message. Worse, it may inhibit all communications, not only from that person but from other employees who will be afraid of a similar response from you.

Because listening can be hard work and is often unpleasant, it is no wonder that in organizations that experience trouble and demotivation among employees, management tries to reduce the flow of communication from employees. They don't want to hear bad news. As a result, a gap grows between how management sees the organization and the perceptions of employees. You cannot afford that kind of gap in your department if you hope to manage effectively. By keeping your channels with employees open, you will be able to anticipate problems, thanks to employees' information, that you might otherwise have not detected until they were full-blown.

Last but not least, your willingness to listen shows your employees that you respect them. No matter how troubled the rest of the organization, you can make a positive impact on the people who work for you by always being prepared to hear what they have to tell you. The information you need to manage will come to you.

MANAGING UPWARD

If your approach to management and motivation is substantially dissimilar to that encouraged and sanctioned by the organizational culture, you yourself will need some protecting. Probably the best person to do that is your boss. But if your boss is more in tune with the culture than you are, the boss may see you as a problem. If you are especially successful as a manager, the boss may see you as a threat. If your employees hold you in high regard and work hard for you when others in the organization are dispirited and demotivated, then your boss may be suspicious of you. The same holds true even if the organization functions healthily, but with a prevailing management style that is different from yours.

Your job is to reduce any threat or suspicion that the boss may feel toward you so that he or she can run interference for you. Here are some recommendations to help you build an alliance with the person you report to, no matter how different he or she may be.

Produce

This has to be the cornerstone of any successful reporting relationship. Your boss may not approve or understand your method of managing the motivation of your employees but, if the bottom line is favorable, he or she is less likely to do anything to impede you. Note the words, *less likely*. Be aware that if you are perceived by higher management as counterculture, even high productivity may not save you.

Keep Your Boss Informed Frequently

If your relationship is somewhat uncomfortable, it's natural for you to reduce the contacts you have with him or her. But that is self-defeating. The boss who isn't sure of what you're doing is likely to feel even more threatened or suspicious. So let the boss know rather regularly what you're up to, and what you plan to do.

Mute Your Self-Praise

In talking about what you're doing, you naturally want to describe significant accomplishments. As you do so, concentrate on the results and skip the part about how exceptional or brilliant you were in bringing them off. Treat your achievements as matter of factly as possible. There is no way, of course, that you can hide your success, but you can avoid rubbing your boss's nose in it.

Soft-Pedal Your Disagreement or Disparate Methods

Look for the things your boss does that you can praise. If you must take issue with your boss, do so in private and in a low-key manner. "I've been thinking about our discussion this morning, and I wondered about something that I thought I should check with you about."

Consult on Your Decisions

This is one of the best ways to reaffirm your subordination and to convey deference. You may have already made a decision, but you can let the boss know you value his or her thinking. There is a risk here, however. The boss, after being consulted, may disagree with your line of reasoning. If that occurs, you ought to give serious consideration to following the advice you've solicited. Perhaps the safest thing to do is to consult your boss on those decisions on which you truly are undecided or in cases where you believe you know the boss's thinking.

Let the Boss Know You Appreciate the Help

Even if the help was minor, acknowledge your appreciation of the time your boss took to assist or advise you. If you achieved the results entirely on your own, let the boss know how grateful you are that you have been given the opportunity and the resources to do a good job. In effect, you are saying, "You've given me the chance to do what I want to do, and I thank you for that."

GETTING POWER FROM YOUR PEOPLE

If you believe that the roots of your demotivation problems are in the management culture of the organization as a whole, you may point the finger at executives up the line and say, in effect, those are the people who are fouling us up. If only they would make the proper decisions, listen to our suggestions, stop interfering with my operations, give more concern to my people, and so on.

That is management by martyrdom. Martyrs, as you know, have no choice but to await their tragic fate. They are powerless.

There's a big difference between being powerless and perceiving yourself to be so. Even in the most autocratic and bureaucratic organizations, managers still have discretion. They can set performance standards for their employees. They can help their people to work more effectively, to get better results from their efforts. They can inspire, guide, direct, and train employees who perform well, even if that reward is a simple, "That was a great job you did." The organization may be chaotic, but managers can run tidy departments. You may feel unrewarded and unappreciated by top management, but you can derive a great sense of achievement and satisfaction from seeing your own people turn in work that is high both in quantity and quality.

There may be many times when you feel that you do not get what you need and want from the people above you. But that does not necessarily mean you are powerless. Look to the people who work for you. Give them what they need and want so they will do a good job for you. Let them know what your standards and goals are. Give them feedback, both positive and negative, while they work to achieve those goals. And when they have done a good job, let them know that you know they've done well.

When subordinates want to perform well for you, they can make you feel and be very powerful indeed.

THE NURTURING MANAGER.

There is another role of a successful manager that is little talked about: nurturer. The role of a nurturing manager is especially important and effective in an environment that is demotivating or is alien to the manager's style. A nurturing manager protects and enhances the growth of the work group, and exhibits caring behavior toward its members. The nurturing manager may not be motivated by sentiment as much as by pragmatism. After all, an effective work group gives much power and prestige to a manager. It provides him or her with a sense of achievement. The manager has done the shaping, the stimulating, and the guiding. The health and vitality of the work group are due in large part to the concern and care of the manager. The nurturing manager provides an atmosphere in which the group flourishes and prospers, in which each member achieves growth according to his or her capacity. A nurtured group takes care of its members—and of its manager.

ACCOMMODATING TO THE CULTURE

If a manager is not in close accord with the organizational culture, its values and style, he or she can still work effectively by:

☐ Developing a work group in which the personal objectives of the members are recognized and their achievement is enhanced.

☐ Muting public knowledge of the differences between the work group and the rest of the organization, even though those differences may have accounted for substantial success of the group.

☐ Cultivating positive working relationships with his or her manager and other managers in which the manager joins with co-workers in working to accomplish organizational objectives, even though the means of accomplishment are different.

Put another way, an organization will tolerate a maverick if the manager has a record of success, does not flaunt his or her differences from the prevailing style and culture, and seeks collaborative rather than competitive working relationships with others.

	Yes	No	Not Sure
1. Organizational culture has to do with the organization's value, priorities, traditions, and structure.	____	____	____
2. Generally the most successful members of the organization are those who share its value, style, and outlook.	____	____	____
3. A manager who does not share in the organizational culture is sometimes isolated by others in the organization.	____	____	____
4. Employees who report to a maverick manager often experience demotivation because of the relative powerlessness of their boss.	____	____	____
5. Unless you are careful and discreet, being a successful manager of motivation in a culture in which most people are demotivated will make you an alien to the culture.	____	____	____
6. If a number of your employees are experiencing demotivation, the explanation could be that you are not adequately communicating your standards, showing appreciation for good work, or disciplining when it is called for.	____	____	____

7. One very important function that you must fulfill is that of protector, defining organizational goals and

	Yes	No	Not Sure
setting priorities if none have been established by higher management.	____	____	____
8. When introducing change, you should try to convey positive expectations that the net effect will be good.	____	____	____
9. If you disagree with the change, then you have an obligation to your employees to let them know.	____	____	____
10. You should try to keep your subordinates as informed as possible as to what is going on in the organization, even though higher management may withhold information.	____	____	____
11. If things are serious in the organization, you should try to put on a cheerful face to keep employees from knowing that things are not well.	____	____	____
12. If you want to know what your employees are thinking and doing, you must be prepared to listen actively and often.	____	____	____
13. When listening, you must keep your emotions in hand even when you hear disturbing information.	____	____	____
14. You must broadcast your willingness to hear news that is unpleasant.	____	____	____
15. If your boss regards you suspiciously or as a threat, you must be prepared to increase your contacts and the information you give him or her.	____	____	____

	Yes	No	Not Sure
16. If you are not considered a true member of the culture, you will most likely experience powerlessness.	___	___	___
17. You should play a nurturing role with your subordinates, protecting them, enhancing their growth, and caring for their well-being.	___	___	___
18. Even if you are a maverick in the culture, you can still survive with a record of success and much discretion.	___	___	___

Answers to Review

1. Yes
2. Yes
3. Yes
4. Yes
5. Yes
6. Yes
7. Yes
8. Yes
9. No. You should keep your disagreement to yourself.
10. Yes
11. No. Don't pretend. That will hurt your credibility with employees. But don't show pessimism either. That will hurt you with higher management.
12. Yes
13. Yes
14. Yes
15. Yes
16. Not sure. You can be empowered by your subordinates if you enable them to work effectively for you.
17. Yes
18. Yes

3

EXPRESSING YOUR
MANAGERIAL NEEDS

As a manager, you have a right to communicate to the people who report to you what you need and want from them. In fact, you have an obligation to do so—to yourself, to your organization, and to your subordinates. As has been pointed out, your people have to know what you expect of them in order to work according to your standards and achieve your objectives. They need to know how well they work according to those standards. When they have—or have not—achieved your objectives, they need to know that as well. Thus, if you are to have an effective work group, your communication is vital when you set goals, evaluate performance, correct performance deficiencies, and recognize achievement. All of this communicating plays a vital role in the motivation of subordinates.

What ?

But *what* you communicate is only one factor. *How* is equally important. You can tell the salesperson that you want more sales calls made, the production worker that you want quotas met regularly, the clerical worker or data processor that you want output increased. But, if in the telling you create confusion or resentment, you might as well have saved your words. You might even be better off if you had said nothing. Resentful employees will give you grudging cooperation, at best, but their feelings toward you and the work could undermine their motivation. To have an effective work group, you need employees who involve themselves in the work you want them to do and commit themselves to achieving your objectives.

how ?

Thus, your mode of behavior in communicating has much to do with whether you get poor, barely adequate, good, or even excellent performance from subordinates.

MANAGERIAL AGGRESSIVENESS

To illustrate, here is a somewhat exasperated sales manager giving feedback to a salesman:

> I've just been through your call reports, and I have to admit I wonder about you. I've told you a hundred times if I've told you once that you are to confine your service calls to after three in the afternoon. Yet, I look at your reports, and there you are making service calls at eleven in the morning, and right after lunch. I know you're not stupid. You certainly can understand this simple message: Don't make service calls during your prime selling time. I guess the answer is that you don't care enough to listen to what I tell you. Well, you'd better start caring. Or else you can go frustrate someone else.

Obviously the sales manager is angry. But he is also being *aggressive*. Aggressiveness, which ironically is sometimes described as a managerial virtue or a characteristic of people on the fast track, disregards the rights and dignity of others. Aggressive statements often put people down, and embarrass or humiliate them.

People who are aggressive often impute undesirable or unpleasant motives to others. (Managers who are truly effective in managing the motivation of employees find it more desirable to deal with employees' behaviors and performance than with their attitudes or motives. In short, they deal with the *what* rather than with the *why*.)

The sales manager may say, "I know you're not stupid," but his other words belie that message. He starts out by telling the salesman that he "wonders" about him. He reminds the salesman that he, the manager, has warned him about making service calls during the day a "hundred times." Then he adds, "You can certainly understand this simple message." The implication is that the manager is making the message so simple that even this salesman can grasp it. So much for the salesman's intelligence. The second putdown is the suggestion that the salesman doesn't "care enough to listen" to the manager's directions. It's one thing to suggest that the salesman has in fact not heard very well. But it's quite another to charge the salesman with not caring to listen.

What are the likely consequences of this aggressive approach? The manager may see some improvement in the salesman's performance. On the other hand, the salesman may continue to do just what he has done and conceal that fact by doing a bit of creative writing in his call reports. The long-term results could be self-defeating. The salesman probably feels resentment over his treatment. The manager may eventually lose him, and if the salesman is a good performer, that's a pity.

It's true that some managers believe in being aggressive because they are "modeling" such behavior after managers whom they regard as successful. In days long past, such a style of manager was labeled "bull of the woods." He was likely to depend on bellowing and intimidating employees to get what he wanted.

More often people who make aggressive statements don't mean to be offensive. It's usually a matter of not knowing how to deal with negative feelings or how to express themselves. Because they do not know how to express wants, needs, and emotions, they suppress their feelings. Later, something will trigger an emotional outburst, and they lose control of what they say (and lose sight of what they really want to accomplish).

If you tend to be aggressive, you could be undermining the effectiveness—or the desire to be effective—of your subordinates. If most of the following statements apply to you and your employees, you may wish to develop a greater awareness of how you communicate with them:

- [ ] People generally seem uncomfortable around you.
- [ ] You suspect that people don't bring you sufficient information about what is going on in the organization.
- [ ] People usually avoid eye contact with you.
- [ ] Employees do not regularly initiate discussion with you.
- [ ] In a staff meeting, you often find yourself working hard to get people to contribute ideas.
- [ ] Your statements to others frequently seem to arouse defensive reactions in them.
- [ ] People, especially your subordinates, are guarded in their conversations with you, causing you to wonder whether they are leveling with you.
- [ ] Other people seldom bring problems to you.
- [ ] When you attempt to be humorous, employees laugh hesitantly.
- [ ] Employees respond to your questions or opinions with brief, quick answers.

NONASSERTIVENESS

The nonassertive manager can hardly be thought of as a manager. Employees who are in conflict bring the problem to the nonassertive manager, and he or she says, "Work it out the best you can." People come to him or her for a decision, and the response is, "Do whatever you think best." Nonassertiveness is abdication. As the aggressive manager tramples the turf of others, the nonassertive person practically invites others to trample his or her turf. Make a strong request of this person, and the result is a cave-in. He or she has no boundaries that are effective in protecting his or her interests. Employees of nonassertive bosses find that neither are their own interests looked after.

Here is how the extremes of the communicating spectrum appear:

Aggressiveness	Nonassertiveness
Totally you, excluding others	Totally others, excluding you

The nonassertive manager does not achieve objectives or maintain standards because no one is quite sure what they are. Working for such a person can be an intensely dissatisfying and demotivating experience.

THE ASSERTIVE MANAGER

An assertive statement conveys what you want without stepping on the other person. For example, let's tune in again on the sales manager who disapproves of some of his salesman's activities:

I've just been through your call reports, and I notice that you've made some service calls at eleven in the morning and right after lunch. You and I have discussed this before, and you'll recall that I asked you to confine service calls to after three in the afternoon. Otherwise you're cutting in on prime selling time. I'm very upset about your continuing to do what I asked you not to do. I want your assurance that you will, except in emergencies, abide by my policy: no service calls until late afternoon. If you continue to make them in the morning and early afternoon, I shall have to consider that in my next performance evaluation of you.

That's a clearcut statement of what the manager wants and how he feels. It's an assertive statement. In contrast to the aggressive remarks quoted earlier, it does not suggest stupidity or indifference on the part of the salesman. It's typically assertive, in that it consists of four elements:

1. *A description of what is going on.* The salesman is making service calls in a time period that the manager has asked him to reserve for sales calls.

2. *An expression of the feelings of the person talking.* The sales manager is upset that the salesman is continuing to do what the manager asked him not to do.

3. *A definition of the change that should take place.* The salesman is to refrain from making service calls until after three in the afternoon.

4. *A clear statement of the benefits to the other person in making the change.* If you don't do as I tell you, the manager asserts, it will be noted in your next appraisal. In other cases, the benefit would not be avoiding pain but enjoying a pleasure. "Pull this off and I'll recommend a promotion (or a raise)."

Assertiveness is conveyed in ways other than the words themselves. Assertive people generally maintain eye contact. Their gestures are natural and proportionate to what they are saying. Their tempo is moderate, not slow and halting or aggressively fast. The tone and volume firm up the meaning of the words. If they are angry, the pitch goes up, and so does the volume. They stand or sit firmly. They don't slouch. Words, posture, and gestures are all an integral part of the message. When you hear an assertive person, you do not receive mixed messages, or see gestures that convey one message while the words convey another.

GETTING RESULTS THROUGH ASSERTIVENESS

You are manufacturing manager in a machine tool company. Not long ago, the production manager who had reported to you for a year (since your promotion) left for another job elsewhere. His assistant moved into the position. Since he took over, you've experienced problems with meeting production deadlines. On your tours of the plant floor, you see some groups working to capacity while others seem to have little to do. It appears to be a problem of scheduling. You speak to your production manager about it, and he agrees to correct the work flow.

One week after your discussion, the problem has not been solved. An important deadline is missed. Once again, you call the manager into your office.

You: I'm getting a lot of flak from the front office because we didn't get this job done on time. The customer is upset. Now I'm upset. You said you'd work the problem out by now.

Manager: Don't get upset with me. I'm on top of the situation. Another couple of days, and there won't be any trouble.

You: That's almost the same thing you said to me last week.

Manager: I know that. But I can't pull off a miracle.

You: I didn't ask for a miracle. You told me the problem was easy, that you'd have it fixed inside of a week. But it isn't.

Manager: I didn't anticipate what happened. I had to take Friday off to get my daughter to the doctor.

You: I'm sorry to hear that. But you and I had an agreement.

Manager: I don't know why you're so hot under the collar. I don't think you have a right to be.

You: It's not a question of whether I have a right to be. I am. I want you to know that. Do you?

Manager: Yes.

You: Okay. Now what about our agreement?

Manager: I told you I'm working on it. I've been having a lot of problems with Tom Mulqueen over in Maintenance. That slowed me up, too.

You: How long has this been going on?

Manager: For a long time.

You: But you knew that when you gave me your assurances. Let me make it very clear. I want our deadlines met. Do you understand that?

Manager: Sure, but ...

You: That's what I want. Now when can you have everything in place? Realistically.

Manager: Give me four days.

You: All right. In four days you'll have revamped your scheduling procedures. If you don't, then that fact will be reflected in your next appraisal—and your salary review. If you succeed, I'll note in your appraisal that you solved a costly problem.

CONFRONTING AND CONTROLLING

In the above conversation, all of the four elements of a genuinely assertive statement are present. You described what was going on, how you felt about it, what change you wanted to take place, and the benefits to the manager in making that change. But you also accomplished the following:

1.   *You confronted the issues.*   There was never a mention of the manager's personality or attitudes. It was strictly, "You promised to change your scheduling, and you didn't." When you stay with the issues in feedback or conflict or evaluating performance, you are more likely to get the subordinate's agreement that a problem exists than if you seem to attack the person.

2.   *You expressed your feelings and insisted that the subordinate accept them.*   He didn't have to agree with them. In fact, he didn't. But in communicating it is important that the other person know how you feel even if he or she doesn't feel the same way—or isn't sure *why* you have the feelings you do. Why you have those feelings is not as essential to good communicating as the fact that you do.

3.   *You controlled the interaction.*   That is not the same as dominating. You guided the discussion to the end you desired. You kept it on track, despite the subordinate's attempt to bring in extraneous issues. You never lost sight of your objective.

BENEFITING FROM BEING ASSERTIVE

Consistent assertive behavior brings you more than the immediate benefits of confronting issues, getting your feelings out, and controlling your interactions with others. Such behavior establishes you as a credible and trustworthy person (and credibility is indispensable in effective management). You acquire a reputation as a person who is straightforward, who says, "This is what I see. This is what I feel. This is what I want." People come to believe they know where they stand with you. Your subordinates especially will take comfort in knowing that you are not a manipulator of people.

Assertiveness thus increases your influence with others. They know that in a transaction with you they can get right down to negotiating with you, discussing what has happened, and what may have to be done about it. They don't have to expend valuable time and energy wondering whether you are being honest with them or playing games with them. (See the Action Plan below.)

Your assertiveness encourages people to want to work with you. They don't have to wonder what your position is on an issue. They don't have to worry about your attacking them personally, since it is known that you stick to the issues. They don't have to try to interpret your real feelings, since you reveal them yourself. You don't try to disguise them or rationalize them.

Being assertive doesn't always win you friends. Many people who trust you won't necessarily like you. After all, when you are assertive, you may frequently tell others what they would rather not hear. But your co-workers, even your subordinates, don't have to like you. If they respect you, they will work with you.

Aggressiveness	Assertiveness	Nonassertiveness
Totally you, excluding others	Primarily you, secondarily others	Totally others, excluding you

AN ACTION PLAN CALLING
FOR ASSERTIVENESS

1. Description of a problem that exists between you and an employee: _____
   _____
   _____
   _____

2. Here are your statements to resolve the problem assertively, covering the four main elements:
   A. A description of what is going on: _____
   _____
   _____
   _____
   _____

   B. How you feel about what is going on: _____
   _____
   _____
   _____
   _____

   C. The change you would like to see take place: _____
   _____
   _____
   _____
   _____

   D. The benefits to the other person from making the change:
   _____
   _____
   _____
   _____

3. You plan to make this assertive statement by (date):
   _____

ADDING A DIMENSION TO ASSERTIVENESS

Assertiveness is not, however, the only alternative behavior to aggressiveness or nonassertiveness. If it were, there would be serious deficiencies in communicating. In every transaction, there are at least two sets of needs and wants, at least two people who would like to assert what is important and of value to each other. If there is to be a transaction, true communication, someone must listen to the assertions. In most cases, there must be a responsive mode of behavior as well as an assertive one. Thus the scale that appears above would look like this:

Aggressiveness	Assertiveness	Responsiveness	Nonassertiveness
Totally you, excluding others	Primarily you, secondarily others	Primarily others, secondarily you	Totally others, excluding you

Responsiveness, therefore, is a legitimate and necessary way to behave in certain situations or at certain times in a discussion. Here is how the two moderate modes of behavior compare.

Assertiveness	Responsiveness
Gives information	Seeks information
Expresses feelings	Accepts the feelings of the other without necessarily agreeing with them
Describes behavior change desired in others	Seeks a change of behavior in self
"Sells" benefits of change to others	"Sells" self on benefits of change

Depending on the results they want, most people choose between assertiveness and responsiveness. When you decide to be responsive, you want information from another person that you think could be useful.

CHOOSING RESPONSIVENESS

As a manager, you may decide to place yourself in a subordinate position of responsiveness when talking with one of your employees in the following kinds of situations:

☐ When you take over an operation that is new to you. You want to learn about the ways things are done, the culture of the organization, and how employees feel about the work and the organization.

☐ When you set goals and want people to express to you what aspects of the work and what potential accomplishments are important to them.

☐ You are counseling an employee on a work-related problem or performance deficiency, and you are not quite sure what might be causing the problem. You have to draw the employee out to find out how he or she views the situation and to get agreement that a problem exists.

☐ An employee has suffered a personal loss or is enduring a crisis in his or her personal life.

☐ When you are confronted by an employee who is in an intensely emotional state, you may feel that for the moment it would not help to counter assertion or aggression with your own assertion.

☐ You are at a meeting and you want to encourage others to assume leadership positions in the group without being intimidated by your presence or your opinions.

☐ You are listening to an employee for whom you have the greatest admiration or respect.

In general you will want to be responsive, as well as assertive, in any kind of interaction in which you suspect that the other person brings knowledge or resources to the discussion that could be useful. It's a learning opportunity for you. To illustrate, the following manager is dissatisfied with a report that she has requested of a subordinate:

Manager: John, I think we need to talk about this report. I'm very surprised by it. It's not the kind of work I've come to expect of you. Frankly, I'm unhappy with it. It's incomplete and, furthermore, in places it just looks thrown together.

Subordinate: Well, I'm unhappy about it, too. More than that, I'm angry.

Manager: Why are you angry?

The manager started by being assertive. She gave information about what was going on and described how she felt about it. She was met by what seemed to be a counter assertion. She encountered a hint of information she didn't have, so she adopted a responsive mode of behavior. She now seeks the information she doesn't have.

Subordinate: Because it seems as if you're piling on the work these days. I know we had to cut back on staff, and I know that I have to do more with less. I also know that you are sort of dumping on me.

Manager: How am I doing that?

Subordinate: Well, take this report. You told me you wanted this done by the first. Then, just last week, you gave me that Lieberman proposal to go over and give my okay to. Right in the middle of that, you come to me and tell me that you'd like more time to go over this report before you have to send it on. So you shorten my deadline by a week. This isn't the first time it has happened. No, I'm not happy with this report, but you said you absolutely had to have it by today, and you have it.

The manager now has more information, and she realizes that it is valid. She goes to the next step in the responsive mode.

Manager: What you're saying is that you'd be able to do better work if I didn't change deadlines on you or interrupt what I've already given you to have you do something else?

Subordinate: Most of the time, that's right. I can make allowances for emergencies usually but, for the most part, I need a schedule that I can depend on. And it's better for me and the work if I can finish one big project before starting another.

Manager: Okay, that's fair. From now on I'll keep a written record of what I assign you. That way, I'll know what you're working on and when it's due.

The manager has defined a change in her behavior for herself. The benefits are clear. She'll most likely get better work out of a valued employee, and she'll have an employee who feels better about working for her.

MANAGING AND RESPONSIVENESS

In managing the motivation of your employees, you realize how important their commitment and involvement are. You want more than grudging acceptance of your goals, a go-along-to-get-along mentality, which is what many managers get from subordinates. No doubt in your work experience you've seen many departments and organizations in which employees responded to managers' orders and assertions with a shrug that says, "If that's what they want, I'll give what I have to give to stay out of trouble."

But when employees can participate in setting goals, when they can make suggestions and offer constructive criticism, when they can contribute their skills, knowledge, and resources to planning and executing, when they can join you in searching for solutions to performance problems, when they, in short, can take credit along with you for successful accomplishments of goals and tasks, they are much more likely to involve themselves and to commit themselves to your and the organization's objectives. They are much more likely to work hard as highly motivated employees. (See the Action Plan following.)

AN ACTION PLAN CALLING FOR
RESPONSIVENESS

1. Description of a problem or a need for discussion that exists between you and an employee: _____

   _____
   _____
   _____
   _____

2. Here are your statements to resolve the problem or to construct the discussion responsively, covering the four main elements.
   A. To seek a description of what is going on: _____

   _____
   _____
   _____
   _____
   _____

   B. To find out how the other person feels about what is going on: _____

   _____
   _____
   _____
   _____
   _____

   C. The change you might make in yourself: _____

   _____
   _____
   _____
   _____
   _____

   D. The benefits to you in making that change: _____

   _____
   _____
   _____
   _____

3. You plan to make this responsive statement by (date): ____

When you as manager are responsive to your subordinates, you are involving them. You are making them team members. You are appealing to the motivating forces in them.

If your predominant mode of behavior is responsive, however, you may find other people often getting what they want without your achieving your best interests.

Predominantly responsive people often share some of the following experiences or characteristics:

- ☐ They have many acquaintances but sense that they lack a satisfying number of substantial relationships.
- ☐ In many of their meaningful relationships, they have the disquieting suspicion that they give much more than they receive.
- ☐ Frequently they have the feeling that they are not in the organizational mainstream.
- ☐ Their ideas may not be taken seriously by the people they work with.
- ☐ Other people tend to offer them unsolicited advice on how to do things.
- ☐ Frequently they hear criticism that they are not firm enough in dealing with others, that they are too easy.
- ☐ They often sense that people don't really listen to them.
- ☐ They sometimes suspect that people try to dominate them.
- ☐ In their dealings with others, they suspect that many people are just being polite.

People who are excessively responsive cheat themselves, because they are hesitant to assert their needs and wants. They have problems in their relationships with others, in gaining respect, in being taken seriously, and in protecting their own boundaries.

COMBINING THE BEST OF TWO MODES

In extreme cases of both behaviors—assertiveness and responsiveness—the result may be what is called a zero-sum game: One person is a clear winner and the other a definite loser. In most healthy situations, each party—including manager and subordinate—would like to experience win–win. Both get at least a part of what they want.

Furthermore, in many interactions people want not only a short-term or immediate result, they hope for some long-range benefits. This is especially true in manager–subordinate relationships. A problem that is solved or an unpleasant situation that is remedied will have a beneficial effect on the relationship in the future.

In a balanced assertive–responsive approach, you exchange information and feelings. You seek a change in behavior jointly, with benefits for both of you. The assertive–responsive approach has the following characteristics:

☐ It acknowledges the rights and feelings of each person in a transaction.

☐ It creates a dialogue in which each person feels comfortable expressing feelings about what is going on.

☐ It recognizes that each person has needs, wants, and resources. The resolution or outcome may but need not be all one person's effort.

Those are characteristics that contribute strongly to building a solid, constructive working relationship. Here's how the scale of modes of behavior would look with the recognition of a separate and distinct assertiveness–responsiveness approach:

Aggressive-ness	Assertive-ness	Assertive-ness–Responsive-ness	Responsive-ness	Nonassertive-ness
Totally you, excluding others	Primarily you, excluding others	Almost equally you and others	Primarily others, secondarily you	Totally others, excluding you

In any normal, healthy interaction between you and others, you are unlikely to give up your primacy entirely. No matter how strongly you wish to be responsive as well as assertive, there will be at least a slight predominance of your assertiveness.

A TIME FOR ASSERTIVENESS

There are times in managing when assertiveness should predominate. For example, you've counseled an employee with respect to a recurring performance problem. You've been responsive and, you believe, patient. But despite the sessions and performance improvement plans, the problem still exists. Then you may feel—and are probably justified in that feeling—that an assertion of what you want from the employee is necessary: "There has been no improvement. I am unhappy about that. I expect you to abide by the performance improvement plan that we discussed and agreed on, and to accomplish it within three months. If you have not overcome the problem by the end of that probationary time, I shall have to terminate you."

There are other circumstances that point to the need for you to assert yourself, which include the following:

☐ *There Is an Immediate Danger or Emergency.* An employee violates a safety regulation and puts others in jeopardy. There is no question that the employee knows the regulation. An assertion in the form of a warning is called for. Or, a crisis exists. Something must be done in a short period of time. Perhaps people are fearful and demoralized. You pull rank: This is what has happened. This is what I want you to do.

☐ *Conflict Has Polarized.* Two of your employees have been feuding. They no longer seem to be able to work out their problems, with or without your help. For the sake of the department's effectiveness and the welfare of those who must work with the combatants, you set the ground rules and make it clear that you expect them to be observed. You can't make them like each other, but you can require that they do the work.

☐ *Employees Don't Know What To Do.* And you do. If they can't bring resources to the work, there may be little point in consulting them. If they don't know what to do or how to do something, they'll probably welcome your stepping in.

MANAGING ASSERTIVELY–RESPONSIVELY

While aggressiveness and nonassertiveness are never appropriate behaviors in managing people, assertiveness, responsiveness, and a combination of the two can be very effective in such functions as setting goals, appraising, criticizing, and counseling. To illustrate the flexibility of a good manager, the following is an interview that takes place between an executive, Steve, and a key manager reporting to him named Frank. The occasion of the interview is a quarterly performance evaluation of Frank. Steve has been reviewing the goals that the two of them had agreed on in the previous quarter.

Steve: I have to say that your record is very good, with one exception.

Frank: I know. The total processing unit.

Steve: Right. You and I agreed three months ago that you would set up a self-contained processing team as a pilot. I got the impression from you that you saw no problem in having the pilot team operative by now. But it hasn't been formed. Has there been any progress at all?

Frank: Well, not as we agreed. I've selected the members of the unit, but that's as far as I've gotten.

Steve: Want to tell me what's going on? Or rather, what's not going on?

Would you describe Steve's mode of behavior up to this point as assertive, responsive, or assertive—responsive?

Steve is describing what he sees is going on, or rather what should be going on, as opposed to what is reality. Then he asks Frank how *Frank* sees the situation, and Frank responds. Both people are therefore giving information. The mode of behavior is *assertive—responsive.*

Frank: I asked Jean Simmons to be the team leader. But then, she was off for a while, sick. That threw my schedule off quite a bit. It's also taking more time than I thought to train Jean's replacement in her regular job as supervisor.

Steve: How long was Jean out?

Frank: About a month, maybe closer to five weeks.

Steve: Did you know when she first reported sick that it would be that serious, that she'd be out that long?

Frank: After the first week or so, I figured Jean wouldn't be back for a while.

Steve: So in view of Jean's absence, what did you decide to do about the pilot program?

Frank: I decided to let it wait.

Steve: Was there anyone else you think might have been able to take over the team leader's spot or who could have been able to train Jean's replacement?

Frank: Looking back, maybe. At the time, I didn't give it much thought. I saw Jean as the best person for the pilot, and I was pretty sure she would be coming back.

Steve: So you didn't have a contingency plan?

Frank: I didn't see a need.

Review this segment of the discussion and describe Steve's behavior as assertive, responsive, or assertive–responsive.

Steve is gathering information. He is therefore predominantly in the *responsive* mode.

Steve: Now that's something I don't understand, that you didn't see a need to have an alternate plan.

Frank: As I said, I knew that Jean was coming back. I had talked with her about the new job, and she was excited about doing it. So I decided not to replace her. That would have been a big blow to her. Besides, although there might have been some-one else who could have done the job, I thought Jean was, all things considered, the best choice.

Steve: I understand that, Frank. But there was also the matter of the schedule we had agreed on.

Frank: Well, Steve, I may have been wrong, but I looked at the options and decided to stay with Jean, even though it might hold up the project a bit. You look as though you don't agree.

Steve: I have some questions about your holding up the project. You and I set an objective, that you would have the self-contained processing team operating by the end of the quarter. You changed that objective on your own, without consulting me. And that makes me angry. This project is very important to me. So is the principle involved here. You changed an objective that we agreed on without even checking with me to get my okay. Frank, for the future, I want you to promise me that you will never change a goal we've agreed on without discussing it with me.

If you describe Steve's mode of behavior as *assertive* you are on target. Taking the data that he has received from Frank, Steve describes the situation and also makes it clear how he feels about what he sees. He gives information and expresses feelings.

Frank: All right, Steve, I understand, and I agree. But I think there's something *you* should understand. I may have been wrong to make the decision entirely on my own, but there have been times in the past three months when you weren't the easiest person in the world to talk to. I don't think I'm rationalizing, but I made some decisions on my own because you gave me the impression that's what you wanted.

Steve: Oh? I don't think I understand.

Frank: About the same time Jean was out, I came to you on some other matters. I wanted to change some work assignments and some schedules. You told me to go ahead and do what I thought best. You just didn't seem to have time to talk to me. Now these were important matters, too. But you couldn't spare the time. I agree with you, looking back, that I was wrong to postpone the pilot project on my own initiative, but you can see where I may have gotten the idea that it was all right with you if I saw a need to do that.

Steve: I see your point, Frank. I had spent a lot of time on my budgets, and they came back to me for reworking. I had to scale them down a bit, and I didn't have much time.

Frank: Right.

Steve: Well, there may be times again when that will happen. And I think it was perfectly acceptable for you to make those changes in assignments and schedules on your own, after I said I couldn't take the time to discuss them.

However, when it comes to an important objective, I have to repeat: I don't want it changed without being consulted. I think the solution to the problem in the future is for you to make it clear whether we're talking about something like the changes you wanted to make in assignments or a goal that we've agreed on. I promise you that I'll make time.

Frank: Understood.

How would you describe what has happened in the last segment of the interview?

Even though Steve is firm in reasserting his policy that no jointly set goal should be changed without his being consulted, the modes of behavior in the preceding segment vary from *responsiveness* to *assertiveness*. Steve seeks information. His acceptance of Frank's feelings is implied. Steve looks for a way to make a change in himself. He promises his subordinate that if Frank makes it clear he wants to talk about a goal, Steve will make room in his schedule for him.

Steve: Now that that's settled, let's talk about our goals for the coming quarter. I am very anxious to get the pilot program underway. Are you still enthusiastic about it?

Frank: I can't see anything holding us back. Jean's excited about it. So am I.

Steve: If this project works out, we'll be changing the whole system and, I hope, save a great deal of money. What remains to be done? How soon can we be operating?

Steve has returned to an *assertive—responsive* mode. He describes what is going on: He wants the program started. His feelings are enthusiastic. He checks with Frank to see what the subordinate's feelings are. Steve describes the possible benefits of success. Then he solicits Frank's help in moving from plan to reality.

Interestingly, Steve has moved from appraisal to counseling to criticism back to setting goals. In doing so, he has varied his behaviors to make them appropriate for the job he wanted to do.

THE VIRTUE OF FLEXIBILITY

Experienced and successful managers are usually good at being assertive. (Not being assertive is probably one of the most common reasons for managerial failure.) They get a lot of practice telling people what they want, need, and expect as they move through the hierarchical levels. As they go higher, they pick up more power, which makes it even easier for them to assert themselves. However, letting people know what you want and getting it may be two quite different matters.

The fact is that the day is fast disappearing when managers can say, "Do this," or "I want that," and be confident that it will all work out exactly as they wish. In today's organizational world, assertiveness, though necessary, is not enough.

Employees want to be respected, treated with esteem, listened to, recognized as having ideas and knowledge about the work they do. They bring talents, strengths, and resources to their jobs. Perhaps most important, they have personal goals that they hope to accomplish through working to help you achieve your and the organization's goals.

You may not always be aware of your subordinates' personal goals. To a large extent, you have to depend upon your observation of people at work to determine what they seem to like and do best. Your observation gives you clues to what motivates your subordinates.

But there's another way you can uncover people's motivating forces: opening yourself up to what people are thinking, feeling, and saying. When you seek information about what they perceive as going on in the job and the organization, about how they feel about the conditions under which they work, and about what changes might help them to perform even better, you advance your knowledge of what drives your people. You take the first steps to enhance the motivating forces within them.

Often, through acting on the information you obtain by being responsive as well as assertive, you find that the most advantageous thing you can do is remove the obstacles to better performance. That is, get yourself and the organization out of their way. At other times, you have to make more profound changes, such as revising procedures, improving the quality of supervision, providing training, or reassigning duties. The important point to keep in mind is that you need the information. The more you have, the better you can generate and evaluate your options.

As a manager, you can't get what you want without the help of others, especially your subordinates. And they won't give you what you need on a consistent basis unless it is important for them to do so. You can't find out what is important to them until you involve them in your thinking, planning, and decision making. (See the Action Plan following.)

AN ACTION PLAN CALLING FOR
ASSERTIVENESS–RESPONSIVENESS

1. Description of a problem or a need for discussion that exists between you and an employee: _____
    _____
    _____
    _____
    _____
    _____

2. Here are your statements to resolve the problem or to construct the discussion assertively–responsively, covering the eight main elements.

    A. A description of what you think is going on: _____
    _____
    _____
    _____
    _____

    A (1) What you plan to say to the other person to find out what he or she believes is going on: _____
    _____
    _____
    _____
    _____

    B. How you feel about what is going on: _____
    _____
    _____
    _____
    _____

    B (1). How you will find out the other person's feelings:
    _____
    _____
    _____

C.   The change you would like to see take place in you:

_____
_____
_____
_____

C (1).   The change you would like to see take place in the other person: _____

_____
_____
_____

D.   The benefits to you in making the change:

_____
_____
_____
_____

D (1).   The benefits to the employee in making the change:

_____
_____
_____
_____

3.   You plan to make this assertive–responsive statement by (date): _____

While the remainder of this book is designed to help you to apply specific and practical techniques to enhance the motivating forces within your subordinates, to encourage them to work harder and more effectively, to make it more likely that they will increase their involvement and commitment, the message in this chapter underlies all of those techniques. For you to be successful in applying them, you must listen as well as talk. You must be as concerned with the feelings of others as you are with your own. You must have a clear idea of what your subordinates need and want of you just as you tell them what you need and want of them. Finally, you must be prepared to show them that there are benefits to their doing what you want.

IDENTIFYING THE COMPONENTS OF ASSERTIVENESS, RESPONSIVENESS, AND ASSERTIVENESS-RESPONSIVENESS

The following exercise is intended to provide a review of this chapter. As you follow the discussion between you and your sales manager to evaluate his performance, identify in the space provided the following modes:

☐ Giving information
☐ Seeking information
☐ Expressing feelings
☐ Accepting feelings
☐ Change desired (in self or other)
☐ Benefits of change

You: Tim, you and I agreed six months ago that you would increase our field sales force by a net of six salespeople, and that gross sales would be pushed up by 20 percent.
What is the component of behavior?   a. _____

Is that your understanding of what we agreed to in the previous evaluation?   b. _____

Tim: Yes.

You: However, during these past six months, the net increase in salespeople has been only three. And the sales volume has gone up less than 10 percent.   c. _____

You: Are my figures correct?   d. _____

Tim: They're correct.

You: Well, I have to say I'm very disappointed at these results. At our first meeting, you and I agreed that these figures were not unrealistic. In fact, you came up with these specific figures. So I gather you're not altogether happy with the results.
                                              e. _____

Tim: I'm very unhappy. I don't, however, think that it is entirely my fault that we didn't make the goals.

You: I believe you are unhappy. Still, the goals we agreed to are important. Unfortunately the previous six months' goals were not met either. So I have to ask you, what has to happen for us to reach these goals?

f. _____

g. _____

h. _____

Tim: I'm training my assistant to accept more of the administrative tasks for me. That will free me to spend more time in the field—about a third more.

You: Okay. Let's set the same goals for the next six months. Is that agreeable with you?

i. _____

j. _____

Tim: Fine.

You: Here's what we'll do. Instead of my waiting six months, I want us to meet every two months and evaluate your progress toward our goals. I'll provide whatever resources I can. However, if we can't make it this time, I want you to know that I shall probably ask for your resignation. If you do make it, I'll consider a small bonus arrangement.

k. _____

l. _____

Answers to Exercise

a. Giving information
b. Seeking information
c. Giving information
d. Seeking information
e. Expressing feelings
f. Accepting feelings
g. Giving information
h. Seeking information
i. Giving information
j. Seeking information
k. Defining change in self and other
l. Benefits of change

REVIEW OF EXPRESSING YOUR MANAGERIAL NEEDS

	Yes	No	Not Sure
1. How you communicate with your employees is as important as what you say.	___	___	___
2. To have an effective work group, you need employees who involve themselves in the work you want them to do and commit themselves to achieving your objectives.	___	___	___
3. Aggressiveness is the mark of a good leader.	___	___	___
4. Managers who are truly effective in managing the motivation of employees find it desirable to deal with employees' behaviors and performance rather than with their attitudes and motives.	___	___	___
5. Aggressive statements are characterized by putting people down, embarrassing, or humiliating them.	___	___	___
6. Often people who make aggressive statements to others do so because they don't know how to deal with their negative feelings or to express themselves.	___	___	___
7. Aggressiveness usually results in short-term change but long-term damage.	___	___	___
8. Employees tend to shun making contacts with an aggressive manager.	___	___	___

		Yes	No	Not Sure
9.	It's acceptable for a manager to be nonassertive when he or she isn't quite sure what decision to make.	___	___	___
10.	The nonassertive manager does not achieve objectives or maintain standards usually because no one is sure of what they are.	___	___	___
11.	An assertive statement conveys what you want without stepping on the other person.	___	___	___
12.	An assertive statement has four elements: a description of what is going on, how you feel about it, the change you want the other person to make, and why that person should make it.	___	___	___
13.	Assertiveness is the most desirable approach in managerial communicating with employees.	___	___	___
14.	A truly assertive statement helps you to confront an issue rather than another person.	___	___	___
15.	Consistent assertive behavior helps to establish you as a credible and trustworthy person.	___	___	___
16.	One drawback to assertiveness is that it is controlling behavior.	___	___	___
17.	You are usually more liked by others when you are assertive.	___	___	___
18.	In a transaction between two people, success is achieved only if one person is assertive and the other is responsive.	___	___	___

	Yes	No	Not Sure
19. Responsiveness is usually not a legitimate way for a manager to behave in communicating with employees.	___	___	___
20. Responsiveness usually means agreeing with the feelings of the other.	___	___	___
21. Responsiveness is often appropriate when you are in the initial phase of taking over an operation that is new to you.	___	___	___
22. When counseling an employee on a work-related problem, you may find that being responsive encourages the employee to give you information that you might otherwise have not learned.	___	___	___
23. Responsiveness is appropriate in any interaction in which you suspect that the other person brings knowledge or resources to the discussion that could be useful to you.	___	___	___
24. When you are responsive to employees, you involve them, an important factor in their motivation.	___	___	___
25. If your predominant mode of behavior is reponsive, you may find other people getting what they want without your achieving your interests.	___	___	___
26. Predominantly responsive people sometimes find that their ideas are not taken seriously by others.	___	___	___

		Yes	No	Not Sure
27.	You will usually find that you should be assertive when counseling an employee on a performance problem on which there has been no corrective action taken.	———	———	———
28.	Aggressiveness and nonassertiveness are never appropriate behaviors in managing people.	———	———	———
29.	Not being assertive is probably one of the most common reasons for managerial failure.	———	———	———
30.	Most successful managers alternate between assertive and responsive behavior, even in the same discussion or interview.	———	———	———

Answers to Review

1. Yes
2. Yes
3. No
4. Yes
5. Yes
6. Yes
7. Yes
8. Yes
9. No
10. Yes
11. Yes
12. Yes
13. No. Depending on the situation, the desirable approach may be assertive, responsive, or assertive–responsive.
14. Yes
15. Yes
16. No. Controlling an interaction means that you guide it to a desired conclusion. You do not force or manipulate it. Controlling can be positive behavior.
17. Not sure. Assertiveness engenders trust and respect, not necessarily feelings of affection.
18. Not sure. This may be true in certain transactions, but often both people assume both modes of behavior at various points.
19. No. It is a legitimate way in certain transactions.
20. No. It means accepting without necessarily agreeing.
21. Yes
22. Yes
23. Yes
24. Yes
25. Yes

26.   Yes
27.   Yes
28.   Yes
29.   Yes
30.   Yes

4

MATCHING PERSONAL AND ORGANIZATIONAL GOALS

For best motivational results, you need to set goals and assign tasks and responsibilities that offer opportunities for employees to achieve their personal goals. In the ideal work setting, employees commit themselves to the accomplishment of organizational goals because by doing so they satisfy their own needs. If you have any authority or discretion in making assignments, delegating responsibility, or promoting employees, you need to know something about employees' personal goals.

You may not have much more than a sense of them. People may not, for their own reasons, be eager to tell you what makes them go. Indeed, they may not be very aware themselves of some of the motivating forces within them. But you can be sure that what people do they do for reasons that seem good and worthwhile to them, even if they keep those reasons to themselves.

What follows are some of the reasons why people commit themselves to work. They may suggest to you some of the motivations of your employees. Be cautioned that the motivations listed below are not categories of people. That is, you cannot fit this person into this motivational category, that person into another. People are far more complex than that. But the checklist may help you to understand the motivational forces in your subordinates and to appeal to them.

Security

Maslow describes this motivational level as encompassing the desire to be secure, to have stability, protection, and freedom from fear. People who are motivated for reasons of security have a strong need for structure and order. You can see that Maslow's description is much more far-reaching than the traditional idea of job security. Time was when many managers assumed that job security was what most people worked for. Today's more enlightened view acknowledges that security is just one of the concerns of people at work. Probably equally strong is the need for structure. Many people who report to you have that need. They want procedures and organization to be well-defined. They are not inclined to take risks that might jeopardize their security. They are at the other end of the spectrum from the entrepreneurial personality. Although they are bureaucratic, every organization needs them. After all someone needs to do the routinized work. Repetition is not likely to turn them off since that kind of thing is comforting. They are usually more apprehensive about change unless you can reassure them that they will not lose structure, stability, or security through that change.

Their assignments and responsibilities should be clear, have fixed and well-defined boundaries, and should not require much individual judgment. Their worlds may be confined, but they tend to respond to your appreciation that they are in command of those worlds.

Life-style

Some employees work to be able to afford material goods or a certain life-style. The work itself may always be of secondary interest, but that does not necessarily mean that they are not prepared, even committed, to doing it well. Quite the contrary. This person is interested in doing well enough to earn raises and to achieve job security, to protect those outside interests that really interest him or her. However, since this employee looks for challenge and fulfillment away from the job, he or she is usually reluctant to take on complicated new responsibilities or substantial risks that may threaten the situation as it is now. You would be ill-advised to push such a person in a new direction without minimizing the consequences of failure.

While this person resembles the employee who works to achieve security, it is possible to "hook" this employee with a task or responsibility that may provide a greater and more satisfying reward system than the one he or she enjoys on the outside. Remember that people will choose the reward that is more valuable than the other options. Thus it is always possible to help this person change focus.

Affiliation

Psychologists talk about affiliation needs, the need to bond with others, to join, and to belong. And some people look to work to satisfy their need to belong. They work well and conscientiously in groups, less efficiently in tasks that require them to be apart from others. (People with strong affiliative needs usually make poor outside salespeople.) It's difficult to make airtight generalizations, but it is frequently true that joiners accept the values of the group of which they are members. Thus, they become involved with the manager's objectives if that's where the energies of the group are directed. Unfortunately, it works the other way, too. You may find that this person is best approached through the work group, not as an individual. That is, you think of the kind of work or task to which the entire group would respond.

This kind of worker can function well in a group, though probably not in a leadership position. Assigning the employee to a committee or a task force or a work team would be in the person's best interests, and probably your own.

If you have a number of people with high social or affiliative needs, then you have to deal with the informal organizations they create or belong to. Set your standards and goals with the organization in mind. If the group members perceive that they can achieve their individual goals through working with you on your goals, then peer pressure will usually ensure that everyone works up to the standards that you've defined.

Esteem

Many people work to achieve their own and others' esteem, which includes yours. Your esteem is probably quite valuable to subordinates, and they will invest themselves to earn it. The main point about people who are motivated by esteem is that they usually accept challenges and risks that are moderate. They need achievement in order to earn that esteem. If the risk is too low, they'll discount it or pass it up. But they aren't necessarily gamblers, willing to take the big plunge for a sizable payoff when the odds are against them.

Esteem-seekers often are moderately competitive. They want more than to be accepted by others: They want respect, and they may believe that respect is gained by winning over others. Therefore this kind of person will usually seek chances to achieve and take on responsibility. But he or she is not a jungle fighter, that is, is not so competitive that in beating others, the employee alienates them. On the other hand, the person who is strongly motivated by self-esteem needs rather than by the need for the esteem of others may be willing to succeed even though the price of success is offending others.

Esteem-seeking people often desire tasks or assignments where they can work alone—competitively—or in group leadership positions that will enable them to influence the directions the groups will take.

The professional person is usually an esteem-motivated employee. He or she tends to be more concerned about professional standing than rank in the organization. If you manage such a person, you'll find high responsiveness to your interest in promoting professional growth and standing. Give this person every opportunity to shine, and you'll have one key to his or her commitment to your interests.

Power

Some people are attracted by power. They tend to be political and to take risks if they believe there is a reasonable chance for payoff. These people will generally do whatever they see as required to gain responsibility for and influence over others. So long as they work for you, they will probably be among your best subordinates. But bear in mind that they will also tend not to be content to work long for you. Moreover, not all power seekers are high performers. Some are empire builders, which takes a lot of energy. They work to acquire people, equipment, space, and prestige, and whatever it costs may detract from their effectiveness in achieving your objectives.

Another kind of power seeker may prove to be a continuing asset to you: the employee who is seeking personal power and freedom. Having power means having options and choices. Having freedom means much the same thing. This kind of employee wants freedom over work, the opportunity to choose the kind of work done and the means to do it. A strict bureaucratic boss may have problems with the personal power-seeking employee, but most managers who can delegate and give employees more freedom will find this person to be a joy.

Be prepared, however, for this person eventually to challenge you. If you know it is going to happen, you can use the person's energy and resources for your benefit. When there is no longer room enough for the two of you "in the same town," let the person seek fanfare elsewhere. He or she will remain a monument to your managerial effectiveness and shrewdness.

Achievement

Harvard professor David C. McClelland has become identified with achievement motivation through his extensive research. McClelland's work began with his attempts to identify people who are motivated to achieve. They do rather than think about doing. The accomplishment, McClelland suggests, is often an end in itself. Achievers want success and the feeling of having done something. They have a deep interest in their work. They appreciate money and other extrinsic rewards, but it is really the successful completion of the work that holds the greatest motivational appeal. However, the extrinsic rewards are enjoyed, and they do indicate success.

People with high achievement motivation tend to set moderate goals for themselves and to work harder when the chances of succeeding are only moderate. They are not interested in attaining objectives that are easy to reach. At the same time, they avoid setting goals that they have only a slim chance of achieving. The goals should be realistic, yet challenging.

Achievers prefer work situations in which they can take personal responsibility for the performance necessary to reach their goals. For this reason, the achiever will not gamble, for gambling is chance. The person with strong achievement motivation will not work easily in a committee or in collaboration with others, since some of the control over the work is in others' hands.

High achievers like to get feedback as to how well they are doing and are responsive to that concrete feedback. McClelland notes that the achiever is more likely to build a machine than to write a book. A machine works or it does not, gives a clear indication of success or a lack of it. A book, on the other hand, may not provide an undeniable success indicator. Besides, the feedback takes too long.

Achievement-motivated people are experimental. They like to try new things. They travel, move around, and seek opportunity much more than people with low achievement motivation.

The implications for the manager of achievement-motivation people are these:

☐ They can be helped to set goals that involve moderate risks, risks that are reasonable and realistic given the employee's ability level and resources.

☐ They need measurements to know how well they are doing, a feedback that comes automatically from progress as well as from others who are in a position to know.

☐ They like to have control over their work so they can take credit for it.

Entrepreneur

This person is a high achiever, high risk taker, very independent. He or she enjoys money and every other indicator of success, especially power. Traditionally entrepreneurs have not been considered good organizational people. They become restless, ambitious, agitators for change. When they find they cannot achieve what they want within the boundaries of the organization, they bolt and found their own company.

If you are fortunate enough to have one of these people working for you, use the advantage while you can. Give the employee protection from bureaucratic interference; reward the subordinate with money and every perquisite you can afford; encourage innovation, because that's what many entrepreneurs are so good at. You'll probably have to smooth over this person's conflicts with other employees, because the entrepreneur is not very sensitive to the feelings of others. He or she tends to think that the entrepreneurial way of thinking and doing is what is important and little else is.

In time, you will lose the entrepreneurial employee. In some organizations, this kind of resource is encouraged to remain by being given responsibility for a profit center, which is run as though it were an independent business. The concept of nurturing the entrepreneurial spirit in the corporate bureaucracy is a daring one, sorely needed in today's competitive climate but often shunned.

DISCOVERING PERSONAL GOALS

Learning about the personal goals of employees isn't always easy. There are about as many kinds of goals as there are people to set them. Still, the manager who recognizes that people have individual needs that they try to satisfy on the job, even if that manager is not always aware of the precise nature of those needs, is usually ahead of those managers who fail to take employees' goals into account when assigning work, providing training, and rewarding accomplishment.

How do you discover what employees prefer? What motivates them in the work they do?

There are three main methods: observation, the record, and interviews.

Observation

In your everyday management, what do you see individuals doing well? There is a strong positive relationship between what people do and what they like to do. There is an alacrity about the way people choose to do certain kinds of tasks. They give priority to some kinds of work over others. You can generally assume that your subordinates' preferences will be evident over time.

Your Records

What do your files show about the work done well by employees? Do you have copies of complimentary memos that you wrote on the completion of assignments or those that call attention to continuing fine work? Do you have copies of past performance appraisals?

The Employees

While observation and records can give you an idea of what some of your subordinates prefer and excel at, you will find that you must supplement this information with data from the employees directly. The reason is that people don't stay the same. What they have done in the past may not be of great interest to them in the future.

When you have built a sufficient level of trust, you can approach the employees with fairly straightforward questions. For example:

- [ ] What aspects of your job do you like most? Least?
- [ ] What functions or parts of your job would you like to spend more time doing, if you could? Less time doing?

☐ What kinds of work and responsibilities are you not doing now that you would like to do, if you had the opportunity?

One additional exercise that takes time but produces valuable data is this: "Describe in detail what your work would be like, would consist of, if you had the job you consider ideal. How would you spend your time?" Such an exercise forces employees to think through their personal values, and to define objectives that they may not have thought through. The conclusions will open a window for you, and they sometimes help employees to realize that what they presently do is much closer to the ideal than they had ever imagined.

One manager has developed a method of obtaining this personal information without disturbing the privacy of employees. Periodically he gives employees a form divided into two sections. The top part of the form gives the employee the opportunity to spell out those goals that the employee wants to achieve through work. There may be any number of personal objectives that the employee might define privately—money, promotion, status, new skills, and so on.

The bottom half is for the employee to translate the personal objectives he or she has just described into action plans, or at least suggested plans. The employee is asked to describe work functions, assignments, responsibilities that would enable him or her to achieve the goals listed in the upper part of the form. The manager sees only the bottom half and discusses it with the employee, if the latter wishes to. The manager then takes the information into account when planning work and training, for example.

Such information can also be useful in setting up coaching sessions, as described in Chapter 12.

TRUST AND ACCEPTANCE

The key word in encouraging employees to open up is *trust*. If you want employees to be genuine about personal objectives and preferences, you have to be extremely careful never to appear to use the information in any way but respectfully. One manager tells of the time he met with an older boss some years back. The senior man wanted to know in what direction the young man was moving. The young man opened up, only to have the older man snort and say, "Now that's foolish. What you really should be thinking more about is. . . ." Then the older man talked for some time about what he thought the junior manager's objectives should be. Obviously, when an employee discusses personal values with you, he or she should not have to worry about being ridiculed.

Accept what you hear, even if you don't agree with it or believe it is realistic. The important thing is that the other person believes it and takes it seriously. You can also take it seriously, even if you don't think the employee's thinking is on target. For example, you might respond, "That's interesting. I would have thought, from observing and working with you, that you might have felt differently. Would you like to hear my conclusions from what I've seen of you?" Then, after you've gotten consent, you may offer your opinions.

Obviously, don't even appear to take what you hear lightly, even if you do find the employee's revelations to be quite at odds with your opinions. Also make every effort to keep the information to yourself. If it must be shared, emphasize discretion. For the employee to hear something from a third party or through the grapevine that he or she thought was to be treated confidentially is to invite the employee's personal vote of no confidence in you.

USING THE INFORMATION

The information that you elicit can be useful in encouraging the employee to think specifically about how the job can offer opportunities to satisfy personal needs and goals. In rare cases, your discussion with employees may uncover a frustration deriving from the awareness that the job really can't offer them the satisfaction they seek. In such a case, you may have to weigh the possibility that the most constructive advice you can give, for these employees and for yourself, is that they prepare to go elsewhere.

More frequently, you can alter duties and responsibilities to bring the work more closely to what the employee needs and wants. Perhaps some duties can be exchanged with or transferred to a co-worker who would value them more. The prescription might involve training and education to equip the employee to take over different responsibilities. It is seldom that nothing can be done over time to enable the employee to achieve some of his or her personal goals while working for you.

EMPLOYEE PREFERENCE QUESTIONNAIRE

1. Please list those aspects, responsibilities, and duties of your job that you like most.

    _____
    _____
    _____
    _____
    _____

    That you like least.

    _____
    _____
    _____
    _____

2. What functions or parts of your job would you like to spend more time doing, if you could?

    _____
    _____
    _____
    _____

    What functions would you like to spend less time doing?

    _____
    _____
    _____
    _____

3. If you had the opportunity, what kinds of work and responsibility would you like to do that you are not now doing?

    _____
    _____
    _____
    _____

4. What skills, knowledge, and experience from training, previous employment, or outside interests do you have that you believe would be useful in your current position or in different areas of responsibility that you would like to assume?

    _____

    _____

    _____

    _____

    _____

EMPLOYEE PERSONAL DATA FORM

Name of employee: _____

Date entered department: _____

Background Information

Education: _____

_____

_____

_____

_____

Previous training: _____

_____

_____

_____

_____

Previous employment: (beginning with most recent)

Dates: _____   Position: _____

Dates: _____   Position: _____

Dates: _____   Position: _____

Dates: _____   Position: _____

Dates: _____   Position: _____

Current Employment Information

Title or position held in this department (beginning with most recent):

Date: _____   Position/title: _____

   Principal responsibilities: _____

_____

_____

Date: _____   Position/title: _____

   Principal responsibilities: _____

_____

_____

Date: _____   Position/title: _____

  Principal duties: _____

_____

_____

Training and education since employee entered the department
or organization:

_____

_____

_____

_____

_____

_____

Outside service, avocations, and hobbies:

_____

_____

_____

Outstanding accomplishments:

_____

_____

_____

_____

_____

_____

Skills Data

List those skills that the employee has demonstrated exceptional
competence in:

_____

_____

_____

_____

List those skills that the employee has demonstrated acceptable or
adequate competence in:

_____

_____

_____

_____

List those skills or experience that the employee's record suggests he or she has applied in previous employment or in which he or she has received training and education (but has not demonstrated in current employment):

_____

_____

_____

_____

List those skills or experience that the employee could be now gaining from outside interests (see above) that might be useful in current or future positions:

_____

_____

_____

_____

Employee Development Data

What kinds of additional responsibilities/opportunities has the employee indicated an interest in?

_____

_____

_____

_____

What kinds of additional responsibilities/opportunities do your observation and records indicate that the employee might become qualified for?

_____

_____

_____

_____

_____

List the additional responsibilities that in your opinion the employee is presently capable of assuming:

_____

_____

_____

_____

_____

_____

REVIEW OF MATCHING PERSONAL
AND ORGANIZATIONAL GOALS

		Yes	No	Not Sure
1.	Employees generally commit themselves to the accomplishment of organizational goals because by doing so they satisfy their own needs.	___	___	___
2.	People who are motivated for reasons of security have a strong need for structure and order.	___	___	___
3.	Most people motivated by security needs are disinclined to take risks.	___	___	___
4.	The employee who is working primarily to support a life-style usually turns in minimally acceptable work.	___	___	___
5.	The employee whose interests are off-the-job may be reluctant to take on complicated new responsibilities or substantial risks that would threaten his or her work situation.	___	___	___
6.	Some employees are motivated to work for the manager's objectives only if the work group they belong to is committed to doing so.	___	___	___
7.	People who are motivated by esteem needs generally seek to avoid even moderate risk because it may threaten that esteem.	___	___	___
8.	Professional employees tend to be motivated by esteem needs.	___	___	___
9.	People with power needs tend to be political and to take risks where they believe there is a reasonable chance for a payoff.	___	___	___

	Yes	No	Not Sure
10. People with high achievement needs tend to seek goals that often are out of their reach.	___	___	___
11. Achievers prefer work situations in which they can take personal responsibility for the performance necessary to reach their goals.	___	___	___
12. You are more likely to keep an entrepreneurial type of person longer if you protect the employee from bureaucratic interference, and encourage and reward innovation.	___	___	___
13. The three main methods of determining employees' personal goals are your observation, records, and reports from others.	___	___	___
14. If you expect employees to open up to you about their personal goals, you must create a climate of trust. They must know that you will use the information respectfully.	___	___	___
15. By using the information you gather about employees' personal goals, you can try to alter their duties and responsibilities to bring the work more closely to what the employees need and want.	___	___	___

Answers to Review

1. Yes

2. Yes

3. Yes

4. Not sure. Some employees whose interests lie outside the job will work quite diligently to ensure that they can afford to continue pursuing their life-style.

5. Yes

6. Yes

7. No. They have a need to earn the esteem of others, which may encourage them to take risks.

8. Yes

9. Yes

10. No. They seek realistic goals that involve moderate risks, according to McClelland, who has done research on achievement motivation.

11. Yes

12. Yes

13. No. The third method is interviews with the employees themselves. Hearsay may bring you some information, but generally it must be verified by one of the three main methods.

14. Yes

15. Yes

5

SETTING GOALS

Many organizations have some kind of formal goal-setting program that extends far down in the hierarchy. Ideally, everyone in the organization, from entry-level people on up, should participate in the setting of objectives for their departments. Programs such as Management by Objectives (MBO) encourage this systemwide approach. Usually in MBO, the goals become the basis for performance appraisals. The employee's evaluation depends in large part on how well he or she attains the objectives that had been set previously, six months or a year before.

There are strong arguments in favor of using goals as the basis for appraisals. Goals have to do with output. They are measurable and verifiable. They provide objective evidence. (Some people define goals and objectives differently. In this book they are used interchangeably.)

Employees set goals naturally, since behavior is goal-directed. The key to productivity and commitment is to establish goals that people find useful. That is, by working to achieve your and the organization's goals they manage to accomplish objectives that are important to them personally.

THE IMPORTANCE OF GOALS

Aside from the important fact that goals determine how people behave (a fact that many managers are still suspicious of, apparently), goals fulfill a number of needs. For example:

- ☐ *They Give Order and Structure.* Maslow defined these as *safety* needs, just above food, drink, sleep, and sex. We all require some order and structure in our lives. Employees seldom work well without structure.

- ☐ *They Measure Progress.* People have a need to be going somewhere with their lives. No one is really happy simply to mark time. When people recognize and work toward goals, they have a sense of movement. They can see the direction they are moving in and the pace.

- ☐ *They Give a Sense of Achievement.* Herzberg identifies achievement as one of the motivators. People take pleasure, satisfaction, and pride in accomplishment.

- ☐ *They Provide Closure.* Most people like something that has limits, that comes to an end. Too many open activities can frustrate, leaving the feeling that one is not going anywhere.

Goals meet one of your most important needs: They create feedback for you. You need to know where people are investing their time and energy, and how well they are investing them. A goal helps you monitor and adjust performance.

CONVEYING YOUR EXPECTATIONS

Setting goals performs another important function for you: conveying your expectations of how your people will perform.

There was a famous experiment a few years ago involving school-children that demonstrated that expectations of performance can have an effect on the performance itself. In the experiment, some of the teachers were to give assignments and express their expectations that the students would do them well. Other teachers, giving the same assignments, would express less confidence or remain noncommittal. Teachers who expressed their belief that their students would do a good job actually did achieve better performances on the whole than teachers who expressed lesser or no expectations.

As a manager, you can have a positive effect on subordinates' performance by letting them know that you expect them to perform according to your standards. Goals are an expression of your expectations. For example, you say, "We agree, then, that by the end of the next quarter, your staff will be able to classify the leads from our advertising campaign by sales district, size of company, type of business, and product interest, and send out no less than 80 percent of the leads to salespeople within 72 hours of receipt. That allows for an extra heavy load of leads, people out sick or on vacation, or some unexpected condition like the computer going down." There's an objective that clearly states what is to be accomplished by what time. It establishes standards of performance.

Managers too often take it for granted that employees know what is to be done, by whom and when; what is an acceptable standard. Take a seemingly simple example of a supermarket. The manager says to stock boys, "When the shelves are empty, fill them with the proper merchandise." But the instructions are not adequate. They do not convey the standards that the manager wants. At what point does the stocker replenish the shelves? When they are half empty? A quarter empty? What happens to any older merchandise on the shelves? Is it left where it is or pushed to the front? Are there occasional other duties, such as working on the cash register when the store is very crowded, that may take precedence over stocking shelves?

Managers often rely on a position description to let employees know what their duties are. But position descriptions may not adequately define standards or priorities.

Goals, then, are an effective way for you to express to subordinates what you expect of them. Goals tell them how their performance will be evaluated, and on what basis they will be rewarded.

CHARACTERISTICS OF EFFECTIVE GOALS

Goals that stimulate the motivating forces in your subordinates, that encourage them to commit themselves to the accomplishment of those goals, should have at least the following three characteristics (they can be remembered more easily by thinking of them as the three Rs of goals). They should be realistic, relevant to the organization, and relate to the person.

Realistic

People can achieve them. What is more important, they perceive that they can reach them. A goal that is too high offers a great deal of risk, perhaps little chance of attainment, and that leads to frustration. When the employee believes that the goal is out of reach, he or she will probably give up.

On the other hand, a goal that is too low, too easily reached, offers little challenge or interest. Goals that are too routine, or extensions of what the employee does now or knows how to do quite competently, invite a ho-hum response.

This is not to say that you shouldn't set goals that are extensions of employees' present activity. They may be necessary. It does mean that your goal setting should not be confined to such routine objectives.

Goals may need to be adjusted upward or downward as the work progresses. That's the value of setting subgoals. If you see that they are being too easily accomplished, then you have an indication that the goal may lose its challenge. It needs to be raised. But if the subgoal is seriously missed, and if the employee is showing frustration, then the goal can be adjusted downward a bit for the next time period. If you don't step in to lower an improbably high goal, you risk demotivation in the employee.

Relevant to the Organization

It helps to be able to show that a particular goal makes a contribution to the organization's success and well-being. In that way employees can relate their efforts to those of others, and they can take legitimate credit in their achievement and that of the organization as a whole.

People who turn out parts for an auto or a large piece of equipment such as the space shuttle can certainly take satisfaction in their contribution if they see how the quality of their work contributes to the whole. People who work in an insurance claims department whose goals have involved shortening the process time for a claim can derive a sense of pride and accomplishment when they see testimonials from agents and policyholders that the shorter turnaround period has made the company more competitive and the policyholders more appreciative of the service.

When you set goals, therefore, relate them to the overall mission and product of the organization.

Relate to the Person

The employee understands what the organization will get from his or her achievement of the goal. What will the employee gain from working to accomplish it? How will achievement satisfy some of the employee's personal goals? Will it mean that one or more internal rewards will be gratified?

You know that you can reward successful achievement (and it's important that your subordinates know that their efforts will be recognized). But this is also time for you to consider what you know of the employee and what he or she regards as valuable. (See Chapter 4 on personal goals, specifically the Employee Personal Data Form, and the discussion of internal rewards in Chapter 6 on making the work more valuable.)

WHY YOUR GOALS AREN'T WORKING

Let's suppose that despite your belief that the goals you've set are in accordance with the three Rs—that is, they are realistic, relevant, and relate personally to employees—you are disappointed that they are not working as well as you'd like. Use the following list to help you to determine what your problem is.

Too Many Goals

People can attend to just so many written goals. Many goals, involving familiar activities or extensions of tasks that are performed regularly, do not have to be restated as goals each period. When something becomes too familiar, it usually becomes unexciting. Too many familiar goals can draw attention from or camouflage an objective that deserves more visibility. If the activity is adequately described in a job description, you don't need to make a big and formal fuss about it at goal-setting time. You might even consider having a "short" goal-setting form for minor changes in routine and perennial tasks. There is generally no need to go through the entire goal-setting and writing process to state them.

Undetermined Priorities

You may not need priorities if the number of goals is manageable and if no unexpected impediments slow progress toward their achievement. However, conditions may change. Suppose your budget were cut, you lost some good people, or a temporary but serious emergency took up time. As a result, your people might have to ration their time and effort. Which goals should get priority treatment? If you don't have the means to achieve all of your goals, you have to make sure that the most important ones receive the most attention.

But even if conditions remain as they were at the time you set the goals, you have to anticipate the human condition. People tend to work at what they like to work at. If they have a choice, they'll choose the tasks and jobs they like most. Hence, the priorities and preferences of your employees might not be your own. If you don't set priorities for the goals you aim for, you may find your people working hardest to achieve a goal that is last in priority but first in popularity.

Too Much Forgiveness

In some organizations, goals that are not achieved are "forgiven." "Let's see, you said you were going to increase unit production from 64,000 to 80,000. But I see that you reached only 66,000. Well, do you want to try again for the 80,000?" That's a very considerate manager speaking, but a self-defeating one. There may well be a good reason for the failure to reach the goal, but it shouldn't be overlooked. It should be explored fully. The subordinate is accountable for the full 80,000. Why wasn't the objective realized? If the failure can be justified, make allowance for it and set a new goal. If it cannot be, then you may have to counsel the subordinate on a deficiency in his or her performance. No one will take a goal seriously if he or she knows that failure to reach it will simply be dismissed or forgiven.

Too Few Subgoals

Your objectives may be set for long-term periods, but people shouldn't have to wait too long to find out what progress they are making. You need to measure progress by setting and tracking subgoals. Your monitoring of those subgoals may show that the original goals were too optimistic or too easily attainable. In both cases they may have to be adjusted so as not to have an adverse effect on motivation. Another important function of subgoals is to give people a sense of achievement while they are still achieving. People need reinforcement to stay motivated and committed.

Narrow "Ownership"

Sometimes managers impose priorities that are important to them but not to their employees. One manager in a research and development function became very concerned about the fact that her employees, all professionals, kept irregular hours. She established a goal that called for 90 percent of the professionals to adjust their working hours within three months so as to be in their offices from nine to five. Many of these professionals worked long hours, much more than 40 hours a week. At the end of three months, working conditions and professional hours were very much what they had been before the goal was set. The manager's priorities were not those of her talented and hardworking subordinates. The professionals continued to work the hours they chose.

Managers may get involved with "ego" goals. For example, one manager volunteered his work group to test a different record-keeping system. The manager believed that taking on the extra work would earn him a certain glory and prestige. But the employees simply saw it as a burden they didn't need. The manager "owned" the goal, but he was never successful in selling his employees on the value of it to them.

As long as employees fail to see the goals as being important to them, they are not likely to commit themselves wholeheartedly.

Withheld Resources

You are most likely an essential resource to your subordinates. If you set goals for employees and then make it difficult for them to take advantage of what help you can offer, employees may resent being exposed on the front line while you take a rear position.

They'll also resent having to achieve goals that require special training or consultation with experts that you are reluctant to provide, perhaps because of budgetary considerations.

Insufficient Accountability

The rule here is to set only goals that you are prepared to follow up. If you set, say, five goals to be achieved by the end of a particular time frame, you must follow them up—all of them. When you do not follow them up, it gives employees the impression that you were not serious about them from the beginning. Once a goal is set, show your interest and concern, which can be done without directing every step.

If it should happen that a particular goal becomes irrelevant because of a change in operation, planning, or priority, let people know about it so they can feel released from the obligation to achieve it. And announce it as quickly as possible. It's not a good idea to wait till the end of the period to tell people that they've been wasting their time.

A managerial failing related to insufficient accountability is forgiveness, discussed earlier. The difference between the two pitfalls is that in forgiveness all the goals are accounted for but deficiencies in achieving them are not.

KINDS OF GOALS

There are four kinds of objectives from which you can choose in a goal-setting session: routine, problem solving, innovative, and personal.

Routine

This is a continuation and extension of what people are already doing. "We sold 20,000 units last year. In order to preserve our share of the market and our profit margin, we need to see 23,000 units this year." Or, "We trained five people for small computer capability in the past period. We need to double that figure this time period." Everyone needs to work a bit more effectively to improve over last period's output. There can be a challenge in that. But if every time you better the previous period's output, you come to expect it. Knowing that you can do it—in fact, that you have done it consistently—lowers the challenge. Too many routine goals cause the goal-setting process to lose its sparkle.

While it may be true that employees have little to say about the quantity of work to be done—such determinations are usually made at a higher level in accordance with organizational strategy and then pushed downward—they may have much to say about how it is to be accomplished. "We have to produce 15 percent more this year with the same (or fewer) number of people. How do you think we can do it?" That implies that goals can stimulate excitement in an otherwise routine objective setting.

Problem Solving

"Our reject rate is 22 percent higher than it was during the same period last year." Or, "Our turnover rate among new hires is one-third up from last year." You have a problem. How can you solve it? It's time to consult the experts, the people who probably know more about the work than anyone else: the people who do it. From their counsel and with their participation, you can set goals involving solutions to the problem. "Our errors in claims payment are up from three percent to seven percent. With taking the first steps you suggest, we'll aim for lowering the rate to five percent in the next three months, then we'll try for three percent again in the next three months." Or you can simply set the quantitative measurement and leave the working out of the methods to the employee, adding excitement and challenge.

Since problem-solving goals can sometimes be long range, you want to be sure to break them down into subgoals in order to be able to evaluate them in each appraisal period.

Innovative

What could be done that hasn't been? What new procedures or shortcuts can be introduced? Could your people construct a model or a prototype? How about a task force to investigate new marketing or manufacturing or distribution methods? The innovation doesn't have to be elaborate. It could involve designing new forms, covering telephones during lunch, the arranging of work stations in a different pattern, or distribution of work in a more efficient manner.

Again your subordinates are in a position to advise you about changes or projects that could be introduced. And they could probably participate in determining the means by which the innovation can be effected.

If possible, each time period and goal-setting session should see at least one innovation for individuals or groups of employees, even if it is small. When your employees have had a part in introducing a successful innovation, their sense of pride and achievement is a powerful reward—and a strong encouragement to repeat their success.

Innovative goal-setting is a potent stimulus to employees' motivations.

Personal

"What are you doing for you?" is a question that you should be asking your subordinates. And you might phrase the question in this way, "What can we (the organization) be helping you do for yourself?" Personal objectives should be part of the goal-setting process. Some managers refer to them as developmental objectives. Whatever the label, their purpose is to encourage and help the employee to become more effective, to do better work, to actualize his or her potential. The goals can include training and education, job rotation, coaching—whatever can improve technical or professional skills, and can prepare the employee for additional responsibilities.

Behavioral objectives can be part of personal or developmental goal-setting, if they work to increase the employee's capability to do the work. For example, you might say to one of your supervisors, "I think you would get a lot more out of the meetings you conduct if you could get more participation from your staff. Let's work on some techniques you might try to encourage people to open up more." In such a case, you offer coaching. But you might also suggest that the employee seek help from seminars, self-study courses, books, or an informal "apprenticeship" with a supervisor who has well-developed leadership skills.

For obvious reasons, personal objectives can be a prime motivating force.

THE GOAL-SETTING SESSION

Ideally, the process of setting goals should be a stimulating one for both you and your subordinates. Looking ahead, determining priority objectives, agreeing on what is important should provide some excitement, especially if you and employees are realistic, believe the objectives are relevant, and can find something in the goals that relates personally.

If the objectives are realistic, they should not threaten. A goal-setting session ought to be an interesting and very natural occasion. In fact, people should look forward to it, if only because the process provides an opportunity to get together with you and talk about matters that are important to both of you. Of course, how openly they talk with you, how much information they volunteer, how much enthusiasm they demonstrate, largely depends on the climate you have created and the degree of trust between you. When employees believe that the manager generally discourages openness and spontaneity, the manager can hardly expect a sudden and substantial change of behavior when discussing goals.

Here are some time-tested recommendations for conducting more profitable goal-setting interviews.

Give Advance Notice

This isn't a necessary reminder if your goal-setting sessions are tied in with periodic appraisals. People usually know when the evaluations come around.

People need time to think about what they regard as important. Unrealistic objectives often result when subordinates have to come up with plans off the top of the head. In giving them notice of the interview, suggest that they think about all four kinds of goals: routine, problem-solving, innovative, and personal. They might come up with some interesting objectives that would not occur to you. And some of their products might be more ambitious than you would have dared suggest.

Provide Essential Information

What changes are going to occur, or have occurred recently, that might alter the nature, quantity, and quality of the objectives? What capital equipment will be added? Will a function be phased out or transferred to another department? What effects will a reorganization have on the amount and type of work? Are there personnel changes that will affect goals? Will budgets be trimmed? What will be the impact of a new product that is to be introduced? What changes in organizational or management structure or overall objectives should be considered in setting your departmental goal?

Obviously, if employees know in advance what opportunities or constraints will affect the future, they'll do a better job of defining desirable objectives.

Allow Plenty of Time for the Meeting

This is a prime time for both of you to learn what is on each other's mind. If it is an appraisal session (see Chapter 11) you'll want to have sufficient opportunity to deal with performance based on previously established goals. Also, the amount of time you set aside for the process is one indicator of how much importance you assign to it. Managers who seem to begrudge the time, who rush through the process, broadcast that they don't assign a high priority to the setting of goals.

The suggested mode of behavior in the setting session is assertive–responsive. You want to convey your expectations, and those of higher management, but you also want to find out what objectives, activities, and values are on the minds of your subordinates. You may discover that the way they see their jobs and priorities is a far cry from the way you see them. This is the time to narrow that gap in role perception.

Employees may bring problems to the meeting that you were only dimly aware of. They may suggest innovations that you hadn't thought of. And they may furnish you with some solid and unexpected clues as to their personal career objectives, information that is useful not only in setting developmental objectives but in coaching for growth (see Chapter 12).

State the Goals

Objectives should be stated clearly and concisely. For example, "Increase sales by 12 percent by December 31." Or, "Have 50 percent of departmental personnel capable of using computer ter-

minals by April 15." Or, "Have around-the-clock telephone claims
reporting system functioning full-time by June 1."

The complaint is often made that it is difficult to quantify objectives for certain kinds of work. Here are some examples of work
that is seemingly hard to quantify and define:

☐ *Creative Department*

Number of new ideas

New applications for products

Dollar values of ideas or applications

Cost savings from innovations

Interest and response to new programs

☐ *Purchasing*

Reductions in complaints

Negotiation time

Vendors' reliability

Lower unit costs

Institution of controls

☐ *Training*

Number of student hours

Percentage of facility usage

Degree of improvement in training delivery

☐ *Analysis*

Flow time

Cost/value ratios

Percentage of analytical errors

Number of reports published

☐ *Market Research*

"By July 1 to have conducted a market study that costs no
more than $60,000 and that will show market penetration in
percentages about product X."

In short, there are any number of ways you can develop indicators and quantify the results of effort if only by thinking in terms of the utilization of people, equipment, and facilities.

How much time should you give to discussing the means by which the objectives are to be reached? Obviously a discussion of means is important if the objectives are new to the employee. Some subordinates prefer an extensive review of means with you, while others will probably become more highly motivated if you leave some development of means to them.

Here is an example of a means or input goal given to an inexperienced editor in a book publishing house: "Your objective for the next three months is to sign contracts with two new authors. This will be done by inviting an average of three prospective writers to lunch per week and by sending at least four letters per week to writers of interesting articles or books."

In most cases, a brief action plan describing means may be helpful. For example, if your objective or output is to increase your market share in a particular area, you might formulate your action or input plan like this: "We will supplement calls to dealers with a four-times-a-year mailing to large volume customers and prospects." However, if your goal is to reduce production costs, you might state your input goals less specifically: "We will do an analysis of overtime activities and costs to find out how we can schedule more work during regular hours."

Your statement of goals should cover the following:

1. What is to be done.
2. Key results that will be accomplished.
3. Constraints, such as time invested or costs.
4. Resources.
5. Means, if necessary.
6. Target date for completion of the goal or subgoal.

You may wish to use the Goal-Setting Data Form that appears at the end of this chapter.

Set Priorities

It's possible that not all the goals can be achieved. If they cannot be achieved, you should set priorities with the employee. Rank the goals. This enables the employee to know the priorities to concentrate on, if it is impossible to do everything.

Get Agreement on the Goals

Make sure that employees understand your statement of goals and their priorities. Ask how they feel about the objectives. For your part, you can elaborate on how each of the goals relates to your own and the overall organizational goals. This may also be the time to discuss fully how each objective relates to the employee. What will the experience of achieving it mean to him or her? How will it contribute to his or her development, advancement, image, and so on? In short, you ought to be prepared to sell to the subordinate the benefits of being committed to these goals.

Follow Up in Writing

First, a written objective serves as a reminder. But just as important, your written follow-up ensures that you and the subordinate have agreed on the same things. You have a contract.

GROUP OBJECTIVES

If you have a task force or a project team or group, you can go through the same process in setting objectives for the whole group. Group goal-setting can take the place of much of the individual process or can supplement it. The group may also define developmental objectives for itself, or you can discuss personal goals with each member.

GOAL-SETTING DATA FORM

1. Name of employee: _____

2. Statement of output goal: _____

   _____

   _____

   _____

   _____

   _____

3. Key result of the accomplishment of the goal (how measured):

   _____

   _____

   _____

   _____

   _____

4. Resources available: _____

   _____

   _____

   _____

5. Constraints to be observed: _____

   _____

   _____

   _____

6. Means, input goal, and plan of action: _____

   _____

   _____

   _____

   _____

7. Target date for completion of the goal or first subgoal:

   _____

8. Proposed target dates for subsequent subgoals:

_____

_____

_____

_____

9. Priority rating: _____

   I have read the above and agree with the plan of action and the goal to be achieved.

                                        _____
                                        Employee's signature

REVIEW OF SETTING GOALS

	Yes	No	Not Sure
1. Goals can be useful for evaluating performance because they are measurable and provide objective evidence of accomplishment.	___	___	___
2. Goals are natural to people.	___	___	___
3. Goals create feedback for you that helps you to monitor and adjust employees' performance.	___	___	___
4. Position descriptions may be used as a substitute for goal-setting.	___	___	___
5. Good goals have three characteristics: They are realistic, relevant, and they relate to the employee.	___	___	___
6. It's good to set goals that are higher than employees can attain so as to provide extra challenge.	___	___	___
7. There are four basic kinds of goals: Routine, problem solving, innovative, and personal.	___	___	___
8. You should always set priorities.	___	___	___
9. Once you set goals, it's best not to make yourself too available, otherwise employees will not work hard to achieve them.	___	___	___
10. If employees fail to achieve goals, you should be understanding and forgive the failures; otherwise you will demotivate them.	___	___	___
11. The best goals are those defined by your employees.	___	___	___

	Yes	No	Not Sure
12. If possible, each goal-setting session should provide for the inclusion of one innovative goal, even if it is a small one.	___	___	___
13. Personal or developmental goals should not be detailed, because it isn't the manager's role to get involved in their attainment.	___	___	___
14. It's best not to give too much advance notice of goal-setting interviews because they are usually high-stress situations.	___	___	___
15. The suggested mode of behavior for you in a goal-setting session is assertive, since you want to underscore the necessity of the employees' achieving the goals.	___	___	___
16. The most efficient goal-setting session is one in which you have defined the goals in advance so that there can be no confusion in the employee's mind.	___	___	___
17. For some kinds of jobs you can't expect to set goals because of the difficulty in quantifying results.	___	___	___
18. The wise manager never trusts employees to develop the means to achieve goals on their own.	___	___	___
19. The wise manager always leaves the development of the means of achievement to the employee.	___	___	___
20. Group goals can be set essentially in the same manner as individual objectives.	___	___	___

Answers to Review

1. Yes
2. Yes
3. Yes
4. No, not usually. They may not be current. They may not allow for problem solving, innovation, and personal development. And they don't always specify standards.
5. Yes
6. No
7. Yes
8. Not sure. If there are not too many goals and they are reasonably manageable, you may not find it necessary to establish priorities. But it is usually a good idea.
9. No
10. No
11. Not sure. There are certain goals relating to organizational strategy that are probably best defined by higher management. However, there is no clear answer on this question.
12. Yes
13. No. The manager should oversee and guide the development of the employee.
14. No. They should not normally be high-stress situations. If they frequently are, something is wrong with the goals.
15. No. Assertive–responsive.
16. No. It should as far as possible be a participative effort.
17. No. A way can be found to measure output for every job.
18. No. If the employee understands the goals and the work, he or she may find it more challenging and motivating to develop the means.
19. No. Some employees may be new to the goals and may not feel confident to develop input goals or action plans.
20. Yes

6

MAKING THE WORK
MORE VALUABLE

You can make the work, task, assignment, or job more valuable to the employee, thereby enhancing the person's motivating forces. The more rewarding the employee finds the work, the more likely he or she will be committed to doing it well.

There are at least three ways in which you can add value to the work:

1. By assigning work that enables the employee to achieve his or her own personal goals.
2. Through helping the employee to identify certain internal rewards, such as a sense of achievement or an increase in self-esteem, that can be obtained through commitment to the work and success in doing it.

3. By reinforcing successful achievement on the part of the employee with an external reward that you grant, such as money, praise, and promotion.

Managers tend to think of their armory of rewards as being limited. But in fact you have a wide and rich variety of ways to recognize good performance, to reinforce it, and to encourage its repetition.

INTERNAL REWARDS

Internal reinforcers are generated within the person. People give themselves their own rewards. Herzberg talks about achievement and progress, reinforcers that occur when the person has achieved a goal, whether it is set by the person or the organization. Because the reinforcement comes from within the person, the manager may think, "There's not much I can do about it." That's not true. Another error a manager may make is believing that it is not necessary to reinforce the employee's sense of achievement. To illustrate, a manager says about an outstanding performer, "She's a real pro. She knows better than anyone else when she does a good job." That may be so, but if the manager does not take steps to enhance the good feelings that the achiever has, he or she may have lost a valuable opportunity to stimulate the employee's motivation.

There are at least two steps a manager can take to increase the value of internally generated rewards. The first is to help the employee to establish attainable goals and measurements so that achievement is evident. The manager takes the second step by helping the employee to recognize the internal rewards for accomplishment. The manager gives the employee something to look forward to. For example, an employee is going through an extensive and difficult breaking-in period. The manager might say, "I know it's tough going now, but once you've gotten through it, you'll find you have a different feeling about yourself and the job. You'll be more relaxed, much more confident about your ability to take on equally demanding challenges." The manager could also add the likelihood that the employee will take a great deal of pleasure in being able to perform confidently. The subordinate just might like the job more, and that's no insignificant reinforcer.

Not only does the manager suggest the kind of reaction the employee will have to emerging successfully from a trying experience, but the manager shows concern for the employee's feelings about himself or herself. It adds to the rapport between manager and employee.

Here are other examples of how a manager can anticipate and highlight those internal rewards that an achieving and well-performing subordinate deserves.

A Sense of Growth

"I'm sure this experience that you are accumulating will be indicative of the tremendous progress you are making." Or, "It must give you a satisfying feeling when you see how you can perform assignments that you could not have handled six months ago."

Status

"You're expanding your know-how to the point where you'll probably be the most versatile person in this department." Or, "You must be very pleased with yourself to be able to show proficiency in so many different functions. You are probably the most multi-skilled person in the department."

Achievement

"If you keep going the way you have been, you'll be the first person in the region to fill the annual quota by May." Or, "I never thought it possible that you would be able to train the administrative assistants to become competent in using the terminals and word processors in such a short time."

Self-Esteem

When you know how important it is to an employee to feel skilled, competent, and professional, you can point out how certain tasks, assignments, and training can lead to a heightened sense of worth. "You're going to feel increasingly valuable to us and to yourself." Or, "You're growing in professionalism from day to day."

Social Needs

It is important for most people to be accepted as members of the group—and to be esteemed by others. A manager can subtly reinforce these desires by suggesting ways in which an employee, through achievement, acquisition of skills, or changes of behavior, can increase that acceptance and esteem by others. Peer approval, esteem, and acceptance of others on the work scene can meet many of a person's social needs. In fact, how co-workers feel about the employee may mean as much to that person as how you feel. "I've been hearing from some of your colleagues good words about how skilled you are getting in running the scheduling sessions. I hear that you can accomplish everything in half the time it used to take." Chances are good that the employee hasn't heard much direct praise from the people who are willing to tell you.

In the above statements, you would be giving the employee positive feedback which, of course, constitutes an external reward. But, more important, you are helping to trigger an internal rewards mechanism in the employee. Don't assume that employees automatically reinforce themselves when they do well. Ironically, they may not have the sense of achievement that you think they have when they have reached an objective or a level of performance. You are in a position to help them define what has to be done and to confirm and recognize what they have in fact done.

Thus, don't leave the internal rewards mechanism to operate on its own. In some employees, it may not be an efficient or precise mechanism.

Usually the most desirable and potent reward is an internal reinforcer backed up by one that is external, coming from you. Money and promotions, of course, are obvious rewards. But you have many other ways to reward an employee for successful completion of a task or assignment and for reaching and maintaining a desired level of performance. The rest of this chapter suggests the wide variety of rewards you have at your disposal.

WORK, A VALUABLE REINFORCER

If, as Herzberg claims, work itself is a motivator, then more work could be the reward for good performance. But you have to make sure that your employees perceive the additional work as a reward for past performance and a chance to grow for the future. The message should not be, "Around here, if you do a good job, they pile on more work." The new work should be interesting and challenging, something that employees prize, or an opportunity for employees to become more valuable to the organization and to themselves.

There are several ways you can use more work as a reward and a motivator.

Job Enlargement

The expansion is achieved by using the employee's present work load as a base and adding to it duties and functions that are appropriate to the same level or category. For example, an inspector responsible for one assembly line is given two. A secretary whose main job has been typing might also be given filing duties. In job enlargement the additional work is by its nature related to what the employee has been doing. Because the new responsibilities are more of the same, employees can develop the suspicion that they have been "punished" for performing well. The result could be demotivation, not only among the employees whose jobs have been enlarged but also among those who see the enlarging as exploitation.

Thus, when you enlarge a job, you have to take special care to make sure that the employee sees it for what you intend it to be: a reinforcer, a recognition of the person's accomplishments. For example, if you add more work, you also increase the person's salary. But that isn't always possible. However, there are other ways to compensate besides money. If you publicize the enlargement, you could be increasing the employee's status. An increase in status is especially appealing to a person who is turned on by competition. You thereby provide the outstanding performer with a chance to show that he or she is clearly an acknowledged superior employee.

Underutilization is another argument for enlarging responsibility. The person is not busy, or has become so adept at fulfilling the original responsibilities that it takes only part of the work schedule to do what formerly required full-time activity. For such an employee, more of the same might be a better option than boredom.

But, in general, to avoid the suspicion of exploitation that attaches to enlargement, couple the additional assignment with praise, publicity, or some perquisites such as a better office, more time off, money, or some other reward that the employee values. Make it a matter of increased status, a recognition of achievement. Appeal to the employee's self-esteem or competitive spirit. Or, if you can justify it, hold out the chance of a promotion if the new work load is handled successfully. Just be very aware that, while job enlargement is a legitimate motivational tool, it may easily be misunderstood or seem exploitive unless you take appropriate steps.

Job Enrichment

Compared to job enlargement, job enrichment is a more obvious way of increasing an employee's value to self and the organization. Another common term for enriching a job is vertical loading (as opposed to the horizontal loading in enlargement). Your message to the employee is, "Because you have performed so well at your level, I shall give you some responsibility that actually belongs at a higher level." It's not a promotion. You're just giving the employee a chance to do more responsible work than normally he or she would be entitled to at his or her grade or level. For example, you assign a capable employee to train a new member of the department, something that a foreman or supervisor would normally do. Or, an employee who regularly submits reports is asked to review the reports of co-workers and prepare a summary of all of them.

Where do you find higher-level responsibilities to enrich a high performer's job? The following checklist can help start your search:

☐ Duties or functions that you perform and that you no longer find interesting or challenging.

☐ Elements of lower-level jobs that you reserved for yourself as you were being promoted but that are more appropriate for your employees to do.

☐ Job functions that you like, would hate to give up, and yet could be performed as well by someone on a lower level. (Giving up something you like is an investment you make in a promising employee.)

☐ Duties and responsibilities that one of your supervisors no longer finds exciting and would be happy to give up in exchange for one of yours.

☐ An innovation in the department that you have long wished for but did not have the time or the personnel to institute formerly.

☐ Components of a higher-level job that was done by someone who retired or resigned without being replaced (if there are several parts to this job, they could conceivably be distributed to several high performers).

In short, you don't have to look very far to find jobs, tasks, and responsibilities that you have been performing that you don't really have to, or some that you are not doing now—indeed no one is—but that you would like to see done.

On the other hand, you can start with the employee rather than with yourself by asking the employee to define the job he or she would find challenging. This will enable you to determine how many of the desired components of that ideal job you can actually provide him or her.

Job enrichment can be a powerful motivational tool for you, and helps you to accomplish other important objectives. For example, by enriching the jobs of your subordinates, you take giant strides toward upgrading the effectiveness of the whole department. Also, you cultivate successors. You become more "available" for advancement since it becomes generally known that you have a capable work group and a potential replacement. But for you, enriching the work of subordinates can lead to making your own work more satisfying and rewarding. By getting rid of some of your work that others can do, you free yourself to tackle challenging problems and to plan innovations that can stamp you as a valuable member of the management team, certainly someone who has the potential to go further than where you are now.

Job Rotation

When employees have turned in good work in one job, consider letting them take on different assignments. In the case of rotation, employees would be learning new skills, dealing with different co-workers, and perhaps showing versatility. There is no question about employees increasing their value to you and the organization. The reason for the change should be understood on that basis: It will increase your worth. Job rotation has great potential motivational value because it periodically puts employees in a learning situation. Employees can be challenged, see progress, feel as if they are advancing. Growth is a stimulator and motivator. And, of course, you are developing a multiskilled, flexible, and adaptable work group.

Committee or Task Force

Putting your high performer on a committee or a task force may be an enriching experience you haven't considered. Membership in a temporary problem-solving group can extend the experience of a good performer. It can be stimulating to sit with other superior employees to solve a significant problem or to launch a project. When you appoint a subordinate to such a group, you broadcast to everyone that the employee is well regarded by management.

For good performers, membership on a committee or a task force provides an opportunity to expand their knowledge, to add to their experience, to learn new skills, and to bolster their self-confidence.

For you, an effective committee or a task force offers a way to solve problems, make profitable decisions, explore and exploit opportunities, and develop methods to expand your human resources.

Your best bet for achieving all of the above results for you and the individuals involved is a group that is:

☐ Formed to accomplish a specific task.

☐ A temporary problem-solving group with the authority and responsibility to do what is necessary to achieve its goal.

☐ Semi-autonomous. The group should be as free as possible to establish its schedule, methods of working, and so on.

Putting people on a committee with an indeterminate mission, little or no responsibility for implementing its work, and with no time schedule can be demotivating. It is usually a waste of good talent. So, assign a problem or a project to the group and, with no more supervision and monitoring than is necessary, let them go to work.

There's a distinction to being asked to work on a project or a problem that the organization regards as important and which, quite possibly, individuals or organizational units have not been able to solve or launch in the past. The distinction is heightened if other members of the committee or task force are also regarded as high performers. It is likely that each person in the group will enjoy more authority than he or she is accustomed to in regular positions, simply because the group has been awarded greater latitude and power than would be available to individuals. The group wields more clout in presenting its solutions and recommendations to management. Participating on a task force brings high visibility with relatively low risk taking.

YOU AS A REWARD

You are one of the most effective rewards you can give for good performance. You may not look at yourself in that light, but it is quite reasonable. If you have established credibility with and respect of your employees, you are a very important figure with them. Because they hold you in esteem, your esteem for them can be a reward that they cherish. For example, if you assign a task or ask an employee to take on a challenging assignment, don't miss the opportunity to let the subordinate know that it is because you esteem his ability that you decided to ask him to do the job. He will then be even more motivated to do a good job so as to justify your confidence in him.

There are other ways that you can position yourself as a reward. Look over the following items to see how many ways you are currently taking advantage of.

Freer Access

Can an employee see you when he or she has a need to? Yes, your schedule may be crowded, and you need time for yourself, to do your work. But there are ways to let certain people know that, even though your schedule is tight and the pressure on you is heavy, you will try to find a way to spend time with them. The message you convey is, "You are very important in this department. What you have to say must therefore be important. I'll manage to make time for you." The result of the message usually is that those people who enjoy freer access to you because of their performance will continue to work so as to merit your esteem.

Informal Relationship

Some managers make it a practice to stop by certain subordinates' offices, desks, or work stations for a chat now and then. The conversation doesn't have to be strictly business. Sometimes, it shouldn't be. A discussion of family, vacation activities, a report in the newspaper, a magazine article, sports, or movies is quite in order. Your informality with the person and your taking the initiative broadcast that you value the relationship you have with that person. If that value is based on the employee's good performance, others will interpret the message: "The boss is closest to people who do a good job."

Consulting

There are perhaps few actions you can take with a subordinate that are more complimentary than to ask for her opinion. It may have to do with an incipient or planned project, a new employee, a restructuring of the department, or some aspect of office decoration. It doesn't have to be adopted. But it must be sincerely sought. You can buttress the impression of sincerity by revisiting the employee later to explain why you couldn't put her suggestion into practice.

Career Counseling

If you are not coaching employees on their growth and development, then it is unlikely that anyone else is. Most employees find that counseling on their career is a rare commodity, especially concerning advice from someone who knows them well, that is, from someone they respect and trust. You occupy a vantage point. You certainly know more than your subordinates about what is happening or about to happen in the organization, the opportunities that are opening up, prerequisites for promotion and certain kinds of jobs, and the career paths that have proved to be more promising. It's possible that many managers don't provide counseling of this type because they know there is a possibility of doing it too well, that because of their guidance they'll lose a valued employee. But that possibility exists always regardless of what you do. In the meantime, your caring counsel can help to ensure continued motivated performance.

Inside Information

There is never enough information in an organization to satisfy employees who are truly involved. In your position, you usually have more of it than employees reporting to you can hope to possess. You don't want to put yourself or others in a bad light by passing along scurrilous gossip, and you don't want to betray confidences. But there is plenty for you to talk about to valued subordinates—imminent announcements about a new product, a relocation of an important executive, promotions that are in the works, an acquisition, and so on. Just be sure that you don't mind that the information is repeated. The employee will relish the opportunity to say that you passed the information along to him or her. Your taking the time to communicate advance or inside information gives the employee extra status.

Your Concern

You can express it on the personal level. For example, you might say, "Look, you've been working awfully hard lately." (Or, "You really knocked yourself out on that special project.") "Why don't you take off early on Friday and enjoy a longer weekend?" Be alert to clues in the employee's behavior that might point to fatigue, worry, boredom, or exuberance. Comment on what you've seen: "It seems to me that you've been looking distracted the last couple of days. Am I right? If I am, is there anything I can do?" That way you show your concern without seeming to meddle. There may in fact be nothing very wrong, but your interest won't go to waste.

Personal Information

You might talk with a key subordinate about a problem you are having at work, or a child who is causing you some concern, or your vacation plans. You don't want to divulge information that would embarrass either of you, but your communicating on a personal level conveys the message: "I value you as a working friend." You thereby strengthen the employee's belief that you esteem him or her.

TRAINING AS A REWARD

Training often carries a negative connotation. Training programs, courses, materials are commonly presented by managers to subordinates as the means to overcome a deficiency. It's probable that such managers are not fully aware of the message. But from the subordinates' viewpoint, the manager may seem to be saying, "You're not doing things the way they ought to be done, so we're going to train you."

Even when there are performance and skills deficiencies, training should be presented in a positive manner. The message should be, "This training will help you to be more effective, that is, to get more of the results you want more often." It is by and large a message arousing defensiveness because it is a rare person who believes that he or she is as effective as he or she wants to be in every situation.

Surprisingly little recognition is given to the reality that people, at least most people, want to grow. They want to become more proficient at what they are good at doing and, in most cases, what they like to do. Herzberg identifies this desire in people as a motivator. Training and education can help people to develop their potential, or in Maslow's terms, to actualize themselves, to become more of what they are capable of becoming.

One manager tells of an experience he had that demonstrates the difference between presenting training as corrective and as a reinforcer. The manager attended a workshop on assertiveness training for managers. During the usual introduction period, when attendees were asked why they were there, most replied that their bosses had recommended that they go. Either they were, in their managers' perceptions, nonassertive or they were aggressive, neither extreme being desirable behavior. Clearly their bosses were saying to them, "You're deficient," or "I don't care for you the way you are. Go change yourself." It's reasonably safe to assume that any behavior change in these people was temporary and superficial. Truth to tell, they probably resented being so labeled and sent to "reform school."

The contrast was provided, for this manager, a short time later when he attended another workshop with an emphasis on public speaking. Most employees would not find this kind of training essential to the performance of their duties. That was true of most of the workshop participants. According to their introductions of themselves, most of them had come to sharpen skills that, while not immediately applicable, could be beneficial to them in years to come.

It doesn't take much imagination to predict how a valued employee would feel if the boss said, "I know of a good workshop on speaking skills. Someday being able to get up before a group and speaking well might be useful. If you'd like to go, we'll foot the bill."

Most training and education that is paid for by the organization is seen as work-related, and understandably so. But don't rule out courses, seminars, workshops, and lectures that broaden the perspective and deepen the thinking of the participants, even if they don't necessarily contribute to the everyday effectiveness of the employee on the job. The more personal the benefit, the greater the probability that the employee will see the training as a reward and reinforcement. Even when the benefit has doubtful pertinence to the job at hand, the manager can find a way to say, "You are valuable to us now. In some way, this will help you to be even more valuable to us."

For you, the ideal training takes place sequentially. That is, each training segment would qualify the employee for more responsibility, and good performance in that greater capacity would lead to more training, and so forth. For example, a manager on a marketing track might go from field management of salespeople to data processing and forecasting. Eventually the manager could enter the world of strategic planning.

MONEY AS A MOTIVATOR

Salary is not a satisfier (motivator), Frederick Herzberg maintains. Periodic surveys that ask employees what they look for in a job or what satisfies them most about work seem to support his research. Money is never one of the highly ranked responses. People identify "interesting work" or the "opportunity to get ahead" as more important to them than money.

Can it be concluded, therefore, that money does not really motivate? No. Money can be perceived by people as a recognition of good performance. It can be a motivator, if three conditions are present:

1. The employee must see a clear link between the work done and the rewarding of money.
2. The money must be given as a reward soon after the performance or often enough, in the case of continuing performance, so that the employee sees the link.
3. The amount must be proportionate to the work done.

A study on the work ethic conducted by the nonprofit Public Agenda Foundation of New York and released in 1983 reported that only 22 percent of American workers believe there is a direct relationship between how hard they work and how much they are paid. Several factors can explain this low percentage:

☐ In the case of unionized workers, individual performance does not determine how much the employee will make except for overtime. But even overtime is not a function of or an indicator of the quality of work done.

☐ Many organizations provide periodic "merit" increases, say, once a year. Thus, an employee who performs outstandingly in a task or assignment in January may have to wait until the following January to receive monetary recognition.

☐ The merit increases may be given to most or all employees in a department, and they may be approximately the same amount.

☐ Many merit increases are so little that the employee cannot regard them as truly proportionate to the performance. It's safe to say that in most organizations it is very difficult for a truly outstanding performer to make very much more money as a result of that performance (which is one reason why people leave organizations to become entrepreneurs).

Thus the average merit increase system can be characterized as too little and too late to serve as a motivator. In some public sector positions, employees wait years for a small increase.

Some organizations permit their managers to set aside a certain amount of money in their budgets each year to distribute as bonuses for superior work. If employees know that their good work will earn them a bonus, they can be motivated by the anticipation of it. *Anticipation*, incidentally, is the key word. Even managers who are stuck with the annual merit increase can get some mileage out of it in the latter months before the increase is given. They might say to highly performing employees, "If you maintain this fine level of work, I'll put you in for the highest merit increase I can get approved." Of course, managers who say that in October have to be somewhat sure that their recommendations will indeed be approved in January.

Once the money has been given, Herzberg argues, it no longer has motivational value. The employee accepts the new level of income as a given. According to Herzberg's reasoning, only the anticipation of more money soon and in a sufficient amount will motivate employees. In that capacity the money becomes a recognition of achievement, which, you'll recall, has been identified in Herzberg's research as a motivator.

What about the periodic studies in which money is ranked usually fourth or fifth as a motivator? They demonstrate rather clearly that most people do not work primarily for money. That shouldn't be a surprise to their managers who also, generally speaking, work for other reasons besides money. The results may also reflect the realistic perspectives of most employees, who know very well that their organizations are not going to provide them with a great deal of money as a reward.

PLAYING FAVORITES

If you follow the principle that good performance deserves to be well rewarded, and that outstanding work should be recognized in an exceptional way, you will eventually ask yourself whether, in the eyes of other employees, you are showing favoritism toward your better-performing subordinates. In the quantity and the quality of their work, in their problem-solving zeal, in their innovative-ness, some people will stand out. To those people you will no doubt consider granting privileges not enjoyed by others: You will want to see that they receive the larger portion of salary increases permitted by your budget. You will want to grant them increased responsibility, to promote them, to make sure they get the choice assignments. You will make efforts to help them achieve more visibility in the organization.

In providing the greatest rewards for the employees who give you the most, you may, admittedly, stir up a lot of grumbling among other employees. They will probably be jealous, even re-sentful, of your special efforts on behalf of some of their colleagues. A certain amount of discontent, of envy, is inevitable. Rather than put themselves out or extend themselves, some employees will rationalize their mediocre performance. They will usually find some external factor, some other person, some rule, regulation, or procedure, that keeps them from doing a good job. Ironically, they may point to your favored treatment of their hardworking co-workers and conclude that there is just no way "to win around here," that their improved performance won't be recognized any-way. After all, you "play favorites."

But, if the grousing is widespread and continuing among your subordinates, it may constitute a clear signal that your perfor-mance standards are not understood. The following recommenda-tions can help you to reduce such grousing but, even more impor-tant, assist you in establishing a strong link between outstanding performance and exceptional treatment.

Extend Favored Treatment Only for Performance

It must be evident to everyone that the rewards go to good per-formers. You may be tempted to extend favors to people who have worked for you for a long time, who are senior in responsibility, who are especially cooperative or whom you like or get along with easily. But that kind of favoritism clouds the issue: The link be-tween performance and favors must be clearly established in the minds of the employees.

Favored Treatment Should Be Given Only for Consistently Outstanding Performance

Giving special treatment on a continuing basis means that the employee who receives it continues to turn in special work. Occasional exceptional performance can be recognized on a one-time basis, as it is done or completed. Through favoritism you want to encourage consistently high performance. That means, of course, that your own measuring and monitoring must be kept up to date. Otherwise you may find yourself continuing to single out an employee for special treatment when that employee's performance is no longer what it was. It is not unusual for employees to coast on their reputations and for managers to reward from inertia. If the outstanding work stops, so does the extra consideration on your part.

Avoid Comparing Employees

Employees who are not among the favored will complain from time to time or will at least drop hints that there is, in their view, discrimination. Avoid any temptation to say, "Well, if you worked like Charlie, you'd get special treatment, too." It's possible that no one can work just like Charlie. Take the opportunity instead to explain your standards and what level of accomplishment above those standards will win the prizes. You may even want to go so far as to counsel the individual on his or her performance deficiencies and potential areas of improvement. Turn the grousing into a hunger for something better.

Be Consistent and Fair in Extending Favored Treatment

There must be some fairly objective way you can define the level and type of performance that merits special attention, privileges, and rights. Stick with that definition. If employees become convinced that you will be fair, that you can be relied on to reward well and consistently, they'll respond favorably.

GIVING PRAISE

Recently managers in a leadership skills workshop were given an action plan: Go back to your work scene, and watch the behavior of your subordinates. When you see someone doing something that merits your approval, stop the employee and praise the action. Tell the employee how much you appreciate what he or she did. The managers were told that the action to be praised and complimented didn't have to be extraordinary. It did have to be effective. For example, it might have been an act of cooperation with another employee, an impressive way of communicating with a customer, a mission that was more than what was required in the job description or above the manager's expressed expectations. The managers were to come back the following week and report on what happened.

To a person, the managers described how pleased the employees were that the managers had observed and appreciated what the employees had done. They were surprised that the employees were grateful for the attention. Several managers told how the employees had thanked them for their positive reinforcement.

Praise is a positive reinforcer that is most available to you. It is also surprisingly seldom used. It is simple, inexpensive, and inexhaustible. Managers who use it well testify to its effectiveness. When it is done right, praise has a ripple effect. Not only does it provide a reward for the person who is performing well, it broadcasts to the entire group that good work will be recognized.

Yet, like the managers in the workshop, most managers do not use praise often. They are surprised when it works well. Why don't managers use praise more often? The answer is probably that many managers are skeptical: They don't believe that it works. They cannot accept that employees are happy with a few well-chosen words. Managers protest, when urged to praise, "If I do that, people will say, 'I'd rather you give me money.'" Yet, when managers adopt the habit of giving verbal positive reinforcement, they find that seldom do people ask for money. They do not discount the praise. Quite the contrary, they value the praise for itself.

There may be other reasons why many managers tend to shy away from praise.

It May Appear Manipulative

The manager may worry about seeming to play a role, somewhat like the proverbial salesperson who is forever "up" and patting people on the back. But there is no "act" involved in praising the work of an employee that definitely deserves praise. If the employee works well, and if the manager and the employee have a trusting relationship, there is nothing phony about saying, enthusiastically, "That was a great job."

Why Praise for Something That Is Supposed To Be Done Well Anyway?

That's the old military attitude. The problem is that unless employees get positive feedback and support from you, they don't always know they're doing the job the way you want it done. If you praise them when they deserve it, employees are more likely to repeat the good work because they know it is what you want and they want your continuing esteem.

Praise May Be Construed as a Promise

The manager says, "You keep up this kind of work, and I'm sure you'll enjoy a good future here." In the employee's mind, the manager fears, this has become a promissory note. The manager is not sure of being able to deliver on that future. Well, chances are, the employee understands that too. If the manager praises in good faith, the employee will accept the fact that whatever the future holds is subject to many variables. Interestingly, even when the manager makes no reference to the future or to any other rewards, he or she may worry that, no matter how vague the wording, the employee will expect something else such as money, as mentioned earlier. For most employees, praise for a job well done does not constitute a contract for the future or for any other thing.

Praise Makes a Manager Vulnerable

Complimenting employees on the quality and quantity of their work may imply or reinforce a manager's dependency on them. But that dependency would seem to be a given. Managers need subordinates. Subordinates surely recognize the relationship. The manager's recognition of it would seem to underline and honor the bond between manager and subordinates.

Managers Get Too Busy to Praise

This is probably the single most frequent problem of managers and the reason why they forget to say "thank you" for the performances they expect. Of course, when they don't get what they want, they seldom forget to say something.

Even the best manager will have a memory slip. One excellent executive tells about the time he asked one of his high performers to take on a rush job. The subordinate completed the work on time and in great fashion. The executive breathed a sigh of relief. The next day he encountered the subordinate in the corridor. The subordinate smiled and said, "You're welcome." Even the best of us can overlook praising.

Once a manager becomes proficient in positively reinforcing through praise, he or she will understand how much easier it is to influence the right kind of behavior while the work is being done than to have to criticize and correct after mistakes and deficiencies have become evident.

Effective positive reinforcement through praise of subordinates will reinforce not only their behavior but yours. When your praise leads to better performance by subordinates, the results will constitute a reward for your efforts. Your use of praise will grow.

A VARIETY OF REWARDS

The verbal praise can be accompanied by written recognition for the employee's personnel file. Even a memo for the person's own file can be valued. If the occasion and achievement warrant it, a memo on the bulletin board, a report circulated, a letter to higher management, an article in the organizational publication, all serve to reinforce your verbal recognition.

There are innumerable other ways to positively reinforce commendable performance. Here are just a few of them.

More Desirable Workplace

What comes to mind, of course, is the corner office. But it doesn't have to be elaborate. There are various hierarchies of values when it comes to where one would like to work—near the door, out of the traffic pattern, in a highly visible place, in a more private location, away from the windows, near the windows, in a location separate from others and the general workplace, in the new part of the building, near your office, and so on.

How about the furnishings? You might be able to authorize a new desk, chair, or rug. One manager was well known for his love of plants, and he was most appreciative when his manager made available an office with southern exposure.

Just make sure the word gets out: First choice goes to the better performers. And don't forget that small things count. Giving a good employee a little extra space around the desk can be significant.

Equipment

A more elaborate calculator, a word processor, typewriter, a two-line or direct access telephone. Ask yourself, "What kind of equipment would make this person's job easier?" That constitutes recognition of performance.

More Freedom

One subordinate is given the chance to set his own working hours. A specialist who has formerly had her work checked by the boss now performs that function herself. These are two examples of subordinates' enjoying more freedom over their work. Other employees have latitude when it comes to selecting their assignments, how they will work, even where they will work: Some subordinates are given the chance to work at home occasionally.

Providing more freedom for an employee—the what, when, how, and where—is a reinforcer too little utilized by managers. That is surprising, especially in view of the probability that many good performers have demonstrated their ability, indeed, often their preference, to work without close supervision. Making that freedom official is a message that high performers will understand and appreciate. The privileges don't have to be extensive. They do, however, have to be regarded by the favored employees and everyone else—including your boss—not as lax management or indifference, but as a reward for service.

Opportunity to Represent You

Give a valuable employee the chance to chair a meeting that you would have otherwise presided over. Or, if there is an interdepartmental meeting where your presence is helpful but not essential, send a favored subordinate instead. You will be represented, and the employee will feel special. Is there a business trip that you feel you must make but don't have time to? Perhaps a knowledgeable employee could fill in for you. It won't be a nuisance trip for him or her. Is someone visiting from the home or a branch office? Let the subordinate take the visitor to lunch or dinner (unless of course the visitor is important enough to feel offended by your not performing the courtesy).

Opportunity to Accompany You

When there is a meeting with higher management, an interdepartmental get-together, a lunch with someone important in the organization, occasionally invite a high performer to go with you. It gives the employee visibility and the feeling of being singled out.

Preference on Selecting Vacation

Where the rule of seniority is not involved, let your more valuable subordinates have first choice on vacation times. If some people have to work holidays and overtime, again, where union rules are not involved, give the best employees the first choice.

Lunch or Dinner

People who work well for you would probably feel honored by your occasional invitation to join you for lunch. For some employees dinner with you may be inconvenient. But if you picked up the dinner tab for a valuable employee and a spouse/friend, you might get a reinforcing message across. Incidentally, you don't necessarily have to pay the check when you invite a subordinate to lunch. The effect will be beneficial if you make a point of inviting your better performers to lunch with you on a fairly regular basis. Your favoritism will be based on their level of performance.

A Token Gift

A plant for the office, a book that you know the person would be interested in, an attractive ornament for the desk would be an inexpensive but effective reminder that you appreciate the kind of work being done for you.

Substitution for You When You're Away

When you leave on a business trip or vacation, you may designate certain key subordinates to oversee tasks or assignments in your absence. Put the authority in writing, not only to make it official but to make it public.

Coaching for Growth

It's in your best interest as well as in the interest of your entire work group to give each employee guidance on developing his or her skills and expanding the employee's knowledge. But you can make a special point of giving favored people more extensive and more frequent attention. Coaching as a managerial function will be treated more in detail later in Chapter 12.

Preferred Assignments

Give favored employees more opportunities to do the kind of work they have shown that they like to do.

"Thank You"

You can get gratifying results from a simple expression of appreciation. Those two words can produce results that belie the words' simplicity. It's safe to say that managers don't use them often enough. When you say them, look the employee in the eye, smile, shake hands if you like, and express the words warmly.

A CLEAR LINK

Your management of employees' motivation would be much simplified if you could know what kind of work appeals to each person's motivating forces and you could make a perfect match between preferences and assignments. But, of course, your knowledge of employees' motivations will always be at least somewhat clouded—as their self-perceptions will be.

You can, however, make up for the lack of perfect knowledge by building in as much value as you can by granting rewards for the kind of performance you want. But in order to achieve the results you desire from your external rewards, you would be well advised to observe the following two recommendations:

1. *Reward consistently.* When you get good performance, recognize it on a consistent basis. That's how you establish, in the minds of subordinates, a clear link between performance and rewards. You want them to believe that "around here, you do a good job, and you get rewarded for it."

2. *Vary the type of recognition.* Review "A Quick Reference Checklist of Available Reinforcers" that follows, to make sure that you are using your full inventory. You don't want your rewards to be too predictable or to become trite. You can be consistent in giving them without diluting their effect because of their sameness.

How to give rewards effectively will be the subject of Chapter 15.

A QUICK REFERENCE CHECKLIST OF AVAILABLE REINFORCERS

1. Expanding the job with responsibilities from the same level (job enlargement).
2. Adding responsibility from a higher level (job enrichment).
3. Rotating the employee among jobs.
4. Assignment to a committee or task force.
5. Freer and quicker access to you.
6. Making a point of chatting, of establishing an informal relationship.
7. Seeking opinions and suggestions.
8. Advising on careers and organizational opportunities.
9. Providing information about the organization that is not confidential but not generally known.
10. Showing your concern for the employee's well-being.
11. Revealing some of your own problems.
12. Training.
13. Education.
14. Coaching.
15. Promising more money.
16. Praising.
17. Promising a promotion.
18. A more desirable office or work station.
19. New or better furnishings.
20. New or better equipment.
21. Giving more freedom to employees to select their own assignments.
22. More freedom to set their own hours.
23. More freedom to choose their own methods of work.
24. Chance to work at home occasionally.
25. Giving opportunities to work without close supervision.
26. A chance to chair a meeting for you.

27.   A chance to represent you at an interdepartmental meeting.
28.   A business trip in your stead.
29.   Taking a client or other visitor to lunch or dinner.
30.   Giving an opportunity to go with you outside the department to a meeting, on a trip, etc.
31.   Preference in selecting vacations or overtime.
32.   Lunch or dinner on the organization.
33.   A party.
34.   A gift—a plant, book, etc.
35.   Oversee tasks and assignments when you're away.
36.   Preferred assignments.
37.   "Thank you."

REVIEW OF MAKING THE WORK MORE VALUABLE

		Yes	No	Not Sure
1.	You can add value to work by assigning tasks that enable employees to achieve their personal goals through doing them.	___	___	___
2.	Internal rewards are generated within the employee.	___	___	___
3.	The manager is not able to influence internal rewards.	___	___	___
4.	The manager can help the employee to recognize his or her internal rewards.	___	___	___
5.	A sense of growth is a powerful internal reward.	___	___	___
6.	The esteem of others is also a valued internal reward.	___	___	___
7.	A manager can suggest ways in which an employee can increase his or her acceptance by peers, a strong internal reward.	___	___	___
8.	Employees automatically reward themselves when they work well.	___	___	___
9.	Usually the most potent reinforcer is an internal reward backed up by one that is external, coming from you.	___	___	___
10.	In some cases additional work can be used as a reward for good performance.	___	___	___

	Yes	No	Not Sure
11. For work to be seen as a reward, it should offer more interest and challenge than the work the employee has been doing.	____	____	____
12. Most employees value job enlargement as a reward for good performance.	____	____	____
13. Generally the way to present job enlargement as a reinforcer is to couple it with some other kind of reward.	____	____	____
14. Another term to describe job enrichment is horizontal loading.	____	____	____
15. In vertical loading the manager adds a higher-level responsibility to an employee's work.	____	____	____
16. One of the fertile areas for finding higher-level responsibility to push down to a lower level is among your tasks.	____	____	____
17. Job enrichment can be a powerful motivational tool for you.	____	____	____
18. Employees may resist job enlargement as exploitive, but they usually welcome enrichment.	____	____	____
19. Job rotation has potential motivational value because it periodically puts the employee in a learning situation.	____	____	____
20. Assigning employees to task forces as a reward for good performance is a reinforcement underutilized by most managers.	____	____	____

	Yes	No	Not Sure
21. Freer access to you, by virtue of your position and authority, can be seen as a reward by your employees.	___	___	___
22. Providing special coaching to an employee on his or her career development is a reward much appreciated by ambitious employees.	___	___	___
23. Positioning yourself as a reward to employees for their good performance requires first that you have established a working relationship of credibility and respect.	___	___	___
24. For best results, training should be presented as a means for helping the employee to be more effective at work.	___	___	___
25. Training as a means to grow and advance on the job can be a desired reward and, therefore, a motivator.	___	___	___
26. Money is not a motivator.	___	___	___
27. When a manager shows favoritism toward some employees, the result is that others are demotivated.	___	___	___
28. It is good managerial practice to provide the greatest rewards for the employees who give you the best performance.	___	___	___
29. Favored treatment should be extended only for consistently outstanding performance.	___	___	___

	Yes	No	Not Sure
30. When an employee who is not favored complains about your favoritism toward another, suggest that he or she emulate the other's performance.	___	___	___
31. It is fair to say that praise is a reinforcer that managers too seldom use effectively.	___	___	___
32. Probably one of the more common reasons why managers do not praise consistently for good performance is that they don't think people really value it as a reward.	___	___	___
33. One danger of using praise as a reinforcer is that the employees who are praised will expect an increase in salary.	___	___	___
34. More control over their own work is a highly prized reward that many employees seek.	___	___	___
35. A simple but sincere "Thank you" can get gratifying results from employees.	___	___	___
36. Two general principles of building value into the work are to reward consistently for good performance and to vary the kinds of recognition.	___	___	___

Answers to Review

1. Yes
2. Yes
3. No
4. Yes
5. Yes
6. No. Self-esteem is the internal reward. The esteem of others is external.
7. Yes
8. Not sure. A manager is well-advised not to assume automatic rewarding by employees.
9. Yes
10. Yes
11. Yes
12. Not sure. Sometimes adding more work to an employee's work load may be seen by the employee as exploitation.
13. Yes
14. No. It is *vertical* loading.
15. Yes
16. Yes
17. Yes
18. Not sure. Some employees may be quite content with their work load and may not welcome additional responsibility.
19. Yes
20. Yes. Task forces are not widely used in American organizations.
21. Not sure. Usually, for employees to see access to you as a reward, there must be a working relationship of credibility and respect.
22. Yes
23. Yes

24. Yes
25. Yes
26. Not sure. The anticipation of more money for good perfor-
    mance may be. Herzberg says that once it has been given,
    however, it has no motivational value. It becomes a dissatis-
    fier.
27. Not sure. They may grumble, but your favoritism may actu-
    ally create stronger motivation in them to do better work
    so as to enjoy your favored treatment.
28. Yes
29. Yes
30. No. Explain your standards. The employee may not be able to
    emulate another's performance but can meet your standards.
31. Yes
32. Yes
33. Not sure. It's doubtful. There is no evidence that people who
    are praised generally expect it to be followed by more money.
34. Yes
35. Yes
36. Yes

7

DELEGATION AS A
MOTIVATIONAL TOOL

You have probably heard that delegation is a good practice, since it helps you to create time for yourself to do those things that are properly yours to do.

That's certainly true.

But look at delegation from the other side: What are the needs and abilities of the employees who report to you? After all, shouldn't delegation be considered in the light of their skills as well as your own interests? Of their desires to grow? Shouldn't what you delegate depend on what they have the capacity to handle and succeed at?

Suppose, though, that they don't have the capability to handle some of the tasks that you perform now. Then perhaps you ought to be asking yourself some hard questions:

☐ Why don't they have that capability?
☐ What do they need to develop it?
☐ What am I doing to help them develop it?

Basically, most people consider that there are at least three aspects of the manager's job:

1. Managing the routine, or what is being done now.
2. Solving problems.
3. Innovating.

Why should you be doing any part of the routine? If it is something your department has been doing, why do you concern yourself with it (except, of course, to make sure the job is being done in the most effective way possible)?

Furthermore, why should you take on all the problems yourself? How much risk is there in letting the employees have a crack at them? Chances are that employees won't foul the situation up any more than it is already, and they may well develop workable solutions.

The same can be said of innovation: If something does not yet exist, no one can ruin it. And it's just possible that some employees can come up with a pretty good way to do what is not now being done.

There's a fourth aspect of your job—in addition to the routine, problem solving, and innovation—that many managers under the stress of everyday deadlines and fighting fires tend to overlook: developing subordinates. Pushing your responsibilities down is a time-tested means to that end. And if it promotes growth in subordinates, then delegation enhances their everyday motivation at the same time.

You might wish to complete the following Should You Delegate Checklist to see whether you could delegate more to subordinates.

SHOULD YOU DELEGATE CHECKLIST

1. Do you take work home often, more often than other managers in comparable situations?   _____   _____

   If your answer is yes, list tasks that you now perform that could be delegated.

   a. Tasks that you do because you like to do them: _____

   _____

   _____

   _____

   _____

   _____

   b. Tasks that you held onto when you had your last promotion, that you brought upward with you: _____

   _____

   _____

   _____

   _____

   c. Tasks that have become so routinized that some of your subordinates can do them:

   _____

   _____

   _____

   _____

   d. Tasks that you formerly liked to do but no longer care to do: _____

   _____

   _____

   _____

Yes   No

 e. Other tasks that could be done by others:

  _____

  _____

  _____

  _____

  _____

2. Do you work longer hours than the people
 you manage?   _____ _____
 If your answer is yes, list below those tasks
 that contribute substantially to your work
 load and components of those tasks that
 might be delegated to others.

 Task: _____

 Components: _____

    _____

    _____

    _____

 Task: _____

 Components: _____

    _____

    _____

    _____

 Task: _____

 Components: _____

    _____

    _____

    _____

3. Do you spend part of your day doing tasks
 for others that they could do on their own? _____ _____
 If your answer is yes, list the actions that
 you can avoid: _____

  _____

  _____

  _____

  _____

  _____

Yes   No

4. Do you lack confidence in the abilities of any
   of your subordinates, which prevents you
   from delegating to those persons?   _____   _____
   If your answer is yes, list the specific steps
   you can take with each subordinate to improve that employee's skills.
   Name: _____
      Steps: _____
             _____
             _____

   Name: _____
      Steps: _____
             _____
             _____

   Name: _____
      Steps: _____
             _____
             _____

5. Are there tasks that you would like to delegate but have not because you have not
   wished to take the time to instruct the subordinate?   _____   _____
   If your answer is yes, list below the subordi-
   nate, the task, and the date by which you
   promise yourself that you will have delegated the task:
   Name: _____
      Task: _____
      Action plan: _____
                   _____
                   _____
                   _____
      Date of completion: _____
   Name: _____
      Task: _____
      Action plan: _____
                   _____
      Date of completion: _____

	Yes	No

6. Do you admit to yourself that you are a perfectionist on details, big and small? _____ _____
   If your answer is yes, list below the tasks that require less than perfection:
   1. _____
   2. _____
   3. _____
   4. _____
   5. _____

   You may have been holding onto the above tasks because you have been demanding perfection. Check off any of the above that you now believe that you can delegate.

7. When you return from an absence, have matters that others thought needed your attention piled up? _____ _____
   If your answer is yes, what actions can you take and with which subordinates, to reduce the amount of work left for your return?
   Name: _____
       Action plan: _____
                  _____
                  _____
                  _____

   Name: _____
       Action plan: _____
                  _____
                  _____
                  _____

   Name: _____
       Action plan: _____
                  _____
                  _____
                  _____

Yes   No

8. Do you feel that your authority results in
   your being able to undertake more work or to
   have a greater sense of responsibility than
   your subordinates could achieve?   _____   _____
   If your answer is yes, how can you increase
   the authority of your key subordinates?
   Name: _____
       Action plan: _____
                    _____
                    _____
                    _____

   Name: _____
       Action plan: _____
                    _____
                    _____
                    _____

9. Do you believe it is impossible to delegate to
   your subordinates because they are just too
   busy?   _____   _____
   If your answer is yes, how can the work load
   be reduced or redistributed?
   Action plan 1: _____
   _____
   _____
   _____

   Action plan 2: _____
   _____
   _____
   _____

   Action plan 3: _____
   _____
   _____
   _____

	Yes	No

10. Have you observed your supervisors per-
    forming tasks that in your opinion they could
    delegate to their subordinates?   ____   ____
    If your answer is yes, list below the supervi-
    sor's name, tasks delegatable, and subordi-
    nate to whom you believe the task could be
    delegated:
    Supervisor: _____
        Task: _____
        Subordinate: _____
    Supervisor: _____
        Task: _____
        Subordinate: _____

If your answers indicate that you do a good job of delegating generally, you may wish to consult the Delegation Update form that appears at the end of the chapter to make sure that on a continuing basis you take advantage of every opportunity to delegate.

BUILDING THROUGH DELEGATION

If you are feeling overworked, for your sake and that of your employees you ought to be delegating more responsibility. Or perhaps you sense that some of your better performers are becoming a bit bored or restless. Maybe some or all of your people have been through a training program, and you are looking for ways to help them apply on the work scene what they learned in the classroom.

In short, it may be the right time to help your employees to stretch themselves, to acquire more experience, sharper skills, and greater knowledge. The result will be increased motivation. Here are some recommendations:

☐ *Don't Limit Delegation to Proven Performers.* If you distribute assignments to everyone, you build a team of versatile performers, a handy group to have when crises or emergencies arise.

☐ *Select Assignments That Stretch, But Not to the Breaking Point.* The purpose is to build your subordinates' confidence in handling unfamiliar assignments. That purpose is ill-served if they fail on the first try.

☐ *Find an Assignment That Will Interest the Individual.* This will motivate the employee to give the job fuller attention. If it is not always possible to choose interesting jobs, it should at least be possible to indicate that successful completion of this task will lead to some kind of valued reward such as a better job, more responsibility, or more money.

☐ *Question Subordinates to Make Sure They Understand What Is To Be Done.* Your questions should be open-ended so that they require a more detailed response than yes or no. Ask questions such as how they regard the job, what it entails, how long it will take, or what they think the final results will be.

☐ *Don't Use the Same Coaching Techniques with Everyone.* Some employees may need only a brief discussion of the general principles involved in carrying out a new type of assignment. Others will need guidance over a period of weeks.

☐ *Give the Subordinates the Responsibility and the Authority to Carry Out the Job.* Part of your job when delegating is to explain and demonstrate. The rest is to leave subordinates alone to carry out the assignment in their own way. If an individual asks for help later—or if it becomes obvious that help is needed—never provide a complete answer or detailed procedure. Instead, help people to think through problems to find their own solutions.

CUTTING RISKS IN DELEGATING

You can't be blamed if you hesitate to delegate to subordinates because you are not quite confident they will do the job in the way you believe it should be done. After all, you are responsible for the results, even when they are completed by those who report to you. How can you ease into delegation comfortably, to build up a subordinate's job without creating an undue risk for yourself? Here are some steps to take:

☐ *Assign Information Gathering.* For example, your department is experiencing too many equipment breakdowns. You decide to ask for new machines. But first you will need downtime figures to back up your request to higher management. Having a subordinate gather those data forces you to explain what figures you need and in what form they should be put. This teaches the subordinate some new things about the department as well as how the boss makes decisions.

☐ *Give Out Parts of Some Jobs.* You get the go-ahead to buy the new equipment and now need to find out what's available. You ask a subordinate to look at options. Again you have to think out and describe what features and benefits to look for.

☐ *Ask for Recommendations.* You feel that the subordinate could make a costly mistake in deciding what equipment to buy. So you ask for three or four recommendations. You pick one, explaining your preference.

☐ *Keep Control Until You Feel a Subordinate Is Ready to Take Over*. For example, instead of picking the new equipment outright, you say to the subordinate, "You make a choice and discuss it with me. I'll retain final approval."

☐ *Schedule Frequent Reports*. When you assign big responsibilities, require the individual to touch base with you frequently until the job is finished. In that way you are never far out of the picture. As you both gain confidence, you can waive this requirement.

☐ *Relinquish Authority Gradually*. Let up as it becomes obvious that the subordinate can handle specific types of responsibility and feels secure in doing so. The person who oversees the purchase and installation of the equipment can be told, for instance, "You handle any decisions involving the replacement of existing equipment. Just check with me before adding any new capability."

DELEGATING WHEN YOU'RE AWAY

When you go away on a business trip or a vacation is an excellent time to delegate. Not only does delegation at this time tell employees that they should be more self-starting and assume more responsibility, but you also reduce tension and worry among them as to how matters should be handled in your absence. Here are some steps for you to consider:

1. *Prepare a list of problems that might arise in your absence.* No one expects you to have a crystal ball, of course, but at the same time, you probably have a fair idea of what problems might arise.

2. *Arrange with subordinates how to handle these contingencies*. Make explicit assignments and grant authority.

3. *Make sure your secretary or another key person knows of these arrangements and assignments.* Make sure that other people in the department also know that your key person is the one to consult if there are any questions about assignments.

4.   *Provide the necessary information for the appropriate subordinate.* Don't leave valuable data locked in your desk where it is inaccessible.

DELEGATING AND STAYING IN CONTROL

No matter how often or much you delegate, you may still feel somewhat nervous when delegating an important task. Remember, you don't have to relinquish all controls. Here are some ways to handle this problem.

Be Honest about Your Anxieties

When you delegate, arrange for periodic reports and consultations. Explain to the employee that you are especially concerned about delegating this task. Set up a reporting and checking schedule at the outset. The employee is less likely to interpret that as negative feedback than he or she might if you impose it after the work begins. The subordinate should get the message that, if the work goes well, your anxieties will abate. You are clearly communicating that the best way to work with you on this task is to keep you in the picture.

Be as Positive as Possible

Make your checkups in a positive manner. For example, "Jane, I happened to come across this report in my files, and I think it covers some of the problems you might be running into." If you make it clear that the subordinate has the choice of whether to use it or not, she shouldn't mind. If she is making progress on the work, most likely your expression of interest will not make her feel uneasy. Rather, she will probably be encouraged to discuss any possible difficulties.

Be Available

If you show that you're willing to supply information or have a discussion with a subordinate about the work in progress, he or she will tend to come to you. Make it clear that you are always there as a resource.

INTERVENING

Some subordinates to whom you have delegated responsibility will be very eager to use you as a resource, to seek your advice or counsel, probably more than you want them to. Sometimes they need the help; at other times they want contact with you. They're in your office with questions such as, "Do you think it will be okay if I . . . ?" or, "I thought I'd better check this out with you." In most cases where you think you are being excessively used as a resource or being sought as a handholder, you must train yourself to toss the problem back in the delegatee's lap at once.

Giving a quick, sound decision based on your long experience may seem like a timesaver. Restrain the urge. Before you furnish the answer, find out whether the subordinate really is in trouble. Encourage thinking with questions that put the burden on the delegatee:

- ☐ "What are the factors you consider important in this situation?"
- ☐ "What alternative steps do you see?"
- ☐ "What are the pros and cons of the option you've chosen?"
- ☐ "Do you think you ought to get more information before you decide?"

Seldom should you take the problem or task back, or provide an easy answer. That takes the growth out of the experience for the subordinate.

RECOGNIZE ACHIEVEMENT

When the job is done well, don't forget to express your appreciation so that the employee's own feelings of success are reinforced. One of the very best ways to continue that reinforcement is to assign another, more challenging bit of work so that the employee feels that he or she is progressing from simple to more complex.

DELEGATION UPDATE

1. Duties newly delegatable because of changed job emphasis:
   a. _____
   b. _____
   c. _____
   d. _____
   e. _____
   f. _____

2. Employees newly capable for the following tasks:
   Task: _____   Employee: _____
   _____   _____
   _____   _____
   _____   _____
   _____   _____

3. Employees potentially capable with certain training:
   Employee: _____
   Task: _____
   Training: _____
   Employee: _____
   Task: _____
   Training: _____

TEST YOUR KNOWLEDGE
OF DELEGATING PRINCIPLES

	Yes	No
1. You should pick only the competent subordinate for delegation.	____	____
2. You should try to enlarge the number of active delegatees.	____	____
3. It is bad practice to delegate more than one duty at a time to a subordinate.	____	____
4. You can delegate a task to an employee who works in another department.	____	____
5. A subordinate's subordinate is a proper candidate for your delegation.	____	____
6. You can use delegation to show approval of an employee's satisfactory performance.	____	____
7. You should withhold delegation from an employee who is not doing well on his or her regular job.	____	____
8. You should delegate work to a new employee.	____	____

Answers to Review

1. No. Since delegation is frequently used as a training device, you may want to give the less competent performer a chance to discover a new, challenging task.

2. Yes. Generally, the more the better for both you and the group. The more widely you delegate, the more you broaden the capabilities of your department. Also, the more subordinates you have trained to take over parts of your job, the less likely you are to be caught short by absenteeism, the promotion of key people, and so on.

3. No. If a job comes up for which one of your subordinates is ideally suited, the fact that he or she may have been delegated another task is not, by itself, a sufficient reason to pass over that employee. But don't overload one or two individuals and neglect all the others.

4. Yes. If you and the employee's manager have arranged for such delegation beforehand, it is acceptable. But never delegate to such an employee unless your co-manager has been informed and given full consent.

5. No. That is bypassing. However, where a subordinate's subordinate is especially well-qualified, there's no reason why the delegation shouldn't be made through the immediate superior.

6. Yes. It can be a reward for good performance. Delegation is an effective way to show the subordinate and the rest of the work group that the employee has your confidence and approval.

7. No. The challenge inherent in many delegated tasks may be an excellent way to shake an employee out of a rut and tap a drive for improvement.

8. No. Ordinarily, it's advisable that new employees master their jobs before you consider them as proper candidates for new assignments for which they may be unprepared.

8

BUILDING THEIR CONFIDENCE

No matter how attractive a goal is, no matter how desirable the reward, people are not likely to try for it unless they see a reasonable chance that they will reach it. Their perceptions of its attainability, of their ability to pull it off, are what count. If you are fortunate enough to have established mutual trust with the subordinate, you may receive clues as to how the employee feels about the job or task when you assign it. The person may be forthright about having certain doubts about his or her chances for success, or of reaching the goals you want. You may get a number of questions about details of this or that aspect of the work. The questions may be so detailed as to surprise you, confident as *you* are that the employee can handle the task. You might be receiving important clues about hesitancy or reservations in the other person.

At other times you have to maintain a sharp eye for a drop in performance standards after you have assigned a task or a responsibility. An experienced writer and editor joined the periodicals staff in a publishing company. At first, she functioned as editor of an important monthly trade publication, working under the supervision of a managing editor. But the new editor seemed to resent having to be closely supervised. Since her credentials were sound, the editor-in-chief appointed her as managing editor of the monthly. After a time, staff writers began to complain that their contributions were not showing up in print, and that no reasons were given for this. The editor-in-chief became unhappy with the layout of the magazine. The editor herself began to call in sick or to keep irregular hours. She became defensive and difficult to communicate with. At staff meetings she reacted strongly to anything that faintly seemed like criticism of her work.

It was a mystery. Finally, the editor-in-chief called in the man who had formerly served as managing editor, before the new editor had taken full responsibility for the magazine. The editor-in-chief asked the experienced editor for his opinion. "I have a hunch," the former managing editor said, "she may be in over her head, and doesn't want to let us know it." He proposed an experiment. He, the former managing editor, would assume a new role, that of executive editor. The managing editor would continue to run the publication, but final editorial approval would come from the executive editor.

Not only did the managing editor not resent the new reporting relationship, she seemed to thrive on it. Ultimate responsibility had been lifted from her shoulders. She appeared to welcome having someone check her work, make suggestions and decisions. The publication showed marked improvement, as did her disposition. She became more confident and less defensive.

The diagnosis had been correct. The new editor had sought management responsibility, yet early on had apparently begun to doubt that she could handle it. Her demotivation showed in the drop in the performance and quality of her work.

AVOIDING ASSUMPTIONS

In making assignments, in asking employees to assume certain responsibilities and new duties, be careful not to assume that subordinates will volunteer that they are worried about their ability to do the job. But sitting back and assuming that employees will sound the alarm is only one mistake you can make. Projecting your own ability or perceptions onto the employee can lead you into dangerous waters. For example, you say to yourself, "Sam has always done well at this kind of thing," or, "Sheila ought to be able to tackle this with the training we've provided her," or, "If I were in Fred's shoes, I could do this tied to a chair with one arm behind my back." You may have good reasons to believe that the employee can indeed do the work well. But what really matters is whether the employee believes the job is doable, that he or she has a fair chance to be successful and to achieve whatever reward there will be in doing the work.

The best time to deal with an employee's perception of the low probability of success is before the work is undertaken. If you have any reason to suspect that the employee may have some questions about his or her ability to do the job as assigned, review the following:

1. Watch for nonverbal clues such as frowning as you talk about the task. Does the employee's face register interest and enthusiasm? Does he or she appear uncertain or nervous?

2. Ask the employee how he or she sees the job. Does it sound interesting? You might put the question this way: "What, in your opinion, is the best way to go about this task?" or, "Do you foresee any problem in doing this?"

3. Monitor the work initially. If you're satisfied that the employee perceives no major problems, then observe from a distance or periodically. If you sit on top of the person, you might convey a message of no confidence. If the employee shows nervousness and if performance flags, then ask questions such as, "Do you feel that there are obstacles to your doing the work the way you think it should be done? If so, how can we get rid of them?" Or, "Is there anything I, or anyone else, can do to help you do a more successful job?"

BE CLEAR ABOUT WHAT YOU WANT

Perhaps one of the most common reasons for employees' fear of failure or their lack of confidence in their ability to succeed is their uncertainty about what you expect. In assigning responsibility or tasks or jobs, you should routinely follow these recommendations.

Define the Task as Precisely as Possible

You probably don't do this as consistently as you should. One of the most frequently encountered managerial deficiencies is taking it for granted that employees know what their managers want. Make your goals as specific as possible. Goals are output. It isn't enough to say, "We're launching a new print advertising campaign and I'd like you to be responsible for handling the inquiries as they come in from potential customers." What does "handle" mean? To the manager giving the assignment, it means that the subordinate is supposed to organize and train a group of people to acknowledge by mail the nearly 10,000 prospect inquiry cards that are expected, and to organize those cards by sales districts so that they can be sent to the company's sales representatives in the field, who will then follow up these letters with personal visits.

Talk as specifically as possible about what you expect to happen as a result of the employees' effort. Not only will you clear up doubts or anxieties in the employees' minds about what you want them to do, you will encourage them to talk to you about aspects that may specifically be troubling them. For example, the employee responsible for handling the inquiry cards may respond, "I'm not sure how we district the cards for salespeople. Where can we get the geographical breakdown so that we know the various sales territories?"

When you have a long-range goal, especially one that is complex, break it down into subgoals: "I want us to put out 5000 units this year. I realize that we have to gear up, train people, get the bugs out. So our subgoal is 800 in the first quarter, 2000 in the second, etc." Breaking down a large or long-range goal lessens the enormousness or complexity of the job in the employees' minds.

Set Standards

Tell *how* you expect the job to be done. For example, when you assign the job of handling the readers' inquiries, you might say,

"I'd like to see all inquiries acknowledged by mail within 24 hours after we receive them. The districting of inquiries should be completed within 72 hours. We'll alert the salespeople that they can expect a new batch of leads every three or four days, certainly once a week."

That spells out exactly how you want the job done. You've also stated what you consider minimally acceptable standards: The salespeople should receive leads no less than once a week.

Standards include a time frame—so much activity within a certain period of time. Specifying the time required is of course easier on short-term or repetitive functions than on those extended over a long period. Even when it is not certain how much time the task will take, it's a good idea to estimate. You may think in terms of six months, while the subordinate worries that you may want it in six weeks. You can thus relieve some anxiety.

Make Your Instructions Clear

Failure to give clear instructions can have frustrating consequences. The employee may hesitate even to start the job or may guess wrongly about what you meant to say but didn't.

1. *Explain what you want and why.* If the job is complicated, break it down into parts and explain each part. But be prepared to show how each part contributes to the whole and, indeed, as has been pointed out, what that whole or final result will be. Use words that are clear to the people being instructed.

2. *Show what you mean.* If you want a report written, show a sample of a similar one. If you are explaining a supervisory responsibility such as criticizing, run through the steps of effective criticism with the supervisor. If you are giving instructions in the use of machinery, let the employees watch you operate it according to the steps you have explained.

3. *Ask them to run through what you've explained and shown.* Get them to tell you what you did and why in each step.

4. *Have them demonstrate or run through.* If it is a procedure, you might ask them to try it themselves under your watchful eye. Or, if the task might take longer and is impractical to perform while

you are there, suggest a trial run. After finishing, the employee can bring the completed task to you for your evaluation. For example, the employee can do the first two or three pages of the report to let you see the format, the organization, the style. If employees prove weak in any area or step, have them repeat that step.

5. *Follow up.*   Check up from time to time to make sure that employees know how to do the job. In the case of a one-time event such as the criticism, have the supervisor report to you on his or her session with the subordinate and the results.

DESCRIBE THE RESOURCES AVAILABLE

Telling subordinates about what help there is available to them can go far to allay doubt or fears that they can't do the work well. Here are some examples.

Authority

If you define responsibility, it's only fair to tell the subordinate how much authority he or she will have in order to do the job. What decisions can be made by the subordinate without checking with you? Does the subordinate have authority to spend money? Can the person requisition materials? Does the subordinate have the power to hire, fire, transfer, or discipline? To what extent will the employee represent you? Can the employee assign, establish procedures, and schedule?

People

If the employee needs the help of others, where are these people to come from? Will they be reporting full-time or part-time? For example, you might say to your supervisor in charge of handling the readers' inquiries, "Talk to Ed Peabody in Personnel and discuss what people you need with him." Or, "Call the temporary help service. We'll use temps on this job." If the subordinate will be sharing employees with another supervisor—as in the case of a task force or project—spell out how much discretion and power he or she has in negotiating with that other manager for the employees' time.

Equipment

What office or production equipment will be needed? How should the employee go about getting it? Will access to a computer be useful? Perhaps you can't make a complete inventory of equipment in advance, but your assurances that reasonable needs will be met can contribute much to an employee's confidence in a successful performance.

Facilities

Where can the work be done? Will a conference room be available for meetings? Should the office layout be rearranged to provide for groupings of employees? You might say, "There's a spare room on the second floor where your team can put together a prototype. And you can lock the door when no one is there."

Experts

You may wish to refer subordinates to advisors or consultants in personnel, training, marketing, and research, both from inside and outside the organization. Explain any limitation and procedures in advance, especially if considerable expense might be involved. There may be other employees or managers who are experienced in the kind of work you want done, and you can steer your subordinates to them for help and guidance.

Precedents and Guidelines

"Two years ago," you say, "we did a similar readers' inquiry program. I think you'll find a file drawer with samples of the acknowledgment we used and some memos on how we got organized. It also seems to me that after the whole thing we put down on paper some suggestions for avoiding the mistakes we made." Experience of others in similar jobs or tasks can be an encouraging launching pad. Your own experience can help you develop guidelines and suggestions. You don't want to spell everything out so completely that there's no challenge left for the subordinate, no room for him or her to bring specialized talents to the work. But you do want the subordinate to be freed from having to reinvent the wheel.

Training

Perhaps specific skills need sharpening, and knowledge and experience need deepening. Often the subordinate will indicate areas of deficiency. For the employee who is being given a budgetary responsibility, a workshop or short training program might be in order.

Training doesn't have to be formal or take place off premises. You might be able to arrange a coaching session with someone else in the organization. Or, perhaps a specialist or another manager might be willing to have your subordinate sit in with him or her for a time to learn how things are done. You might even ask a more experienced employee in your department to show the subordinate the ropes.

YOUR ROLE

The role you play could be influential in the success of an employee, and in the degree of motivation that person experiences in taking on a commitment. Some optional roles for you to follow.

Coach

From time to time you may have to perform a coaching function, especially when a subordinate becomes overwhelmed or debilitated by a feeling of inadequacy (as opposed to an actual incompetence that calls for counseling). Many people have these fears when they confront a task or a type of work that is different from what they've been accustomed to, or when encountering obstacles to progress. That's the time for you to schedule a session in which you can review together any factors that the employee fears are contributing to the problems—real, imaginary, or anticipated. With your·help encourage the employee to develop some solutions or preventive measures.

Supporter

What are some of the talents, skills, or knowledge that led you to select the employee for this responsibility that created the base of confidence that you have in this person? You may have to review the person's work history to demonstrate that he or she has the wherewithal to handle the challenges, perhaps even through a parallel experience that hadn't been recognized earlier.

Access to You

You might emphasize that you are ready to provide whatever resources or moral support the employee might require in a problem situation. When the employee needs you, you explain, you'll be ready. That assurance may be all that is necessary. You may not have to provide the backup, just the promise of it.

Collaborator

You upgrade yourself from a resource to an active partner. There may be times when your experience, skills, and knowledge are needed, or would really push the project along. The problem is that the employee may find it hard to see you as an equal partner. Furthermore, you would be seen as getting more glory if the work is successful, simply because you are more visible. At the same time, your participation in the task gives it more importance and prestige. A possible compromise is for you to say, "You and I will work until you have things under control. Then you're on your own." Or, you might add, "Thereafter I'll come in only when you want." The implication is that you'll let the subordinate have the greater sense of achievement and glory.

SPECIAL EFFORTS YOU CAN MAKE

Many of the above steps you would take when you assign most kinds of tasks, jobs, and responsibilities. The following recommendations apply in special cases, where the assignment carries with it unusual importance or there are organizational constraints that must be loosened.

Relief from Other Duties

The individual task by itself may not be too heavy but the total work load may look formidable. State your priorities: "If you feel that you have too much on your plate at the moment, I'll understand. But the things that count right now are. . . ." You may have to distribute some of the employee's normal duties to other employees for the duration of the special task.

Remove Organizational Barriers

In most organizations horizontal communications are not as strong as vertical lines. Employees often find communicating and cooperating across functional lines of authority difficult. It would seem so easy and desirable for a supervisor in one department to be able to pick up the telephone and say to his or her counterpart in another department, "Mike, we have a rush request coming through. How about shortcutting the paperwork on it. Start processing it, and I'll have the completed papers to you day after tomorrow." In most cases, Mike needs approval from his boss, who probably would prefer to hear from yours.

If there is going to be this chain of requests in the subordinate's future, you may be able to set up special arrangements with the other department head so that your subordinate doesn't have to ask for approval each time he or she needs it. You may have to be explicit about how far the arrangements extend: "If you see a time problem developing, call Mike and explain it. But that shortcut extends only to this job and that department."

In cases where the employee must requisition supplies and equipment, you will want to consider the feasibility of delegating special authority to the subordinate to submit such requisitions and have them honored.

Break the Job into Smaller Units

Perhaps the job as a whole looks more formidable than necessary. Find a way of defining the job in stages or discrete units. The subordinate might respond by indicating at which stages help will be required and what kind. By breaking the job down into steps, parts, or stages, you can help the subordinate build confidence and enjoy a sense of achievement as each step is completed.

Have a Flexible Timetable

If an employee feels the pressure of a deadline to the point at which anxious feelings are threatening performance, you may feel it is necessary to expand the time in which the work is to be done. If you can permit a flexible schedule, you can say, "This is the time period I anticipated, but if you think more time is needed, I'm willing to discuss it." To give yourself the leeway to do this, you may want to make allowances in time when you set the schedule. You may also want to keep the fact that you do have a flexible schedule to yourself. Still, there are tasks that are uncertain in their dimensions. You may have no precedents to guide you. That uncertainty will probably cause tension in the subordinate to whom the work has been delegated. You may ease the tension, therefore, by saying, "My estimate is that the job will take six weeks, but I've built more time into the schedule just in case. I don't want you to feel in six weeks as if you have your back against the wall."

You may have to play an active and continuing role to ensure that deadlines are met, however. That's one reason why it is useful to have intermediate goals to help you check on progress. If the subordinate is not following the schedule that you believe is reasonable (for your purposes), don't communicate your stress before you make sure that the employee sees the time period as reasonable. You may have to negotiate. But once you have negotiated a deadline, insist that the employee stick to it. Some employees, though, seem unable to gauge the time required for certain tasks.

You may have to monitor—discreetly, perhaps—the performance of the tasks.

Some people, probably most people, need deadlines in order to organize their work. Open-ended schedules often result in procrastination. You may need to negotiate a deadline that both of you can accept. Both of you should look at the variables that might hamper progress toward the deadline (and the employee may have a better idea of the number of variables). Once you have agreed on the time limit, insist that the deadline be met, unless of course some significant variable occurs that you hadn't anticipated.

But it's not wise to play games in setting deadlines. For example, you know that one of your employees has a tendency to procrastinate. You set a short deadline so that you will be able to put the pressure on him, yet you'll still be able to extend it if you have to. The employee will soon learn, after the deadline has been extended two or three times, that the time limit you set initially doesn't have to be worried about. The subordinate will ignore it and frustrate your intentions.

YOUR ROLE AS PROTECTOR

In your role as protector, a role incidentally that many managers deny is appropriate, you head off any interference from others that might hamper your subordinate's effectiveness. It seems as though it is a natural function of a manager—and indeed it is. But managers often resist playing it, although their subordinates expect it of them. For example, excessive and conflicting goals and priorities may come down from the higher echelons of an organization. The job of a manager is to establish the relative importance of the goals and to define priorities if they do not exist clearly. Employees can easily be demotivated in the confusion that results when they are not sure of what they should be doing. Managers who simply pass through what comes down from the top usually wind up complaining that they get mediocre performance from subordinates.

Managers have more power to protect employees from interference and impediments than employees have. It's a difficult but necessary role for a manager at times. In one department the supervisors are accustomed to calling on one another freely for help when their work load becomes excessive. It is a practical way of keeping the work loads fairly distributed. One supervisor receives a special assignment from her boss and, at the same time, is approached by another supervisor for help. In such a case the boss would step in, explain why the supervisor could not fulfill her usual role as temporary help, then look for other ways to provide assistance for the overburdened supervisor.

There are other more complex and delicate situations in which you might be called on to provide protection for a subordinate. You have a boss, for instance, who sometimes bypasses you to give work directly to your subordinates. You have the option of talking to your boss and explaining why this practice is inadvisable, not to say disruptive, or of asking your subordinates to bring any such assignments to you for redistribution, if necessary. There is nothing more demotivating for a subordinate than to have a full load of responsibility from you and then to receive more work from a higher manager who does not seem to concern himself or herself with your, and the employee's, priorities.

Conflict between your employee and someone in another department with whom your subordinate must deal on a frequent basis can have a debilitating effect on performance and on the subordinate's motivation. The conflict interferes with the employee's ability to do the job successfully. Of course, there are generally two sides to a conflict. You can go to the manager of the other feuding employee and complain. But it's generally best, before you automatically assume the role of protector, to investigate the matter within your own department and try to defuse the situation from your side. Here are recommendations to follow:

1. *Try to uncover as many facts as posssible.* You've probably been getting a self-serving version. Look around. Ask for documentation, if any. You may want to make some inquiries of other employees who have had to deal with the other department or this particular employee.

2. *Discuss alternatives.* Encourage the employee to come up with suggestions that from your point of view might increase the

chances of building more cooperation between the combatants. Since the employee's tendency at this point may be to blame the other person for all of the obstacles, you may have to be patient and persist in explaining that what you want to know at this stage is what would constitute cooperation in your subordinate's eyes.

3.   *Ask what the subordinate can do to reduce or eliminate the friction.* Again, you may have to be persistent in asking the question, because in the subordinate's eyes, there is nothing he can do. He probably feels the other person will have to make all the changes. But eventually you should be able to uncover certain areas in which your subordinate, by giving a bit here and there, could work around the other's "obstacles."

4.   *Talk to the manager.*   You are now dealing from a position of strength because you have taken the first steps toward creating a more cooperative atmosphere. You have taken action to protect your subordinate from outside interference without increasing an antagonism between the two departments that could only disrupt performance more.

FEUDING SUBORDINATES

Conflicts between subordinates can create the threat of demotivation in them and sometimes in others who have to work with them. Employees quite reasonably suspect that, when conflict exists, it is harder to get the work done according to the standards that have been established.

When conflicts between subordinates are problem- or procedures-centered, you can usually aid in their resolution by getting the disputants to work with you on a desirable alternative to the existing situation. But some feuds between subordinates are not so clear-cut or amenable to a rational solution. They may actually be personality-centered, or involve issues where there is no obvious right or wrong. Your concern is how much—and when—to intervene in the conflict.

You intervene when the feud in any way interferes with the effectiveness of anyone in the department. You should not intervene to try to get the combatants to like each other. They're entitled not to like each other. That's an issue between them until the feud relates to work. Therefore, when you have to become involved because an aspect of the quarrel interferes with work, keep their personalities out of your intervention. Concentrate on the problem they have created and insist upon finding a solution for that. If some aspects of their behaviors is causing the disruption, describe what you find undesirable or obstructive, and offer to work with them to develop alternative behaviors that help get the work done right.

You can follow these steps:

1. Describe the behavior or the problem that has a negative impact on the work.
2. Get their agreement that a problem exists and that their behaviors are disruptive and inappropriate.
3. Enlist their aid in looking for a solution to the problem or in finding different ways to behave with each other that won't get in the way of the work.
4. Follow up to see that changes are taking place. If they are not, you may have to be more insistent, perhaps even threaten some disciplinary action.
5. Express your appreciation when the desired changes take place.

SHOULD YOU BE A RESCUER?

One fairly sure way of helping employees to anticipate successful achievement of goals is to be accessible to them should they run into difficulties they can't manage by themselves. People will probably be more willing and therefore motivated to take on jobs, tasks, responsibilities, and challenges if they know that you will rescue them.

But if they begin to perceive that you rescue too quickly, that perception could lead to problems for you as well as them. If you are busy solving problems for others, you'll find little time to take care of your own. Also, encouraging openness from employees may make you suffer. Of course, you want to encourage them to be candid with you about how they see their ability to do the work. But if they know that you'll step in at the slightest hint of trouble, they'll have little incentive to level with you.

Finally, in time the subordinates' motivation will suffer. If you rescue them on a fairly regular basis, they'll have to accept you as a partner in the achievement. To put it candidly, your rescuing them will rob them of the chance to feel good about what they've done.

Thus, an important job for you is to help employees to develop a higher expectation of achievement in an assignment or a continuing function. You want them to find greater motivation in taking risks and accepting new challenges. You want to encourage, nurture, support, and coach them to come up with their own answers to problems, and to develop and apply their own resources.

You must be especially wary of any attempts to delegate work up to you. When a subordinate brings a problem to you, be careful not to say such things as, "Leave this with me, and I'll get back to you later on it," or "Let me think about it." If your response is similar to these, you have let the subordinate transfer his or her problem.

Sometimes accepting problems or work from subordinates seems as if it might be the easiest way to take care of the immediate situation but, as has been suggested, it will only cause complications in the long run. Taking problems out of the hands of subordinates makes you an automatic rescuer. It diminishes their growth and your effectiveness.

When you are approached by an employee with a problem, take the following steps:

1. *Place the responsibility where you want it.*   You may want to say to the employee, "Okay, Janet, let's see what we can do with this problem right now. Maybe we can both see it more clearly. But when we're finished working on it, I want you to come up with the finished product."

2. *Set a timetable for the other person.*   Don't let the subordinate simply walk out of the office with the half-finished work. Get a commitment that what you've started will get finished. For example, you might say, "Have we looked at all the questions? We don't

have an answer yet, but we're closer to it, don't you think? How about keeping me informed about your progress? Why don't you check back with me the day after tomorrow?" The schedule for reporting back to you reinforces the fact that you expect the subordinate to assume responsibility for the problem once more.

3. *Let go of it.* Even when you've handled the situation adroitly, you may still have a lingering anxiety that the subordinate doesn't know how to deal with the problem. Or you may experience some guilt feelings because you didn't do more. Since the whole idea is to give the subordinate an opportunity to come up with the result, answer, or understanding, the logical next step is for you to forget about the problem temporarily. You've made a note of when the subordinate is to report back to you. Now turn your attention away from that problem to your own.

	Yes	No	Not Sure
1. People's perceptions of the attainability of a reward determine how motivated they are to go after it.	____	____	____
2. You should be careful not to assume that employees who anticipate difficulty will volunteer their fears.	____	____	____
3. The best time to deal with an employee's perception of the low probability of success is before the work is undertaken.	____	____	____
4. One of the common reasons for employees' fears of failure is their uncertainty about what you expect.	____	____	____
5. One way to increase the employee's confidence of success is to define the task as precisely as possible.	____	____	____
6. You may find it helpful to set standards as you assign work.	____	____	____
7. In assigning work or a task, take care to describe the resources available to the employee to help him or her to be successful.	____	____	____
8. The role you play may be influential in the success of an employee, hence in the degree of motivation the person has to do the work well.	____	____	____
9. You must take care not to project onto the employee your confidence in being able to do the work.	____	____	____
10. You should stand by as rescuer for employees who encounter diffi-			

	Yes	No	Not Sure
culty with the work. Being available will help them avoid demotivation.	⎯⎯	⎯⎯	⎯⎯
11. When an employee brings a problem to you, make sure you work with the employee to solve the problem.	⎯⎯	⎯⎯	⎯⎯
12. When the understanding is that the other person has to come up with the answer to a problem, you have to be able to let it go and to let the employee bear the whole responsibility.	⎯⎯	⎯⎯	⎯⎯

Answers to Review

1. Yes
2. Yes
3. Yes
4. Yes
5. Yes
6. Yes
7. Yes
8. Yes
9. Yes
10. Not sure. You want to be available to help, but you don't want to be thought of as an automatic rescuer.
11. Not sure. You may want to help the employee understand the problem, but you may also want to insist that the employee have full responsibility for solving it.
12. Yes

9

SITUATIONAL INFLUENCES

A third factor that has to be considered when people choose to act in a certain way or to commit themselves to a course of action is the situation surrounding the action and behavior. The conditions under which the action is taken or the work is done can affect the value of the reward or the person's confidence in being able to gain that reward.

For example, if you are a skier, you may find yourself with little motivation to go out on the slopes when the temperature is 30 degrees below zero. The reward, in this case the pleasure of skiing, is somewhat diminished by the possibility that you will wind up at the bottom of the hill half-frozen. You may also have reason to worry about your ability to perform well in such frigid temperatures.

Situational factors exert influence in everyday minor choices. You walk into a restaurant for lunch. On the menu you see two items that appeal to you, a cheeseburger at $4.95 and a sliced steak sandwich at $9.95. Both have value to you until you compare prices. You may have enough money for either, but when you think about what you might also be able to buy with the $5 differential, suddenly the sliced steak sandwich doesn't retain its value.

Situational considerations, and their effect on the value or attainability of the reward, have an influence at every stage and on every decision of your life.

There are four categories of situational factors that affect value and attainability: the work environment or atmosphere, the people involved, the location in which the work is done, and personal circumstances. What works or may be desirable in one situation, under one set of conditions, may be undesirable in another situation. But employees consider at least one of these factors when weighing choices or making commitments to the work, or to the manager's or the organization's objectives. It follows that you have to take these factors into consideration when you ask for commitments from employees, when you assign work, tasks, and responsibilities, and when you are concerned about the disappointing performance of an employee.

THE WORK ENVIRONMENT OR ATMOSPHERE

A few years ago a young insurance manager accepted a transfer from a Midwestern office to one located in Manhattan. The move was an indicator of the young manager's success. Although his title was the same, his new responsibility and visibility were vastly increased. Despite his outstanding record of success and proven talents, he found he could not function well in New York City. He experienced a pronounced demotivation. Eventually he put in for a transfer back to the Midwest, even though it meant he would not rise above his present level in the company.

In the Midwest, he had found that business was conducted on a more relaxed, friendly basis. One key to his excellent record was that he related well personally with those he did business with. In the community he acquired a reputation for being trustworthy and knowledgeable. People wanted to do business with him.

New York City was a very different environment in which to work. Personal relationships count, but they usually take longer to establish than in other parts of the country. Competition is intense. A new face often meets the question, "What can you do for us that these other 20 companies can't do?" His conclusion: "It isn't fun for me to do business in a cutthroat environment." Even though the opportunities to make money and get promoted were considerable, the young manager decided that he couldn't be effective under such conditions. He also discovered that, for him, the rewards of doing his work covered much more than money. He felt rewarded by his relationships as well.

An example of how the work environment can differ radically in the same organization was provided by a publishing company a decade or so ago. At that time, before wage and salary policies had to be closely scrutinized to avoid the risk of discrimination suits, the two divisions of the company had widely varying compensation structures. Editors in both divisions did essentially the same kind of work but on different publications. Division A was acknowledged to be the prestige part of the company because of the type of publications it produced. But because of the management style that prevailed in that division, it was characterized by poor communication and lack of cooperation between departments. In fact, competitiveness was so fierce that co-workers often withheld information from one another. There was a great deal of backbiting. Antagonism ran high. Because of the prestige attached to the division, salaries on an average tended to be higher than in the other division.

In contrast to the autocratic style practiced in Division A, the style prevalent in Division B was democratic. Working relationships were friendly and open. Although there was a mild competitiveness between co-workers, people in the division cooperated freely with one another. Their products were not "flagship" publications, but the people on the staff took pride in their work. They admitted to feeling resentful that the editors in the other division enjoyed more money, more "glory," and that the promotions came more readily there than in their own division. Still, many of the editors who were interviewed said that, given the opportunity to transfer, they would be reluctant to do so. The conditions that existed in Division A detracted from the rewards to be gained from working there or made the work more difficult to accomplish.

What constitutes a valuable reward or excessive difficulty in attaining it varies from person to person. There are people who flourish in a highly competitive, rather impersonal environment. Generally, however, most people prefer to work in a climate that is collaborative, with people supporting rather than fighting or undermining one another. Excessive conflict can interfere with results. Managers can reduce tension and anxiety in employees by making efforts to apply similar standards to everyone, to reward the results that they want, and to discourage behavior that is unreasonably political, competitive, and partisan.

When you put a subordinate in an atmosphere that is tense, combative, and constrictive, you shouldn't be surprised when the employee experiences reduced motivation.

PHYSICAL ENVIRONMENT

The physical surroundings also have to be taken into consideration in assigning work and anticipating how people will perform in them. Production managers will tell you that people tend to work better in a plant that is kept neat and orderly, in which housekeeping is strictly enforced. A secretary who has been working in a carpeted space with three others is transferred to an open area in which 50 other people work. It is plainly furnished, has tile floors, and is cramped and noisy. She may work less efficiently than before. An employee who tends to be claustrophobic will probably be unable to perform in a small, closed-in space, as will a salesperson assigned to an inner city territory that is rundown, dirty, and probably perceived as dangerous as well.

It's safe to say that most people would prefer a physical environment that is clean, attractive, and comfortable. In transferring employees from a surrounding that is unattractive to one that is more congenial, you may well find that the person will find coming to work more rewarding.

However, making an environment clean and comfortable will probably not *by itself* stimulate motivation where there is little or no perception of gaining a reward that is valued. Pleasant physical surroundings can add to the motivational factors that are already working. At least, the congenial physical environment will not detract from them.

You have only to visit certain organizations that have spent a lot of money to landscape their offices and yet have concerned themselves little with the truths of employee motivation to observe how wretchedly people can perform in the midst of beauty.

PEOPLE INVOLVED

A bright young woman with an M.B.A. degree from an Ivy League school was recently offered by her company a promotion that would involve her moving from Chicago to San Francisco. The recent purchase of a company on the West Coast meant that the company's western distribution system would have to be redesigned. She was to be given the responsibility for the work. It was an assignment that would last perhaps a year, with the glory of successful completion extending much beyond that time. However, the West Coast division manager, to whom she would report during that year, was highly prejudiced against M.B.A.s, especially those held by fast-track female employees. The young woman had heard how the executive belittled the work of talented female subordinates, how he withheld resources, and had even raided the staffs of woman managers.

The young woman turned down this plum of an assignment, suspecting that the attitude and obnoxious behavior of the older man would exact a toll on her that she was not prepared to pay, no matter how high the reward that she might gain through implementing a workable distribution system. In her case, the situational factor probably reduced the value of the reward as well as her hopes of attaining it.

On the other hand, in another company, a similarly bright young woman was offered an opportunity to work in the Atlanta regional office. Two of her co-workers had declined the same offer, The regional manager in Atlanta was known to be hard-driving, very demanding, somewhat irascible—but fair. He was an acknowledged genius. He knew the business and the organization. People who had worked well for him emerged with honors and distinction. Clearly he was a molder and director of talent, and the company recognized him as such. They also rewarded his alumni. This young woman took the challenge. The rewards for successful performance under this exacting manager were enhanced.

You can probably observe this phenomenon at work in your own organization. People work well for supervisor Tom, but they perform less well for supervisor Jim, although both supervisors are technically or professionally qualified. So far as employees perceive it, however, the value of the reward for working for Tom, and the chances of being successful in the job, are greater.

THE LOCATION OF THE WORK

Many New York-based corporations discovered long ago that managers no longer necessarily heed the invitation to relocate to the big city. True, it is the center of much action, but it is considered to be expensive, unsafe, dirty, and inconvenient to commute to and from.

Many young engineers through the years have been approached to take jobs with the oil companies in the Middle East. The money is excellent and the benefits considerable. Yet the prospect of living in those societies for a period of time reduces the value of the work for many people.

From time to time people in the advertising and publishing fields are offered fine jobs in those fields outside New York City, generally acknowledged to be the hub of such activity. No matter how attractive the inducements are, many hesitate because they fear getting out of the mainstream; once removed, it will be difficult to get back in.

Of course, geographical location can enhance the value, also. An employee who is devoted to skiing would find living in the American Northeast or the Mountain West a distinct plus. Some people like to be near the water or the excitement of a large metropolitan area, inconvenience and expense notwithstanding. Some locations acquire a special attractiveness. For example, in one company, three branch offices, located in Chicago, Atlanta, and Dallas, are notably the final field assignments for young potentials. After one of these three offices, the next step is a high-level management position in the United States or abroad.

The location doesn't have to be far removed or radically different to affect the employee's perception of the job. For example, your home office is located in Philadelphia, and the Philadelphia branch office is physically part of the home office. Because of the need to expand the central operating office, a decision is made to place the branch office in another part of the city. Some managers would look upon the move as a challenge, with excitement, because the separation means more independence in functioning and decision making. Others might view it as a minus: They'll be removed from the seat of power. They'll lose influence and status, as well as visibility.

PERSONAL CONSIDERATIONS

For personal reasons, the employee may feel that the work has lost some of its value or that he or she is not up to doing it. Marital problems, worry about children, poor health, or midlife crisis, for example, all can affect the employee's view of the work. Any one of these factors can impede the employee's performance. They may explain why an employee who should be able to do the tasks, who should welcome the opportunity to do them, may show reluctance.

A Chicago marketing executive discovered this when he asked a brilliant young subordinate to take on a troubleshooting assignment in the field. The subordinate had spent a number of years in the field, had accumulated an enviable record of accomplishments, and was now in the home office being prepared for more significant responsibility. The executive describes the problem: "Our Dallas office was in bad shape. We'd had a high management turnover there. The territories needed restructuring. Our salespeople were poorly trained in product knowledge, and pretty much having to depend on themselves. Morale had hit bottom."

The executive called in the subordinate, Carl, and described the situation. Then he asked Carl to spend a few months in Dallas getting things in shape. "It was," the executive says, "a situation made to order for him. I knew he could do it. We didn't have a promotion ready for him, but after he got through in Dallas, he'd have plenty of visibility and I'd have no problem convincing top management to make a good position for him."

Much to the executive's surprise, Carl begged off the temporary assignment. It took some probing to produce the explanation. Carl and his wife were in the process of divorcing. Custody of the children had become a big issue. Carl wanted custody and he didn't want to be away for an extended period of time lest his wife use his absence to argue that she should have the children.

Your judgment must rule in cases where you suspect that personal reasons are creating or contributing to an adverse situation. Your relationship with the employee may be such that the employee feels comfortable in leveling with you. You at least have a right to know that personal reasons are the explanation, even if you don't know exactly what they are. Despite whatever sympathy you may have, you have goals and standards that demand priority. Counseling (see Chapter 13) is probably the best way to approach this problem. You may also have to be ready to refer the person to someone else who is more professionally qualified.

TAKING THE SITUATION INTO ACCOUNT

You can't always adjust the situation so that it enhances the value of the reward for doing the work or increases the employee's confidence in being able to do it well. But you can't afford to overlook the influence of the conditions surrounding the performance, that is, you can't if you want your employees to maintain a high level of motivation. Some managers tend not to think of the situational influence—and pay for it in decreased motivation and productivity.

If you are reasonably sure that the employee values the task or assignment or job, that the employee feels fairly confident of his or her ability to do it, but you encounter a lack of enthusiasm or expressions of doubt or indecision at the time of assignment, then the logical place to look for the reasons is in the conditions. Some incisive questioning at that time could save you much grief later on.

Having made the assignment without having received a hint of an employee's doubts or reservations, you wonder why the presumed ability is not being applied. Again you question whether the working conditions have eroded the employee's motivation. It's almost inevitable that some relocations don't work out, that some people will have personality conflicts, that some employees will find a new environment incompatible, or that they will develop personal problems that could not have been foreseen when the changes were made. What can you do then?

You have to ask yourself some hard questions. Can you make the situation better without seriously disrupting the operation? Without incurring undue expense? Can you tolerate the lower level of motivation and productivity? If you go to much expense and trouble to correct the situation, will it be a worthwhile investment for retaining a valuable employee?

If you find that you cannot do much about the situation, you have other options. There are steps you can take to increase the value or the expectation of success that will sufficiently overcome or at least to lessen the influence of an adverse situation.

INCREASING THE VALUE

If you were trying to persuade the young woman to take on the job in San Francisco (and thereby report to the chauvinistic manager), you might want to make her aware of the internal as well as the external rewards that would be forthcoming as a result of her taking the risk and being successful: "If you can prove that you can work with him, you'll come off as heroic not only to management but to yourself. You'll have every right to be confident in your ability to take on the toughest assignments." Or you might be less subtle and say, if possible, "We'll increase your pay to make up for the trouble." If you can't raise her pay immediately, promise her that you'll put in for an increase the moment she is through with the assignment. Add a bit of extra value right away by suggesting that you'll let the president know that she has accepted this difficult assignment despite the obvious drawbacks. After all, the obnoxious executive must have acquired a reputation!

One manager wanted to discourage a reassignment. For some time he had enjoyed the exceptional abilities of a bright young assistant. The assistant, however, wanted no part of home office life. He was ambitious for a field assignment. When one opened up that the young man was interested in, the manager asked him to stay on for an extra year with his department. He gave him a special title and a nice office.

The point is that you need not give up without putting up a good fight. You may be able to find some reward that will increase the value of the work sufficiently to neutralize the situational factors. At a recent conference on productivity, one organization boasted of its success in getting people to work in a very monotonous job that had low status and appeal. They routinely offered to transfer anyone out of it after four months, at which time boredom began to erode the effectiveness of most people. Incidentally, just having the option seemed to be enough for some of the people assigned to the boring work. They continued to do a fine job and didn't ask for the transfer.

INCREASING EXPECTATION OF SUCCESS

If you suspect that situational factors are causing the employee to worry about whether he or she can do the job, you'll want to step in with all the assistance and confidence-building resources at your disposal. You might want to review Chapter 8 for the checklist on increasing employees' expectations of success.

One of the most important steps you can take, if it is possible, is to let the subordinate suggest to you how the task or job can be changed to make it more attractive and doable. You may be surprised to find that you can make more alterations than you suspected. Your attentiveness to the problem and your concern for the employee will give the person much needed support.

LIVING WITH THE SITUATION

You are not necessarily powerless when you cannot increase the value of the expectations of employees. Even though the situation is unpleasant, you may still be able to achieve a high level of motivation from employees if you take one or more of the following steps.

Assign a Time Limit

People tend to respond well to a bad situation if they know that there will be an end to it. That's one reason why the company that hired people for boring work, mentioned earlier, was successful. If you can say something such as, "Do this for the remainder of the year, and we'll see that you get a new assignment," you are likely to get the level of cooperation you need. If you cannot be definite, make an estimate. But in either case, be sure that, in the absence of unforeseeable circumstances, you can deliver. Otherwise, you will have a demotivated employee as well as a person who may no longer trust you.

Extra Support

For example, you can offer more access to you: "Look, when the work is getting you down, call me. It's okay if you just want to talk." This kind of special consideration can help subordinates through tough jobs and adverse circumstances.

Make a Special Plea

Sometimes it may come down to your asking the employee to do you a favor: "Jeannette, this job is very important to me. I'm asking you to do this, even though I know you're not excited about it. Believe me, I won't forget that you've done me a favor." Making an occasional, personal plea for a favor is perfectly in line. But then, of course, you must not forget it.

PERSON TO PERSON, ONE TO ONE

While it is true that you must consider the situational factors in
making assignments and in evaluating performance, it could be a
mistake to assume that an employee will regard a situation as
unfavorable or unpleasant because you do or because other employees have found it so. You will find people who like monotonous
jobs. You will also encounter employees who derive excitement
and satisfaction from taking on tasks that others shy away from.

Therefore, when you look at the situation, take care not to
project your feelings or the judgments of others onto every employee. Bear in mind that the practice of management is person to
person, one to one. You may generalize about principles, but you
must deal with people individually.

REVIEW OF SITUATIONAL INFLUENCES

	Yes	No	Not Sure
1. The conditions under which the work is performed can affect the value of the reward.	___	___	___
2. The person may perceive difficulties in being able to do the work if he or she sees the conditions as adverse.	___	___	___
3. Situational influences are present at almost every level of decision or course of action.	___	___	___
4. When you assign work or add responsibility, you need to take the situational influences into account in anticipating the motivation of employees.	___	___	___
5. What constitutes a valuable reward or excessive difficulty in attaining it varies from person to person.	___	___	___
6. When you assign a subordinate to an atmosphere that is fiercely competitive, you can expect the employee to respond to the combative atmosphere by increasing his or her competitiveness.	___	___	___
7. Most people probably prefer a physical environment that is clean, attractive, and comfortable.	___	___	___
8. Turning an unpleasant environment—one that is dirty and cluttered—into a clean and attractive surrounding usually has a positive effect on motivation.	___	___	___

		Yes	No	Not Sure
9.	Geographical location can add to or detract from the value of the work.	___	___	___
10.	If you cannot enhance the situation, you should try to add more value to the work.	___	___	___
11.	When you cannot add value to the work, you can achieve good results by telling the employee that there is really no alternative.	___	___	___
12.	Assigning time limits and providing extra support will sometimes serve to overcome the negative influences that a situation creates.	___	___	___

Answers to Review

1. Yes
2. Yes
3. Yes
4. Yes
5. Yes
6. Not sure. Some people will be turned off and experience demotivation. It's safe to say most people seek an environment that is agreeable and collaborative.
7. Yes
8. Not sure. It may have no effect on motivation.
9. Yes
10. Yes
11. Not sure. It's a negative approach that may come across as a lack of caring.
12. Yes

10

THE IMPORTANCE
OF FEEDBACK

Your feedback to employees on how well they are working—or how poorly—is essential to motivation. Most people want to do well on the job. Not only do they want to do well, but they want to have the feeling that tomorrow they will do even better than today. Few employees like the thought of standing still. Your feedback, therefore, is a guidepost. It tells your subordinates where they are relative to where they might or should be.

Your feedback is an encouragement. Whether you give constructive criticism or positive reinforcement, your message can be, "I know you can do better and that you want to do better. Also, I know I can help you do better." Employees will then look forward to getting more positive reinforcement from you. Each time they hear from you, especially if each occasion of feedback indicates clear progress and growth, they feel spurred on.

Your feedback is a reward and a recognition of their good performance. Rewards, as has been so often stated in this book, constitute psychological reinforcement. When behavior is reinforced, it is more likely to be repeated than if it is not.

But you need feedback, too, for your own purposes. Feedback from employees alerts you to what may be going wrong in your department. You may discover that there is a gap between how employees see their jobs and how you see them. There may be conflicts emerging between certain employees that could interfere with their effectiveness or that of others who have to work with them. You may get clues that the organization of the department or of the workflow is not adequate. Employees' feedback can tell you of the deficiencies in the supervision they receive from the people who report to you or of the interference they get from co-workers outside the department. You may hear of low morale, uncertainty, anxiety, or any other emotions or factors that can erode the effectiveness of your subordinates.

But, just as important, you need to hear what you are doing right. You can no more operate in a vacuum than can your employees. What you learn that you are doing right, you can repeat and refine. Chances are you don't get enough feedback from your boss not as much as you would like. Let your employees make up some of the feedback you are missing. You need rewards too. You need that shot in the arm. You can benefit from having guideposts.

CONTROLLING THE DISCUSSION

For best results in an interview with an employee, you should maintain control. In the minds of many people, controlling has a negative connotation. But it needn't have. The essence of control is knowing the direction in which you would like the discussion or interview to go and taking the appropriate steps to guide it there. Control is not the same thing as domination. When a person dominates a discussion, he or she is usually the only one who achieves satisfaction, and that satisfaction is often gained at the expense of the other person. Dominators have an agenda and an objective. Achieving a goal takes priority in their minds. Thus dominators force a decision, interrupt others, argue, manipulate; by position, authority, or overwhelming personality, they push everyone else along a predetermined path to a preconceived destination.

The key word in the definition of controlling is *guiding*. You don't push or force or trick people into going where you want them to go or doing what you want done. You have a general sense of what you want to happen. For example, if you are giving negative feedback through appraising, criticism, coaching, and counseling, you know what you want to have happen as a result: more effective performance.

But always remember that you have a partner in the transaction: the employee. Your subordinate wants something out of the discussion, too. In most transactions, your success will proceed from the recognition that the other person has needs and interests that want to be recognized and satisfied. The other person has a dignity that resists being affronted or neglected. The other person is bringing certain knowledge, strengths, and resources to the transaction. You need to be able to capitalize on what the other person can contribute. (You may find it helpful to review Chapter 3 on assertiveness–responsiveness.)

The control that a successful manager maintains is subtle. You work to keep the discussion on the track, headed in the general direction you want it to go. When the talk strays, you find a way to get it back on course. If the disruption is not serious, you know how to exercise patience and seize the right moment to intervene. If the "disruption" turns out to be enlightening, you know how to listen carefully, without letting defensive reactions close your filters.

You always show respect for the other person, even if you object to that person's behavior or ways of working. You encourage the participation of the other in the interview. Although you know how to involve the other in what is going on, you keep in mind how valuable it is to have an informative, succinct, and purposeful interview.

FOUR KEY QUESTIONS

Maintaining an awareness of what you want from, and what is
happening in, an interview is fundamental to gaining and maintaining control. Becoming accustomed to answering the following
four questions can help you develop your awareness of the purpose of the transaction and increase the likelihood that you will be
successful in guiding the discussion where you want it to go, to the
benefit of both of you.

1. *What do I want from this transaction?*   Whether the discussion
   or the interview is casual (a periodic and relaxed review of
   what is going on) or serious and structured (an appraisal or
   counseling session) you want something to happen as a
   result. You seek information, agreement, cooperation, commitment, and some form of action. Having your objective
   fixed clearly in mind will help you to stay on course during
   the interview. It will also assist you in being articulate
   about what you want.
      There are probably other things you would like to accom-
   plish through a good discussion or interview. No doubt you
   would like acceptance by the other person that you are a
   manager who is pleasant and satisfying to work with. You
   would like to be admired and respected. You hope that your
   sincerity, honesty, and good faith come through during the
   session. You would like this occasion to be the beginning, or
   the continuation, of a mutually beneficial working relationship between you and the other person.
      The more clearly you define for yourself the primary and
   secondary objectives of the transaction, the greater is the
   probability that you will be successful. The better you understand what you want, the better the chances that you can
   communicate your understanding to the subordinate. Also,
   the more honest you are in admitting all those secondary
   objectives—respect, the impression of sincerity, admiration,
   and trust—the more likely that you will act in such a way that
   the employee will respond favorably.

2. *What do I think the other person would like?* Obviously subordinates want to spend time wisely and to learn something from the conversation or interview. They may look for an opportunity to give you information or explanations. If they sense that they are not being effective on the job and are not in your favor, they would undoubtedly like to know how to change in a way that they as well as you would find acceptable. They would like to feel that it is possible to rely on and trust you. They may hope that you gain a favorable impression of them as a result of what has gone on between you. It's possible that they would like to offer suggestions on improving the effectiveness of the department—or of you personally. Finally they would like to believe that their professionalism, prestige, standing, feeling of self-worth, and other needs have been enhanced by the transaction.

3. *What is going on at this moment?* It is important not to be so preoccupied with what you are saying and doing that you lose sight of the clues that the other person is giving. Is the other person interested, absorbed, following, thinking about what you are saying? Or do you get the impression that the employee is bored, focused internally, annoyed, or indifferent? Are you being as effective as you could be? Do you believe that you have made it clear why the interview or discussion is being held and what you want as a result? Are you trying to relate to the listener? How can you get a reaction or some participation? Does the other have knowledge, opinions, or experience that you should try to tap at this point? Has the other person contributed, and have you listened carefully? Have you learned from those contributions?

   If you don't have an idea of what is going on at all times with the other person and with yourself, then you are not in control of the situation. Both of you could be going nowhere.

4. *How does what is going on between us help both of us to get what we want?* If you want your discussion to lead to some kind of action, you must sense the effectiveness of what is happening right now in the transaction. How does what is happening contribute to getting what each of you wants? If you don't

know how what is happening now makes a contribution, the conversation may veer off track and never get back on. To be truly in control of the situation, you must be able to relate what is happening at a given moment to your objectives or understand how the current situation is leading away from them.

As a manager giving feedback, your objective is to influence others—their thinking, their decisions, their actions, and possibly even their values. The four questions we have just discussed you must learn to ask of yourself automatically. If you do not really define for yourself what you want from the transaction, then you will probably have to settle for what you get (and that may be what the employee wants from you—leniency, "forgiveness," tolerance, more consideration, etc.). Disciplining yourself to answer these questions helps you to notice how the other person is reacting and to pose questions or statements that get the other person involved.

In the transactions that you initiate, you are the persuader. It may be that you want the person to correct a fault, to take on a difficult or undesirable assignment, or to adopt your methods. The point is that *you* choose what action you want. A continuing awareness of what is going on at the moment will help you to get it.

ADOPTING THE EMPLOYEE'S OBJECTIVE

Losing control can often result in your adopting the other person's agenda or objective. You start out to "sell" your standards, your procedures, whatever it is that you want, and wind up being an unwitting buyer. Undoubtedly it has happened to you many times. For example, you took your car to the garage for repairs. When you left it, you emphasized how important it was for you to have the car back in two days. The service manager agreed to repair it by then. But when you came to pick it up, the service manager said, "Sorry, we'll have to keep it another day." You responded, probably with annoyance, "But I told you I had to have it today, and you agreed."

"Yes," he said, "but I've had two men out with the flu. I couldn't anticipate that. I'm sorry."

If you accepted his excuses, the service manager made a sale. You lost control of the situation. You hadn't intended to buy, but you did. You wanted your car, but instead you got a sad story. What the service manager was actually saying to you was, "I have a problem. Here, I want you to own it too."

Employees will ask you to own their problems. For example, an employee can't get to work on time. She says her babysitter often comes to the house late. That is a problem for her, of course. But what about your problem? You want her to be at work on time.

You want an important report by Tuesday. But by Tuesday, you haven't received it. You ask the employee to account for the failure. Well, she tells you, the person who was supposed to provide her with some of the important data she needed for the report was out sick one day, and had a rush job to do the next, and so on. She wants you to buy her problems. If you do, it won't help you to get your report.

Another employee has been falling below quota. You call him in for a conference. He tells you that, despite your opinions and records, he has been doing more than his share. He certainly works harder than some of the other people, and he feels less appreciated. First thing you know, if you lose control, he will have convinced you that he is a victim of your biases, that you ought to make allowances for his performance.

The more you are aware of what is going on and of others' attempts to influence you, the better prepared you are to get what you want. Stay in control. Remember where you want the process to go. Some people assume that you are going to accept their bill of goods, and they don't expect you to refuse.

One way to resist the sale is to look at the other person and listen. Then you ask, "Yes?" You're indicating that you have heard but are not accepting the proposition. The burden remains clearly on the other person. The attempt to switch the burden to you has failed.

Probably the other person's response will be like this: "Well, that's why I can't do such-and-such." Your rejoinder: "I don't know that. What I hear is that you have a problem. I also have a problem. I know you'd like to solve your problem, but so would I."

You have now clearly stated that you are not willing to buy. The next step is to decide jointly what can be done to solve your problem.

INVOLVING OTHERS

When you seek to involve others, to encourage them to express their needs and wants, to give you feedback, and to participate in finding a solution to problems and deficiencies, you convey a message of respect for the other people. You exhibit a win–win mentality rather than a win–lose. Let us both get something out of this, you say. You won't make much progress if the employee suspects you want to beat them down.

The idea that the boss's voice is the only voice that counts doesn't work well these days. Today's manager must be more of a coordinator and a developer than a dictator. Nothing will do a manager in faster than to display the attitude, "I get what I want regardless of what others want," or worse,"I get what I want any way I can."

Here are a few of the ways in which you as a manager can demonstrate to your employees that you respect them, even though you may be giving them negative feedback on their performance.

Accept Opinions

The employee probably has reasons, explanations, and excuses for behavior that is not acceptable to you. Listen. Don't respond in a "yes, but" manner. That's interpreted as, "I hear what you're saying, but you're all wrong." Use a "yes, and" response: "I understand that you feel that is a consideration. I'd like to give you another one." Instead of appearing to put the employee down, you accept that the person believes what he or she is saying, then you answer with your opinion. For example, certain employees may resist adopting the techniques and procedures you have instituted, wanting to do it their own way. They give you an impassioned defense of their ability to handle the job, a history of past accomplishments, their conviction that they work better in their own way. You acknowledge that they in fact believe all those things, and you believe certain things as well, specifically, that everyone else in the department, through using your recommendations, has increased productivity by 10 percent. You want them to turn in the same results.

However full of holes another person's comments might be, assume that the person takes them seriously and act accordingly. The worst thing you can do in an exchange with an employee is to make him or her feel wrong and foolish.

Accept Feelings

In any human interaction, feelings come into play. There may be joy, anger, suspicion, impatience, mistrust, fear, affection, and so on. It is probable that in a negative feedback session, the emotions also will be negative. You have to be prepared to accept the anger, fear, anxiety that you see in the employee who is on the receiving end of the feedback, even though you don't see a reason for it, or think it is unjustified. For example, you are talking to an employee about a problem you've pointed out to her before. The employee seems confused and angry in the current session. Your reaction, quite understandably, is that she has no right to be surprised, confused, and angry—at least, not surprised and confused. But the fact is that she does feel this way, and it is simpler for you to accept that fact. Otherwise you'll spend the whole time arguing about her justification for feeling the way she does. Or, you'll create such a barrier of resentment in the employee because you deny her the right to have human feelings that you'll cease to be effective.

When you accept that another person feels a certain way, you are not necessarily agreeing with those feelings. You are not saying, "If I were in your shoes, I would feel that way, too." You are simply acknowledging that the other person feels a certain way. If you want to overcome negative feelings in another, give more reasons why the person should feel differently. Say, in effect, "Yes, you're angry because I criticize you now, but if you accept my counsel, you will feel much more secure and happy with yourself." That positive approach is more productive than trying to argue the employee out of the feelings he or she has. Extend to the other person the same privilege you claim for yourself: You have a right to your feelings. So does the other person.

Avoid Behavioral or Attitudinal Labels

If the employee seems resistant to your criticism or counsel, the worst thing you can say is, "You're stubborn," or, "Why are you fighting me?" Or, if the employee has a flushed face and clenched fists, you don't say, "I don't see why you are so angry." Putting labels on behaviors is risky, and characterizing someone's attitudes is usually seen as obnoxious behavior by the other person. If the person resists the label, then you get trapped into debating whose perceptions are right instead of discussing matters of substance. Remember that each person is an expert in his or her own feelings and perceptions. Thus, if you want to call attention to the other person's feelings or behavior, do so by acknowledging your own perceptions: "I sense that something I've said has upset you." In that way, you put your own perceptions on the line rather than the other person's behavior. The other person can't argue against your interpretation any more than you can label the other person. The employee's response will be less defensive.

Take Responsibility for Misunderstanding

If the employee shows that he or she doesn't fully understand you or if the person's response is clearly off the track, be careful not to say, "You're wrong," or "You didn't understand me." Take responsibility for the error, even though you believe you were clear.

If the employee's response to you is way off, you may be tempted to say, "You're not listening to me." That may be true. But it could also be true that you didn't say what you thought you did. Where there is a possibility that there has been a failure, initially assume that it is your responsibility. It is a generous gesture that often pays off in the other person's increased goodwill.

This advice isn't given to make you into a nice person, although it probably will have that effect. It's really quite pragmatic, in that the more you can reduce the other person's negative feelings and resistance, the more impact you can achieve.

If you repeat yourself and are convinced that you have used indisputably clear language, then you might want to be stronger in admonishing the other person to listen with special care to what you are saying. You don't always have to take responsibility for misunderstanding when it strikes you as possible that the other person is being unusually deaf to your meaning or is possibly playing a game with you.

Look for Options

There is no one best way to get results. Be aware of options in every situation. For example, you start a counseling session with the belief that the employee needs to be shown ways to overcome a performance deficiency. During the interview you come to suspect that the employee would perform better in a capacity you never previously thought of. Even though you know that the present inadequacy could be overcome, it gradually becomes clear that your investment would pay off more handsomely if the responsibilities were changed.

A notable example of this unexpected option was an employee who performed in a mediocre fashion. Her boss stewed about how to upgrade the quality and the quantity of her work. Meanwhile there was a task in the department that was onerous and, as a result, was rotated, everyone in the work group taking his or her turn at it. The manager, in a stroke of inspiration, asked the mediocre-performing employee whether she would like to take the unpleasant job on a permanent basis. She accepted, did a much better job than the part-timers, and was very happy with her new responsibility.

Every dialogue is different; every dialogue generates options. As you listen, you might say to yourself, "That's something I hadn't considered." It has possibilities. Options are things to say, actions to take, and decisions to follow. Being open to them and becoming aware of them defines the flexible mentality. It gives you a lot of room for movement.

LISTENING ACTIVELY

Few human acts convey as much respect and consideration to another person as does listening well. There is probably no other thing you can do in an interview that will encourage the other person's involvement as much as taking care to listen. If you want to achieve a maximum impact on the employee, you must listen as well as talk effectively. Here are some recommendations to follow.

Maintain Eye Contact

It's not easy to do. In fact, most people require training in it, or at least a heightened awareness of its importance. No doubt you've talked to people who looked away frequently, past your shoulder or down at something on a desk. It probably made you feel as if what you were saying was not of much interest and that, in fact, you were not of importance to the other person. When you make eye contact throughout a discussion, you not only visually convey respect for what the other person is saying, you listen better. You can see the person's expressions, gestures, and other body language. Furthermore, you increase the probability that you will get more respect when you talk.

Avoid Interruptions

You have undoubtedly found yourself talking to another person who couldn't seem to wait until you finished speaking. Such a person doesn't seem to listen to your words, looking instead for a cue to break in or for a break in your conversation. You take it as a putdown. Give the other person time to articulate. Don't try to complete sentences the person is slow to finish. When you try to guess what the other person is saying, you create resentment, slow the process down, and generally obscure the direction the conversation is taking.

Watch Your Body Language

There are at least three things many people do that they believe encourage another person to talk, but that, in fact, the talker may see as somewhat threatening. The first is leaning forward. You may believe that it shows that you are attentive, but the talker may see you as ready to pounce into the conversation just as soon as he or she draws a breath.

Another bodily communication is smiling. You may consider your smile to be friendly and encouraging, but the other person might see it as taking lightly what he or she is saying, as if you find it all very amusing. Also, refrain from nodding frequently and saying, "Right," "I see," and "Unh-hunh." If you say these phrases constantly, you may grow tiresome, and the talker may wonder whether you are in fact listening or trying to show that you are listening while your mind is elsewhere.

It's also a good idea not to frown strenuously. That conveys skepticism.

Ask Encouraging Questions

If the person seems to find it difficult to talk, help by asking questions that show that you want to hear more. Here are a few of the questions that you can pose:

- ☐ "That's very interesting. Can you say more?"
- ☐ "Would you explain a bit more about that?"
- ☐ "Would you care to elaborate?"
- ☐ "I'm not sure I understand fully. Can you tell me more?"
- ☐ "Why do you suppose that is true?"
- ☐ "Is there anything else you can add?"
- ☐ "What happened then?"

Your encouraging responses don't have to be made up only of questions. From time to time you can nod slightly and say, "Go on." Or, "I'm listening." "Take your time." "I'd like to hear more if you're willing to talk about it." These are aids in what is referred to often as nondirective interviewing. You're not leading the other person in a direction of your choosing, but rather encouraging him or her to tell you what he or she wants to.

Avoid Shutoff and Gratuitous Comments

Some responses, such as the following, can discourage further communicating:

Judgment: "That was wrong," or, "You shouldn't have done that."

Free and probably unasked-for advice: "If I were you. . . ."

Putdown: "That wasn't very smart."

Ridicule: "Where in the world did you get that idea?"

Diversion: "That reminds me of the time. . . . "

Sarcasm: "Go on. Nothing you'd say at this point would surprise me."

Analyze While the Person Is Talking

Ask yourself such questions as the following to help you process what the talker is communicating:

☐ What is this person really trying to say?

☐ Where does the information lead?

☐ What is the connection between what I am told now and what I was told a while ago?

☐ What else do I need to know?

Limit Distractions

It's all too easy to fall prey to distractions: allowing your mind to wander, reading mail while the person is talking, and accepting phone calls, for example. If you're engaged in a serious conversation with an employee, shut the door so you can't be distracted by people passing or talking outside. Ask someone else to take your phone calls. Keep your eyes from straying to the top of your desk.

Provide Closure

People need to close out a subject. Make sure you have finished the conversation before going on to something else. For instance, the employee says, "I really think that we ought to consider getting Engineering more involved on a day-to-day basis from the outset."

You reply, "Yeah. Oh, that reminds me, you and I have a meeting with Miller tomorrow afternoon."

It would be much better if you said: "Right. I think that's a good idea. I'll make a note. Oh, before you go, I want to remind you. . . ." You closed out one topic before jumping to another.

There is little you can do that is more complimentary to another person than to listen to what he or she has to say. There is little you can do that encourages the other person to open up more than listening. Few people do it well.

THE POWER OF PAUSES

When you are communicating, don't rely heavily on lots of words. Sometimes you can get your message across with greater impact by using pauses. Here are some examples.

The Pause To Get Agreement

When you write, you set off the important points by using para-graphs. In speaking, you can do the same thing with pauses, providing time for a point to hit home. "John, I needed these figures last Friday so I could work up the report over the weekend. It was due to my boss yesterday. He didn't get it so. . . ." You don't have to finish that statement. In his mind John will do it for you. John was at fault for not giving you the figures. The boss didn't get them when he wanted them. Now you're both in trouble.

The pause to get agreement is sometimes more effective than telling the other person.

The Pause for Calm

If an employee reacts emotionally to something you have said or done, a quick-on-the-trigger rebuttal from you will not have a calming effect. But a stretch of silence could help that person to hear the words that have just been spoken emotionally and provide him or her with the chance to reevaluate the tone of those remarks—and perhaps reconsider the remarks themselves.

The Pause To Impress

You say to the employee, "This is not the first time we've had to talk about this." Then, instead of reminding the subordinate about the previous times you've had to call him or her on the carpet, you just let silence take over. You'll probably get a nod and "I know."

Keeping your face and posture relaxed plays a large part in the effective use of the pause. Even an unplanned pause—when you're caught by surprise and at a momentary loss for words—can be turned to good effect if you immediately react by relaxing instead of betraying your discomfort or confusion with signs of tension.

MUFFLING YOUR IMPACT

Sometimes, through fear, tension, or embarrassment, you may muffle the impact of your message and make it less effective. Here is a checklist to help you determine whether you are communicating clearly and directly or, in fact, are avoiding dealing with the other person in the transaction:

☐ Are you talking in general terms instead of asking specifically for what you want and expect? A common example is the manager who sends out memos or gives speeches to the entire department about absenteeism rather than taking action with individual offenders.

☐ Are you talking in terms of what ought to be rather than what is? Do you say, "We really have to get those 10 people on board," instead of, "We don't have those 10 people yet, and I'm upset about it."

☐ Are you sending mixed messages by saying one thing but looking another? Keeping a smile on your face when you are bursting with anger is a good example of a mixed message. If you are angry, show it. The employee will get a stronger impact.

☐ Are you saying "we" or "one" to mask the truth: "*I* would like," "I want," "I think," are more direct.

☐ Are you looking at the desk or over the other person's head while talking to him or her?

DEALING WITH AN EMPLOYEE'S OPPOSITION

You call an employee in for counseling. You have the data on which to base your criticism. But to your surprise, the employee also comes prepared with data. They show that you have been partly to blame for the performance deficiency. Don't respond too quickly, even if you think the employee is wrong. It may not be easy when someone is opposing or disputing you. But you will eventually be more effective if you take your time and follow these recommendations:

1. *Relax.* You may not be able to relax internally, but assume a relaxed position. Sit back in your chair. Cross your legs. That suggests less tension than keeping both feet on the floor. Keep your facial expression attentive but free of frowns. When you look relaxed, you not only appear confident, but you make it easier for others to discuss their opposition in front of you. You want all the information you can get before you rebut. At that point, you don't want any surprises left. Your pose of relaxation may throw the employee off balance, and encourage him or her to be less emotional. Chances are he or she came prepared for your defensiveness. And you aren't defensive, not so far as the employee can see.

2. *Listen.* Listening becomes very difficult to do when you are convinced that you have the arguments to demolish the other

person's position or when you are angry and anxious to lash out. But without listening, you don't learn what is important, and you may shut off the other person. You don't want to cause the employee to stop talking, because you will then be responsible for the person's suppression of the grievance as well as the emotions accompanying it.

Maintain frequent eye contact while you listen, so that the other person knows that you value what is being said. What you hear can provide you with the means of persuading the employee that he or she is not correct.

3. *Accept.* As has been stated elsewhere, you don't have to buy the substance of the opposition. You can say, "I can understand why you would see that as a problem," or, "I can understand why you would feel that way." There's no point in retorting with something such as, "That's ridiculous," or, "Why in the world would you feel that way?" The other person will not care to have his or her feelings discounted.

4. *Answer.* First, check with the employee to make sure you understand the complaint or opposition: "If I heard you right, you are angry because in the middle of the project I shortened the deadline. Am I right?"

The person answers that your understanding is correct.

You say, "I realize that we can't go back to the time and reverse my decision. Would you feel a bit better if I explained to you why I had to do that?" Chances are the employee will listen. After all, you've performed the same courtesy. Don't try to overwhelm him or her with a long, weighty argument. Choose what you believe is an effective answer to the complaint, state it succinctly, then test the reaction: "Do you understand now why I had to make that decision?"

When you run into opposition by an employee, don't be thrown by what seem to be negative feelings and reactions. Opposition implies involvement, even interest, on the part of the other person and certainly gives you an opportunity to respond and to persuade the other person of the rightness of the course of action you chose.

THE ANGRY EMPLOYEE

Sometimes an employee's opposition is expressed in an unpleasant manner. For example, you suddenly find yourself on the receiving end of an employee's anger. Being a target is an unpleasant feeling. But if you retaliate, you'll undoubtedly make things worse. The employee may stop showing but not necessarily feeling the anger. And suppressed anger can affect performance as well as morale.

There are managers who would move quickly to shut the anger off, even though the feelings remain unresolved. Those managers may feel as if their position and authority are threatened. But if you respond to the attack with dignity and self-confidence, you will have no problem retaining your managerial status in the eyes of others. And that will probably be especially true of the person who is expressing anger. Consider the following steps.

Suspect That the Anger Is a Symptom of a Greater Problem

Don't immediately and automatically assume that the employee is voicing a dislike of you, as a person or as a manager. The real target may be working conditions, personal problems, or a combination of both. A blown temper is almost always a sign of emotional overload and must be probed with caution.

Let the Employee Get It All Out Before You Start Probing

Allow the angry employee to sit or pace, do anything except threaten violence. Just watch, remain quiet, and encourage him or her to get it all out. After the angry feelings have been expressed, you may just want time to think it over. Suggest that the two of you get together later in the day.

The purpose of the delaying tactic is to allow time for the subordinate to reflect and to regain composure. When the two of you meet again, don't talk about the display of anger but rather about what might have caused it. If the employee wants to apologize, suggest that analyzing the problem is most important. You may want to accept the apology just to get the incident out of the way. But what you really want to do at this point is to enlist the employee's help in probing into his or her frustrations.

Keep the Discussion Private

Carry on your discussion behind closed doors. Suggest that both of you agree to keep what is said confidential. The employee who boasts to others about telling you off isn't doing either of you a favor.

Divert Your Emotions as Much as Possible

You're probably going to have an emotional reaction. Expend your energy on helping the employee to find out for himself or herself what really caused the disturbance. If the reason is legitimate and in your department, it's possible that you can change the situation and the irritant. If it's not work-related, at least you've helped the employee to find out something about himself or herself. And you may have provided a safety valve for a potentially explosive emotion.

COMMUNICATING EFFECTIVELY AND PERSUASIVELY

When you give feedback to employees, you want something to happen as a result of the interchange. Bear in mind that the result you want doesn't always automatically come about just because you expect or want it. In almost any transaction some persuading is involved. Whether you are assigning work, criticizing, or counseling, remember that the following rules of persuasion usually apply: Know your "product," know your prospect, involve your prospect, ask for action, and be prepared to handle opposition.

Know Your Product

What project, procedure, and action are you hoping to get accepted? Perhaps you want an employee to change behavior, adopt a different method, or take on more responsibility. Whatever you are selling, know what you have to offer. What are the strengths and the benefits of your product? You need to be precise about your needs and wants in the transaction.

Know Your Prospect

You should know something of the employee's needs and wants if you are to be truly effective. That information is helpful if you want to translate what you want into benefits that are attractive to the other person. Why should the other person want to agree to a change of behavior, try the method you propose, and accept greater responsibility? It's probably not going to come about simply because it is something you want. How would you describe those benefits? What kind of words would you use? Is this a good time for your prospect to hear what you have to say? For example, is the prospect depressed, in which case you might not want to talk about a change of behavior? Or does the employee feel overloaded, in which event you could hardly speak of taking on even more work?

How detailed should you be? Can you briefly sketch or must you be thorough? Should your approach be formal or informal? The answers to the above questions are to be found in your knowledge of the person. Remember that effective management is one-to-one, person-to-person.

Remember also that persuasion does not occur entirely on a rational level. The employee responds to you emotionally and intuitively as well. If you are to be successful, you must anticipate some of these responses. Will the person be anxious? Does the employee have a tendency to accept assignments without thinking them through? Does the employee have an ambition or a self-image that would make what you propose attractive?

People have biases, psychological sets, and preconceptions that you must be aware of and be able to address. Managers who try to communicate only on a rational level are frustrated frequently by their lack of success in having an effect on others.

Involve Your Prospect

In most cases, communication cannot flow one way. The other person brings biases, ideas, strengths, wants, and needs to the transaction. You need to hear them if they affect your getting what you want. Besides, you need to get feedback on how well you are doing in your persuasion. So take the employee's reaction temperature from time to time. Ask questions such as, "Am I being clear?" or, "Do you find this interesting?" or, "Does what I am saying make sense?"

Another reason why you need to get the other person involved is that many people have trouble listening. They are not trained to listen well. They tend to hear only part of what you say, or what they wish to hear, which may be quite different from what you are saying. Through questions and invitations to respond, you can find out what the other person has heard.

Ask for Action

Don't assume that the employee knows exactly what you want to happen as a result of the interview. Spell it out. No doubt you want some kind of change. Be specific. You don't want the employee to leave your office confused or mistaken. Asking for action also provides closure for you both. Closure is natural and desired.

Be Prepared to Handle Opposition

Even though you are the boss, the employee may still resist complying with your requests or orders. If the change requires that the employee do something new, he or she may oppose it. Many people show opposition to new ideas, techniques, responsibilities, and ways of working.

Some managers take employees' opposition personally and, in some cases, perhaps that interpretation is justified. But unless you have cause to believe that a particular employee is strongly biased against you, don't react too negatively to the resistance. Look at the resistance in a positive way: In expressing opposition, the employee may reveal that he or she doesn't clearly understand what you want. Or the employee may come up with a solution that you find better than yours. A resistant employee is at least an involved employee.

Being persuasive is knowing the techniques, what makes them work, and applying them effectively. The techniques themselves are rather simple. But thinking them and applying them are more complicated. "Thinking them" means being aware of them, having the intention to use them, and using them skillfully.

Employees these days are much more receptive to a "sell" style in managers than a "tell" approach. When you use persuasive, assertive–responsive techniques in communicating your expectations to employees, you are not only achieving your immediate wants and needs, you are building a foundation of respect between the employees and you. A firm foundation of respect means a productive, long-term working relationship.

POSITIVE MESSAGES

Managers who have positive attitudes about their employees usually achieve greater results than managers who tend to be somewhat pessimistic and negative. Certainly being positive in a feedback session gives you advantages. It gives you freedom to be flexible in the way you achieve that outcome. You do not get locked into a particular scenario, which may not be appropriate to the person and to the situation. When you are giving an employee feedback, you create a dialogue with the employee; you believe that the employee wants a solution to the problem, and therefore, you are open to whatever options emerge from that dialogue.

When you think positively, you say to yourself, "Both of us want something good to happen as a result of this interview." Then you remain open to whatever opportunities come your way to achieve something positive. You open doors for yourself, as opposed to closing them, when you try to follow a negative scenario that you have created.

Being positive has a favorable impact on others. Positive messages beget positive responses. Positive messages gain you the respect and trust of employees, necessary for continuing effectiveness. Unsure people often dwell on the negative. For example, some managers think they do their jobs merely by pointing out what is wrong with a work situation and what is deficient about the way employees do the work. But the positive manager seeks to find out what can be done to correct it. There's a vast difference between "won't work" and "can do." Most people prefer to be around people who can do. The person who dwells on what will work, what is right about this, rather than on what is not right, broadcasts an optimistic self-confidence that inspires confidence in others.

You'll find that the confidence you show as a positive person often makes good things happen for you. When you put out the messages, through your words, your expressions, your gestures, and the tone of your voice, that this is the way you think things should go, you'll often find others swinging around to your way of thinking.

YOUR FEEDBACK SKILLS INVENTORY

To determine how effective you are at giving and receiving feedback, score yourself on the following scale:

5—*Always*
4—*Frequently*
3—*Occasionally*
2—*Seldom*
1—*Never*

1. I look for opportunities to tell employees how they are performing.   5   4   3   2   1

2. In my discussions with employees, I try to control the transaction.   5   4   3   2   1

3. I recognize that the employee in discussions with me has needs and wants that I should acknowledge.   5   4   3   2   1

4. In a serious discussion or an interview with an employee, I make sure I know what I want from it.   5   4   3   2   1

5. In such a discussion, I ask myself what I think the employee would like from the exchange.   5   4   3   2   1

6. During a transaction, I frequently examine my behavior in terms of my being effective, that is, getting what I want.   5   4   3   2   1

7. When I give feedback, I work to influence the thinking and the actions of my subordinates.   5   4   3   2   1

8. In the transactions that I initiate with employees, I consider myself the persuader, trying to get the action I want from them.   5   4   3   2   1

9. When I give negative feedback to an employee, I remain alert to the possibility that the other person will try to get me off the course of action I have chosen.   5   4   3   2   1

10. In feedback situations, I work to involve employees in finding a solution to problems.   5   4   3   2   1

11. I realize that, even as boss, in communicating with employees my voice is not the only one that counts in their minds.   5   4   3   2   1

12. Even when criticizing an employee, I try to show that I respect him or her even though I disapprove of the person's actions.   5   4   3   2   1

13. In negative feedback transactions, I accept the employee's opinion or belief in his or her explanation without necessarily agreeing that it is justified.   5   4   3   2   1

14. However full of holes I believe a person's comments might be in a negative feedback exchange, I assume that the person takes them seriously.   5   4   3   2   1

15. I avoid responding to an employee's explanation of inadequate performance with a "yes, but" answer.   5   4   3   2   1

16. I respect the fact that an employee who is being criticized or counseled will probably have negative feelings.   5   4   3   2   1

17. I accept the employee's belief, when angry or embarrassed during my criticism, that he or she has a right to have those feelings.   5   4   3   2   1

18. I know the difference between accepting someone's emotions and agreeing with them.   5   4   3   2   1

19. In feedback situations I avoid talking about the employee's attitudes.   5   4   3   2   1

20. If a misunderstanding occurs during a feedback discussion with an employee, I take the blame for it.   5   4   3   2   1

21. I listen to employees in every feedback situation because I realize that every dialogue is different and represents an opportunity for me to learn something about the employee or about the department.   5   4   3   2   1

22. In dialogues with employees, I believe that listening is often just as important as talking.   5   4   3   2   1

23. When I listen, I practice making and maintaining eye contact.   5   4   3   2   1

24. When I listen to an employee, I make sure I don't interrupt.   5   4   3   2   1

25. In active listening, I try to sit back and look attentive without smiling or frowning.   5   4   3   2   1

26. When an employee seems to find it difficult to talk in a criticism, appraisal, or counseling situation, I try to ask encouraging questions to get him or her to open up.   5   4   3   2   1

27. While an employee is talking to me in a feedback situation, I try to analyze what the person is saying according to what I need to know, where the information leads me, and what connection it has with what I've already been told.   5   4   3   2   1

28. I make sure to limit distractions while an employee talks to me.   5   4   3   2   1

29. I frequently use pauses to emphasize my points when I give feedback to an employee.   5   4   3   2   1

30. When I give feedback, I make sure I am specific in telling the employee what I expect.   5   4   3   2   1

31. When I feel anger, I let my expression and tone of voice reveal the fact. I do not try to hide it.   5   4   3   2   1

32. When I receive an employee's opposition when I criticize or counsel, I try to relax and listen before I respond.   5   4   3   2   1

33. Before I respond to an employee's opposition during a feedback session, I first check with the employee to make sure I understand the person's meaning.   5   4   3   2   1

34. When an employee argues with or opposes my criticism or counseling, I interpret the opposition as a sign of involvement in the transaction.   5   4   3   2   1

35. When an employee shows anger with me, I remind myself that it may be a symptom of a greater problem than the one the person seems to be discussing with me now.   5   4   3   2   1

36. I let an angry employee get all the anger out before I try to deal with whatever has caused it.   5   4   3   2   1

37. When I start to give feedback to an employee, I know exactly what it is that I want the employee to do or to understand.   5   4   3   2   1

38. I believe it is important to know as much as I can about the employee before I start a feedback session.   5 4 3 2 1

39. I realize how important it is to involve the employee in the feedback session by asking questions to determine how much the other person is hearing of what I say.   5 4 3 2 1

40. I assume that it is my responsibility to spell out exactly what I want of the employee as a result of the feedback interview.   5 4 3 2 1

41. When an employee expresses opposition to my feedback, I consider the possibility that he or she doesn't clearly understand what I seek.   5 4 3 2 1

42. I consciously use persuasive techniques when I give feedback rather than assuming that the employee will accept what I say simply because I am the boss.   5 4 3 2 1

43. I believe in being positive in a feedback interview and that the employee also wants something good to result from the session.   5 4 3 2 1

44. I subscribe to the belief that when I convey the conviction that things ought to go a certain way, I increase the probability that they will in fact go that way.   5 4 3 2 1

Scoring the Inventory

If your score is more than

<u>198</u> you know that you are highly effective in your feedback interviews.

<u>154</u> you are generally effective but may occasionally be disappointed that you do not achieve your way or the consequences you want.

<u>110</u> you enter into feedback sessions with employees not as confident of your success as you want to be.

If your score is lower than <u>110</u> , you need serious review of the feedback and communications techniques in this chapter and in Chapter 3.

11

APPRAISING PERFORMANCE

Does your appraisal system work well for you? Does it tell you which employees are performing well and which are not? Does it reveal weaknesses in your goal setting and work assignments? Do your appraisals provide reasonably objective indicators of where and with whom you should invest the major part of your time and energy to get the best results and the most improvement? Can you estimate, from your evaluations, what kind of performance you can expect in the next six months, barring unforeseeable circumstances?

Many managers would have difficulty answering the above questions in a positive way. Their appraisal systems do not provide them with the necessary workable data. In fact, some of the most elaborate and carefully constructed systems produce much information that has relatively little use.

TRAIT-BASED EVALUATION

Some appraisal systems require managers to evaluate personality characteristics, traits, and attitudes. Too often, they guess. Managers are asked to rate what they cannot see, to measure what defies measurement, or to judge factors that may have little to do with performance. For example, a manager may have to attempt to determine the degree of an employee's maturity. What constitutes maturity? Not many years ago, many people defined maturity as the ability to control feelings and emotions. Individuals who expressed how they felt, who became angry, wept, and showed intense emotion were often labeled immature. Today, most people have quite different views on the expression of feelings. It is widely regarded as healthier—and perhaps more mature—to display them than to bottle them up.

Other managers might try to define maturity as the ability to get along well with everyone. Yet some people get along well by paying a tremendous price. For example, they don't do anything to upset anyone. People who fear to make even a ripple don't make substantial contributions to the operation. They may be reluctant to come up with new and different ideas. They are agreeable to other people's ideas when perhaps they shouldn't be. Not only do they avoid even constructive conflict but they urge the suppression of it in others.

You encounter some of the same difficulties when you attempt to measure intelligence. There are different types of intelligence, and many ways in which it is demonstrated. It is unreasonable to ask a manager to estimate intelligence when even much psychological testing of intelligence has been shown to be irrelevant.

MANAGERIAL RESISTANCE

Another reason why appraisal systems often fail to deliver helpful information is the resistance that managers generate toward them. There are several reasons for this resistance.

Managers Are Uncomfortable Playing Judge

When they have to interpret attitudes or traits, or when they have to render verdicts on performance, or give an employee a grade or numerical rating, they worry about making a wrong judgment. They fear either being or seeming to be arbitrary. Furthermore, the relationship they have with an employee during the appraising process may be quite unlike their everyday dealings. In fact, the role they must assume in evaluating in their minds may undermine the valuable and constructive working relationship they have tried hard to build all year.

Appraisal Seems Like Confrontation

If managers are not well trained in appraising or if they do not understand the reasons for the system, they may wind up presenting evaluation information to employees in a fragmented, awkward way that has a negative effect on employees. In the face of employees' resentment or anger managers may learn to dread the experience.

Appraisal Takes Time

When you consider the time necessary to prepare for the appraisal, to gather the documentation, and to conduct the interview, it may seem too much of an intrusion on the managers' schedules. As a result, they may give minimum concern to the evaluation, with the bottom line being that much useful information is left out.

Too Few Discernible Results

A poorly conceived and planned evaluation probably provides little guidance to employees. If the manager defaults on showing employees how they must change to become more effective, he or she is bound to be disappointed by the lack of results. Why spend a lot of time on appraisal if nothing really happens?

Higher Management Doesn't Take the System Seriously

In one company, an appraisal system was installed with much publicity and seriousness. The managers were to follow a prescribed procedure. First, they would fill out an evaluation form. They were then to review it with the employee, who would agree or disagree. If the employee disagreed with any aspect of the evaluation, he or she was given the privilege of submitting a written rebuttal. After the form was signed by both employee and manager, it was sent to higher management, along with any rebuttals. After two years, it was decided that the entire procedure took too much time. The evaluations were to be sent to higher management levels before the employees saw them. The shortcut saved time but broadcast that management had little interest in fairness and completeness.

Managers also tend to perceive that higher management doesn't take the system seriously if they receive no feedback on the appraisals. If year after year managers go through the evaluation procedures but never have received any indication that anyone on a higher level has reviewed them or made personnel decisions on the basis of them, they cannot be blamed for believing that appraisal is an academic exercise.

MANAGERIAL BIAS

A third reason why appraisal systems can produce disappointing results has to do with the bias of the appraisers. No matter how well the system itself is designed, the managers who use it are subject to certain shortcomings, because of the halo effect, leniency and strictness, averaging, and personal bias.

Halo Effect

Raters may allow one characteristic of an employee to have an excessive influence on their ratings of all other factors. Sam is a loyal employee, a quality that his boss admires. He has been working in the company for 28 years. He always does what he is told; he never questions or objects. Sam's work is mediocre, but he gets great evaluations.

The quality that is given disproportionate value may also be one that the reviewer dislikes: the horns effect. Phyllis is outspoken and does not hesitate to criticize her manager's judgment when she believes it is wrong. Phyllis performs in an outstanding manner. All that she requires is that her work have a rationale. Her manager rates her work as needing improvement. He also uses the word "uncooperative" in describing her.

Leniency and Strictness

Some managers tend to be overly generous in their ratings. They give unwarranted high marks, often out of fear that they will make a mistake by being too harsh. They may also fear confrontation. They don't want to upset any employee.

Other managers go to the other extreme by rating employees with unnecessary harshness. They don't want to seem too easy in their judgments. No one higher up in the organization will be able to call them pushovers. Instead, these strict managers hope that people up the line will admire them for their high standards.

Excessive leniency or strictness generally stems from differing personal standards that individual managers have. Department-to-department ratings that vary from extremely high to extremely low can seriously impair an appraisal program. They can also have a detrimental effect on employee motivation. People who automatically earn high ratings won't have anything to shoot for, and won't really grow and progress on the job. People who never get top ratings may just give up.

Averaging

Some raters like to play it safe. They avoid placing employees at the extreme ends of the scale but consistently give them average evaluations. In that way they believe they can avoid making errors of judgment and being unfair to anyone. Averaging may also be attributed to the supervisor's own standards, against which most employees may be just average performers. Whatever the reason, the rater who uses averaging does an inadequate job of observing how individual employees are performing. When appraisal time arrives, they do not really know whether employees have done well or not. It is best, they reason, to give them all average scores.

Personal Bias

This distortion factor differs from the halo effect in that it involves more general feelings of liking or disliking that often have little to do with performance. The manager may feel a special rapport with the employee, may admire the person, in fact, may envy the employee and wish that he or she were more like the employee. It is perfectly all right for managers to like some employees more than others, and to feel closer or more empathetic with some than with others, but these personal feelings should not affect the manager's view of the employee's performance. In those organizations in which one hears frequently, "Around here it's not what you know but who," it's probably true that bias is widely operative.

Bias that is based on personal feelings toward individuals is not as serious, however, as discrimination against people who are of a different race, ethnic group, religion, age, sex, national origin, etc. That sort of bias, when it influences appraisals, can be illegal and lead to expensive headaches for both the biased manager and the organization who backs the manager up.

APPRAISERS' EFFECTIVENESS

Although it may be true that subjective elements can never be entirely neutralized, it is possible to encourage and to help appraisers to develop greater objectivity in their evaluations of employees' performance. Here are some of the steps you can take with your managers.

Train Them

In some organizations, managers are simply handed the appraisal form when the system is installed or when they become managers.

Managers need to know what performance factors are being evaluated. They need to see what a good evaluation form looks like, and could certainly use help in planning and conducting an effective appraisal interview. The training doesn't have to be extensive or expensive. If the system is already in place, more experienced managers could discuss their knowledge of the system and their ways of using it. Model evaluations, rendered anonymous, of course, could give new managers some idea of the standards of performance that you want. Role playing could help managers acquire the skills to talk constructively with employees about their performance. The training would serve to underscore the seriousness with which management regards the appraisal system.

Present the System Positively

No doubt managers will strive to be more conscientious and accurate about performance evaluations if they see the role of the system in the organization's overall growth and progress. Appraisal is, to begin with, an important part of the management of motivation. Employees should look forward to appraisal time as information time: They will be able to find out how they are performing. Specifically, it confirms their feelings that they are doing well or not. It points to specific areas in which they are doing well and to how they could do even better.

Managers need information from employees about how the employees see their tasks—difficult, too easy, unnecessarily complicated, without purpose, and so on. An appraisal system provides controls that show what is or is not going according to plan. The information helps measure progress toward the goals that were set earlier. What may emerge from the evaluation is the realization that the plan is not workable and that the goals need to be changed.

A good feedback system such as appraisal has the benefit of uncovering problems and obstacles. It provides opportunities for managers and their subordinates to find solutions to the problems that prevent them from working well. (There may be times when the subordinates know more about a problem than their managers do and can come up with more solutions.)

There is also a long-range payoff for the managers who conduct appraisals well: The manager confirms his or her dedication to good performance. The manager wants results—for himself or herself, for the organization, for the employees themselves. Appraisals that are professionally done say to subordinates, "You see, I mean it when I talk about the need to help everyone be effective on the job."

It is through the feedback that comes through appraisal sessions that managers come to know better just what their subordinates' resources are. No matter how long you may have worked with an individual, you are safe in assuming that there are still parts of that person you don't know or know well. There may even be aspects of a person that he or she is not well aware of. Thus a good appraisal can provide learning for both of you.

Appraisals of performance provide the organization with an inventory of employee skills: Who is doing what, has done what, and may be capable of doing what? Organizations need these data in order to plan for growth.

Reward Good Evaluations

From the outset, make it clear to managers that they themselves will be evaluated on the basis of their performance appraisals of their subordinates. Each appraiser should have his or her appraisals reviewed by the next-level manager. Even if the higher manager doesn't know the appraised employees well, the manager will still be able to note patterns in the appraiser's evaluations that could signal bias, for example. The manager could repeatedly emphasize certain points, characteristics, or behaviors to the exclusion of others—or at least deemphasize other equally valuable performance characteristics. Labels are telltale. The manager who frequently characterizes a certain subordinate as "negative" tells much about himself or herself. A review of the manager's appraisals through the years might pick up the fact that the manager was not dealing effectively with that subordinate.

In a few organizations employees evaluate their appraisers on their skills at evaluating performance. Several low ratings would surely alert the appraiser's boss that something was wrong. But to be truly effective, in most organizations subordinates would have to evaluate their boss in a confidential manner if any significantly honest data were to be developed. Employees would probably worry about reprisal if their boss were to see negative evaluations.

TIMING OF APPRAISALS

Evaluation should take place at least once a year. New employees need to be appraised more often, such as every six months for the first year. Appraisals should be scheduled so that employees know when they will occur. When they are not scheduled, there is a temptation for the appraiser to postpone them under the pressure of everyday responsibilities. Or the manager might act on impulse instead of preparing carefully. For example, a manager may become annoyed with an employee and decide that now is as good a time as ever to do some appraising. Appraising should not take the place of on-the-spot criticism or counseling. It is also not grudge time.

Both employee and appraiser should have ample time to get their thoughts and records together for a constructive appraisal session.

CHARACTERISTICS OF EFFECTIVE APPRAISALS

A good appraisal program should be based on the following guidelines.

It Should Confine Itself as Much as Possible to Work-Related Criteria

What are the functions, actions, and behaviors exhibited during work? What are the indicators or measurements of a job done well—or not so well? Typical examples of job-related criteria are the amount of work done, whether deadlines are met, and the quality and accuracy of the work performed. The appraisal should minimize reliance on traits and personal characteristics. Measuring "enthusiasm," "initiative," and "commitment" is precarious. As has already been suggested, traits are hard to see and to judge.

Appraisal Forms Should Be Simple

Managers and employees should be able to understand how the evaluation is to take place, and what the factors in appraisal are. If appraisal forms and procedures are too complicated, managers may give short shrift to them. The more complicated they are, the greater are the chances of error and misjudgment. Lack of clarity leads to confusion, and confusion breeds mistrust. Everything about appraisals should be open, aboveboard, and easy to understand. They should inspire trust, not suspicion. Both good and bad performance should be readily apparent from looking at the appraisal forms. They shouldn't have to be deciphered.

The Program Must Be Applied Uniformly

Organizations that use multiple appraisal systems, or different systems for different divisions or categories of employees, should be careful that all employees in a given group are evaluated by the same system. When employees doing the same kind of work are evaluated according to different tests, forms, and procedures, the variances in individual employees' evaluations may depend more on the system used than on work performance. Moreover, it would be unfair, and perhaps discriminatory, to compare two employees' performance when those employees have not been appraised using the same criteria. Informal appraisals, without written instruments or guidelines, are dangerous. To leave the criteria and timing up to the appraiser is to invite legal problems and seriously undermine the reliability of the appraisal.

The Appraisal Should Work

Simply put, the appraisal should give you the information you need to manage. How realistic are the goals you set, and the work assignments you give out? How well is each employee performing? Who needs what help or training? Who is heading into a major performance problem? How effective is your work group as a whole? Who is showing progress from one appraisal period to another?

In general, the evaluation procedure should meet the objectives mapped out for it when it was put into operation.

Questions that cannot be validated by actual performance results or activities should be avoided. At least they should be recognized as risky. A good example is the requirement that the appraiser estimate how far in the organization he or she believes a particular employee can rise. It seems laudable to identify the potential of employees, but asking appraisers to do so on a personal estimate that is on a highly unscientific basis does not hold the promise of obtaining useful information.

THE APPRAISERS

In most organizations the person who does the appraising is the employee's immediate supervisor. Again, in many organizations, the supervisor or manager fills out the appraisal form, then schedules a meeting with the employee so that the two of them can review and discuss the appraisal.

There are optional appraisal methods. For example, the manager and employee each review a blank appraisal form independently, then meet to arrive at an agreement. They then fill out the form together. Any lingering disagreements are noted.

In another variation the manager fills out a form in advance, and the employee does the same. Then they meet to try to arrive at one form that incorporates the assessment of both. Or they each submit a form simultaneously to be reviewed by a higher manager.

Whether you regard the appraisal process as being based on negotiation with employees has much to do with how you perceive your role as manager and your style. But there is no question of the desirability of letting the employee have a voice in the appraisal. On points of performance where there is pronounced disagreement between the employee and you, you should consider inviting the employee to submit evidence that you have misjudged.

No discussion of appraisal methods would be complete without a reference to peer evaluation. Using co-workers to appraise the performance of one another is practiced in few organizations. But it makes a great deal of sense. Co-workers often know the true value of an employee's contribution better than the manager. Their evaluations can make a useful supplement to the manager's, and they can serve to offset the bias that the manager may feel for or against the employee. Of course, it must be acknowledged that the co-workers themselves may be biased against or in favor of a particular employee. Still, the greater the number of people who are evaluating, the greater the chances that a total, more objective appraisal will result.

MEASUREMENTS FOR APPRAISING

One common form of appraisal involves identifying various functions of the job and standards of performance that are to be met. For example, a salesperson might be measured on the number of new business calls per week, or on the number of home-office prospect leads supplied that are followed up within one week, say, after receipt. A secretary might be evaluated on accuracy, quantity of daily output, and efficiency of filing. The salesperson's manager would be rated on recruiting, completing reports on time, time spent with salespeople in the field, training, and the like. A supervisor would be evaluated on scheduling work, number of rejects or inaccuracies, and productivity.

It's useful to tie in the functions or activities with goals. That is, each appraisal period, manager and subordinate sit down and define goals that are to be achieved during the next period. (The process is described in Chapter 5.) Generally the goals are of four types.

1. *Routine.* These goals are extensions of the activities currently performed. "By the end of six months, the unit will have increased production from the present 2000 to 2250. Subgoal: The increase will be in steps of 300 for each of the first five months, and 450 the remaining month." Or, "For the next six months, sales calls on new business will be increased on an average of three per week."

2. *Problem solving.* Perhaps absenteeism is high. The goal is expressed this way: "Through employee orientation and stricter supervisory monitoring, absenteeism will be reduced by 20 percent by the end of six months." Or, "Insurance claims payment will be expedited, cutting an average of two days from the time period required presently to process payment."

3. *Innovation.* "To have three persons trained to use the computer terminals that will be installed by September 1." Or, "To redesign the work flow and division of responsibility to achieve the same efficiency with two fewer employees by November 15th."

4. *Personal development.* This category may be more difficult to quantify, but it is no less important than the other kinds of goals. What is the employee doing to develop professional or work skills, to increase his or her value to the operation? This goal can be measured by the completion of a training program, a course, the earning of a certificate of proficiency. Or it might be measured by the acquisition of additional or higher level skills that the employee can demonstrate at the end of the appraisal period. It's possible that the employee can demonstrate greater knowledge of the work or of the field by submitting to an examination, perhaps by peers.

One of the chief advantages of using goals to evaluate performance is that you can look at the results and say, "You've completed 85 percent of the goal," or "You've exceeded the goal by 20 percent." Using these data, you can then determine how realistic or attainable the goals are, what will be required to reach them if they have not been attained, and what new objectives should be set for the upcoming period.

If you appraise by behaviors or functions, you can evaluate the quality and quantity by using a scale such as the following:

Outstanding		Very good		Adequate				Poor	
10	9	8	7	6	5	4	3	2	1

The combination of grades of performance and numbers can make the evaluation more specific. However, the rating should be explained. Below each scale, there should be a few lines for the manager to explain the basis for the rating. For example, the manager gives a subordinate, a production supervisor, an "outstanding." The explanation: "The newly installed equipment had a breakdown ratio of nearly 40 percent. This was in large part because maintenance had to be called, the malfunction diagnosed, and then repaired. Time elapsed was approximately two days. He trained the operators to recognize causes of malfunctioning so they could diagnose the problem, and in some cases perform immediate repairs. Average downtime has been cut to three hours."

Of course, no scale will eliminate the possibility of arbitrariness. Does one give a 5 or a 6, a 7 or 8? At least the explanation amplifies the reasons that went into the judgment. Some appraisal systems try to reduce arbitrariness by becoming less specific. For example, performance is rated as "satisfactory" or "unsatisfactory." But satisfactory performance can range from minimally acceptable to exceptional. Everyone doing at least acceptable work gets thrown together. There is no room for plaudits. There is no provision for suggesting ways to improve for people who have indeed much room for it.

Other methods involve rating employees "on the curve" by comparing performance, behaviorally anchored rating scales that attempt to describe effective and ineffective performance, and various weight checklists.

Whatever the scale used, the preferred appraisal should have the following characteristics:

1.   *It should concern itself with behaviors and job functions.*   Attitudes and personality traits are treacherous, and they probably won't provide sufficient documentation for legal purposes.

2.   *The form should require an explanation for the rating given.*

3.   *The appraisal should show clearly any performance deficiency and what actions will be taken to correct it.*

NEW EMPLOYEES

Even though you appraise new employees six months, or even three months, after employment, you can't afford to wait for this period of time to pass before giving needed feedback. You don't want the employee to flounder through the first appraisal period, then suffer a negative appraisal. Therefore, with employees new to the job and your department, take the following steps:

1. *Set performance goals and standards from the outset.* You want to make sure that the employee has a clear perception of all of his or her duties and the priorities among them.

2. *Criticize when necessary.* When the employee makes a mistake or suffers a failure in performance, give the employee immediate feedback. Ask the new employee to diagnose the failure. Did the person misunderstand the responsibilities? Was it a simple error?

3. *Document the conversation.* It might be useful to provide a written summary, for the employee as well as for the file, of the feedback and the corrective action recommended. Such a memo clarifies and reinforces your verbal message and serves as documentation in case you later have to terminate the employee.

4. *Repeat the procedure if the mistake or failure is repeated.* Be thorough in investigating what is happening or not happening. Is it one or all facets of the job that are going wrong?

If you follow the above steps conscientiously for new employees, you will have no surprises for them at appraisal time. Your remedial action will have saved you also much valuable time.

PREPARING FOR THE INTERVIEW

Your frame of mind as you plan for the appraisal interview should be as positive as possible. You should see the process as an important means to help the employee to become more effective on the job, something that both of you want. Before the interview takes place, follow these steps:

1. *Assemble your records.* You'll probably want the appropriate job analysis or description with which you can compare what the employee actually did. You'll want to have the previous evaluation handy so that you can compare the actual performance

against the objectives that were set then. Collect the documenta-tion of any criticism or warnings that you wrote during the period to be appraised.

2. *Give the employee notice.* There is no recommended time period, but you should allow time for the employee to gather whatever records or documentation he or she has.

3. *Choose the time and place.* Since you want uninterrupted time, schedule the session in concert with the employee. Neither of you wants to be rushed or distracted. Depending on the person to be appraised, you may take one hour or three.

CONDUCTING THE INTERVIEW

The following suggestions might be useful in helping you to con-duct the appraisal interview.

Invite the Employee To Become Involved in the Process

The worst thing you can do is simply sit there, deliver your eval-uation to a silent employee, then terminate the interview. You want the employee to learn. You want to be sure that he or she learns. The appraisal time could also be a learning opportunity for you. The employee may give you feedback that you could find beneficial.

From the outset, make it clear that you want a dialogue, that you don't want to give a speech, that you regard the appraisal process to be one of the most important events of the year, if not the most important. To that end, you have blocked out a lot of time so that everything that needs to be said will be said.

Get the Employee's Perception of the Quality and Quantity of Work During the Appraisal Period

This is also a step that involves the employee. In addition, having the employee give his or her own evaluation helps you to compare your perception of what was done—or not done—with the em-ployee's.

Offer Your Evaluation

Reinforce those perceptions of the employee with which you agree, and explain why you differ on any aspect of the evaluation. The more documentation you have on the points where you disagree, the better off you will be. Your written evaluation, incidentally, should conform rather closely to the feedback you have given the employee during the appraisal period. If it varies considerably, then you must in all honesty ask yourself why you haven't been more complete in your oral feedback or why you are presenting the information now. Ideally, there should be no major surprises for the employee at the time of the written evaluation. To withhold important performance information during the period and then to offer it in a written appraisal puts the employee at a severe disadvantage and could impair the working relationship between you. It will certainly undermine the trust that the employee has felt for you.

Your evaluation of the employee will gain more immediate acceptance if, in addition to being predictable, it stresses the positive. Talk about constructive ways the employee can achieve better results from the work. Don't dwell too much on the past. Say, "I know you want to be more effective than you have been, so let's look to the future and different ways of doing things."

Deal with the here and now. Past appraisals are usually of little relevance (see page 278). If the problems they refer to still exist, those problems are part of the current evaluation. Reciting a long list of past mistakes or deficiencies will demoralize the employee and cause him or her to think, "What's the use?"

☐ *Develop an Action Plan Jointly.* Choose goals that are realistic and specific. Don't focus on every area that may benefit from improvement. Select those that are most important. Solicit the employee's views. Whatever you develop, be sure that both of you agree on goals selected and their respective priorities.

☐ *Allow Employees to Make Written Contributions.* They may want to expand on what you have said. They may want to dissent. They may want to appeal to the higher reviewer.

☐   *Have Them Sign the Review.* That shows that they have read it.

☐   *Summarize and Close.* Thank the employee for his or her participation. Summarize the main points. Schedule follow-up dates, if necessary. Ask the employee if there are any unfinished matters, or if he or she has any further comments. If not, conclude the interview.

☐   *Write a Summary for the Employee.* You may wish to give the employee a copy of the written appraisal, if such is the custom. Otherwise, write a summary of the points discussed and the action plan agreed on, one for the employee and one for your file.

REFERRING TO OLD APPRAISALS

When an employee has demonstrated the same performance problems over a period of time, say, two or more appraisal periods, you are quite within your rights to refer to past appraisals to document continuity of performance. After all, if you did not call attention to an uncorrected problem or deficiency, you could undermine your credibility and seriousness.

But there are at least three occasions when you should be careful about referring back to old data: when you get new responsibility, when you have a new employee, and when you get angry.

New Responsibility

When you move into a position, and you don't know the employees, you should be wary of previous appraisals. You might have to discuss the most recent one with employees, especially if you have not been in the new job long enough to shape your own evaluations. But tread lightly. Don't accept another manager's evaluations automatically. Discuss the most recent evaluations, but put them in as nonthreatening light as possible by asking the employees to comment on them. You wouldn't want to say such things as, "Well, apparently, you're difficult to get along with," or, "You're very slipshod when it comes to finishing your work."

Those were perceptions of your predecessor, who is no longer around (and even if he or she were, you wouldn't want to rely too heavily on that person's perceptions). Instead, you might say, "I notice that you've had some difficulties in keeping the quality of your work at a high level. Would you like to tell me about it?"

New Employee

When a new employee transfers into your department at appraisal time, you may want to suggest that the interview be conducted in two sections, if possible. The evaluation for the previous period should be done by the new employee's old boss. The second section, in which you establish objectives for the forthcoming period, should be conducted by you. Again, as for the new responsibility described in the above section, you should be careful about assuming that another's perceptions are to be adopted. If you must discuss the prior evaluations, do so in a relaxed, friendly way, affording the employee much opportunity to tell you about them.

Your Anger

It is possible that the employee has disappointed you or demonstrated a massive failure. You are upset. The temptation is to go back to prior evaluations and really "load it on." No matter how discouraged you may be, resist the temptation. Don't dig through prior appraisals to develop a laundry list. Deal only with those performance characteristics or deficiencies that have manifested themselves in the most recent period. If they are continuations from prior periods, it may be acceptable to refer back to show that they still exist—and are still uncorrected. Otherwise use discretion.

OBSTACLES TO A GOOD APPRAISAL INTERVIEW

Ideally the appraisal interview should come at regular, scheduled intervals. But there may be situations that militate against having the interview when it is normally conducted and suggest you postpone it for a time. Here are some examples.

Heavy Work Pressure

The employee is working unusually hard to complete a task or assignment. If you perceive that she might feel anxiety and stress simply by having to take two hours or so out of the day to sit through an appraisal interview, then you might advise her that you will reschedule it when the pressure is lighter or has returned to normal. You do not want her to sit in your office worried about what is going on—or not going on—back at her work station. She will be distracted, and the appraisal interview will not have impact.

Personal Problems

The employee has recently lost a member of the family. Perhaps a family member is seriously ill. If you sense that he is heavily burdened and temporarily distracted by personal concerns, you may want to hold off the appraisal; you may feel that the employee has all he can do just to keep up with the work flow. There can be no hard-and-fast rule on this matter. You have to make individual judgments depending on such considerations as length and severity of the problem, the employee's tolerance and ability to cope, the current level of performance (if it continues at a normally high level, then you might feel free to go ahead), and so on.

Health

If an employee's poor health has affected her ability to work well, you will probably want to defer the interview until she is functioning fairly close to normal. A physical or mental debilitation is probably quite enough for her to handle without the anxieties created by an appraisal interview when her recent work record has not been great.

Change of Responsibilities

Say the employee has recently been promoted to a supervisory position, and you have to appraise him for the time during which he worked at the former responsibility. You may want to defer the interview for a short time; if you must conduct it at the regular time, be careful not to appraise performance characteristics that have not yet had time to mature and show themselves. Stick to the old, prepromotion levels of work. Preferably, you will let the employee settle in for a time, then hold an appraisal. You may decide to hold a second appraisal, the first having concerned itself with the old responsibilities, the new appraisal with the more recent position.

APPRAISING AND REWARDING

The question is perennial: Should the manager discuss rewards during the appraisal interview? To elaborate, should the manager say something to the employee such as, "To sum up, your performance has been so impressive that I have put in for a 10 percent merit increase for you?" Or, "I'm sorry that because you did not achieve your goals, I can't offer you more money at this time."

On the positive side, those who advocate tying rewards directly to performance suggest that the appraisal time is a natural opportunity to show employees that good performance, as described and recorded on the appraisal form, will get rewarded, but poor performance will not. The argument has much logical appeal.

Those who answer that the conversation about performance and the discussion of rewards, even though related, should be conducted separately argue that the question of the amount of reward can distract the employee from hearing what she needs to hear about the details of performance. If she is sitting through the appraisal interview wondering whether the good performance that the manager is describing will lead to this or that amount, she is not concentrating on the appraisal process and feedback.

You might consider separating the two discussions, since the distraction argument makes a lot of sense. But you can say at the end of the interview, "As you can understand, your appraisal will play a role in my decision as to your merit increase. We'll get together in a couple of weeks, after I've made my recommendation and gotten it approved, so that I can tell you what you'll be earning next period."

You might also want to announce at the beginning of the interview that you will not be discussing merit increases during the session. That will probably increase the chances that the employee will hear you better.

Separating the two gives you two opportunities to recognize the good performance instead of one.

PREDICTABLE APPRAISALS

Ideally, what goes on in an appraisal interview should be predictable. If the evaluation involves goals that have been set, when standards are clear, when criteria are performance-related, there should be little mystery about what is to take place. After all, if performance has been deficient, the employee should have received appropriate feedback. Thus, except for a relatively new employee, the session should not produce major surprises.

Except in the case of failing performance, the appraisal process should not produce significant stress. In fact, employees who are performing well might even look forward to evaluation as confirmation of their own opinions about the work they've done. The chance to talk about the future, to set interesting new goals, is appealing—or should be. Appraisal thus plays a vital role in guiding employees toward greater effectiveness in the achievement of their and the organization's goals. Appraisal makes an important contribution to the management of motivation. (Use the checklist at the end of this chapter to help you measure your appraisal system's effectiveness.)

However, the good feelings in both appraiser and appraised should not encourage them to overlook or "forgive" expectations or objectives that have not been met. Underachievement of agreed-on goals could be an indicator of trouble, either in the employee or in the goals themselves.

Performance appraisals constitute just one phase of an effective feedback program. Other components are coaching, counseling, and on-the-spot, informal reinforcement or criticism. Each component has its own purpose, even when they are combined as, for example, when the manager decides at the time of appraisal to counsel an employee who has a serious performance problem. Most managers, most of the time, perform some of these functions. Some managers, some of the time, perform all of them. All managers should perform all four feedback functions in a conscientious, consistent, and systematic manner.

If you don't regularly appraise, coach, counsel, criticize, and reinforce, you run the danger of not meeting your own or your subordinates' needs. Without feedback, both you and your subordinates operate, to some extent, blindly and by chance.

REVIEW OF APPRAISING PERFORMANCE

		Yes	No	Not Sure
1.	The best appraisals measure personality traits as well as performance.	____	____	____
2.	Some managers are uncomfortable with appraisals because they feel as if they are sitting in judgment on employees.	____	____	____
3.	The bias of managers is a major reason why appraisals produce disappointing results.	____	____	____
4.	Managers should understand that appraisals can be an important part of the motivation system.	____	____	____
5.	The performance evaluation process should take place at least once a year.	____	____	____
6.	A good appraisal program should confine itself to work-related criteria.	____	____	____
7.	Simplicity of the system usually contributes substantially to its success.	____	____	____
8.	Many organizations feel it is a sound step to tie the evaluations to some form of managing by objectives.	____	____	____
9.	Peer evaluations can be useful in offsetting any bias on the part of the manager.	____	____	____
10.	Appraisals should concern themselves with behaviors rather than attitudes.	____	____	____

		Yes	No	Not Sure
11.	It is customary in many organizations to appraise new employees on a more frequent basis than employees who have been there longer.	____	____	____
12.	You should not give the employee notice of the appraisal interview because you will only stimulate tension and anxiety.	____	____	____
13.	During the appraisal interview you will want to limit the employee's comments so as not to turn the session into an argument.	____	____	____
14.	The best appraisal sessions are those that hold no surprises for the employee.	____	____	____
15.	To prevent any argument on the part of the employee, you may want to have on hand older appraisals in case you have to refer to them.	____	____	____
16.	It's a good idea to relate the session to reward. That way you are linking performance with rewards.	____	____	____
17.	You can't go wrong in making appraisals if you apply an average rating to everyone.	____	____	____
18.	Intelligence and maturity are valuable indicators on the appraisal form.	____	____	____
19.	If higher management doesn't seem to take the system seriously, managers will probably not either.	____	____	____
20.	It's better to evaluate too strictly than too leniently.	____	____	____

Answers to Review

1. No. Traits are very difficult to measure.
2. Yes
3. Yes
4. Yes
5. Yes
6. Yes
7. Yes
8. Yes
9. Yes
10. Yes
11. Yes
12. No. You should give the employee notice so that he has time to think about his performance, failures, successes, and objectives for the next period of time.
13. No. The employee is a partner in the session, and as such deserves the chance to make any contribution she can. If the appraisal is based on objectives, there should be little or no argument.
14. Yes
15. Not sure. Unless there is a continuing performance deficiency, you might be well-advised not to seem to overwhelm the employee with historical data.
16. No. If the employee is sitting there concerned with the reward, he or she probably isn't giving full attention to the appraisal.
17. No. You can go wrong. Your better performers will be cheated by an average rating, and the poorer workers will not have their deficiencies brought to light.
18. No. It is probably impossible for a manager to measure them objectively.
19. Yes
20. No. Appraisals should be as accurate as possible. They should not involve guesswork or arbitrariness.

A CHECKLIST TO HELP YOU MEASURE THE EFFECTIVENESS OF YOUR PERFORMANCE APPRAISAL SYSTEM

		Yes	No
1.	Appraisers should be trained in the evaluation process.	___	___
2.	Appraisers set aside as much time as is necessary to complete the evaluation.	___	___
3.	Higher management takes the appraisal process seriously and insists on data that are as accurate as possible.	___	___
4.	The evaluation system is presented positively as a means to help employees to be more effective.	___	___
5.	Good evaluations lead to rewards.	___	___
6.	The evaluation process should take place at least once a year.	___	___
7.	Appraisals should confine themselves to work-related criteria.	___	___
8.	Appraisal forms should be simple and easy to use.	___	___
9.	Appraisal programs should be applied uniformly to all employees in a given group.	___	___
10.	The appraisal program should give management the data it is looking for.	___	___
11.	Questions on appraisals should be validated by actual performance results or activities.	___	___
12.	Questions should concern themselves with behaviors and job functions.	___	___
13.	The appraisal form should require an explanation for the evaluation given.	___	___

	Yes	No
14. The employee to be appraised should be given ample notice of the interview so as to be able to collect data and records.	____	____
15. The appraiser should hold the interview without interruptions.	____	____
16. The employee's perception of the quality and quantity of the work done should be part of the interview.	____	____
17. Appraiser and employee should develop an action plan jointly for the next period.	____	____
18. Employees should be invited to make written comments on the form.	____	____
19. The employee should sign the form.	____	____
20. The appraisal should be reviewed by a third party.	____	____
21. Discussions of rewards for good performance should take place separately.	____	____
22. All expectations or objectives that have not been met should be accounted for and explained.	____	____

The more answered "yes," the more effective your appraisal program is likely to be in the management of employees' motivation.

12

COACHING

Coaching can be short-term or long-term. Short-term coaching is problem-centered. An employee has a problem or has run into a difficulty in performing well. It could be that the employee has undertaken or been assigned a task that he or she does not know well enough to complete independently. Through coaching you help the subordinate to find a solution to the problem or a new and better way to perform the task. This kind of coaching may be initiated by the employee who recognizes a need for help or by you when you spot a need to intervene. Short-term coaching is not the same as counseling, which is the culmination of one or more other steps to correct a performance deficiency. In fact, coaching may be one of those preliminary steps.

Long-term coaching, which will be dealt with later in the chapter, is extended to help the employee to grow and develop. It does not assume that there is a present performance problem, but that employees want to do better or do more. They want a sense of advancing on the job and in their career.

Both kinds of coaching have as their purpose helping employees to be more effective, but one concerns itself with now and the other with the months and years to come.

Salespeople especially are accustomed to the *now* kind of coaching. In sales it is called "curbstone coaching." After the manager and salesperson have called on a prospect or a customer, they sit in the car or over a cup of coffee to analyze the interview. If the call was successful, they examine the relative strength of the tactics that the salesperson used during the presentation. If no order resulted, they will try to isolate the reason why the interview didn't work.

A SUPERVISORY PROBLEM

Frank, a supervisor, asks his boss, Tony, for some time to talk about some difficulties Frank has been having with one of his subordinates, Ken. Ken has been in the department for about 12 years, while Frank is relatively new as a supervisor.

Frank: Ken is a real problem to me. He's turning out less and less work. Many times what he does has to be returned for redoing. Some of the others are beginning to complain.

Tony: What do you mean when you say "many times"?

Frank: I've been keeping track. About one out of four jobs goes back.

Tony: You've spoken to him about it?

Frank: Yes. He seemed quite surprised to hear that his work was below par. He said he thought he had been doing okay.

Tony: Let's see the records you've been keeping. What did he say when you showed him these?

Frank: He said he's been doing the cost reports the same way he did them when Paul was his supervisor, and that Paul never complained, and he doesn't know why I make things so tough on him.

Tony: Is it true that he's doing everything the way he always did?

Observation

There are two mistakes Tony has made with this question. First, it asks for a yes or no answer. That kind of question seldom conveys much usable information, especially if the purpose is to encourage the other person to volunteer information. In coaching you need information from the person having the problem in order to make conclusions that can guide you toward a solution. The second problem is that the question calls for a judgment that may masquerade as objective. Frank cannot know for sure whether Ken has indeed been doing things as he always has. A better alternative is:

Tony: What's your feeling about his answer?

Frank: Well, I realize that he and Paul worked together for a long time, and they had a good friendship. I came along and took over from Paul. I suspect that Ken resents that. In fact, I'd go so far as to say I think Ken thought he'd get Paul's job.

Observation

In asking the question in the way he did, Tony learns more of what worries Frank, and what may well be impeding his ability to deal with the problem Ken has created.

Tony: Well, could be. What do you recommend be done about the performance?

Observation

Many problem-solving discussions spend too much time analyzing the reasons for the problem. Most people occasionally like to play detective or psychiatrist. However, Tony, while not discounting the possibility that Frank's analysis offers some explanation for Ken's behavior, quite properly directs his supervisor's attention to thinking about solutions.

Frank: I could tell Ken that he's not working for Paul anymore, and that he has to learn to do the work according to my standards.

Tony: That is an option. What will you do if he just goes along as he has been?

Frank: Fire him.

Tony: Well, that is another resort, a last resort. Let's look at some other options.

Observation

Tony is wisely avoiding an either-or approach to a solution. Most people, especially in a severe problem situation, do not take time to consider how many options they really have. He encourages Frank to look at alternative solutions.

Tony: If you could get Ken to meet your standards, how would you feel about his staying on?

Frank: I'd be happy to have him stay. I'm not out to get rid of him.

Observation

Tony's question is very important in light of what Frank considered to be the source of Ken's resentment. It may have been that Frank has been a bit hesitant to deal with the older man and that he would have been more comfortable if Ken were to leave. But now Frank has committed himself to Ken's staying on, provided he meets standards.

Tony: Then what do you think the next step is?

Frank: I suppose I ought to sit down with Ken and tell him what I expect from him from now on. That's probably something I should have done a long time ago. But Ken's been here so long. I guess I always took it for granted he knew what to do.

Tony: Maybe he did know what to do—as far as Paul was concerned. Now he needs to know what you expect. Okay, I suggest that you and I meet again after Ken and you agree that he can and will do what you expect.

Later, after Frank and Ken have talked, Frank reports back to his boss.

Tony: I'm glad to hear it. Do you anticipate any obstacles? Do you believe Ken is going to have any problems meeting those objectives?

Frank: I think that in certain areas Ken needs some refresher training. Some of the others in the section have developed better work methods.

Tony: What would happen if one of your better people tutored Ken?

Frank: Well, he has more overall knowledge than most. He would probably resent being tutored.

Tony: You mean, in some ways the others could learn from Ken. Now, what does that suggest?

Frank: We ought to set it up so there's an exchange. Hey, we could schedule a few seminar-type meetings for the whole department, a sort of refresher for everyone. Ken has an awful lot of stuff stored in his head. Maybe he might open up. And then he'd listen to the others. I hope.

Tony: Everyone might come out ahead. And that approach would lessen the threat to Ken.

If Frank reflects on his session with his boss, he'll realize that not only has Tony helped him to work out an immediate problem, but he has also implicitly given Frank some pointers in working out problems in general.

A COACHING SEQUENCE

In problem-centered coaching you may find it helpful to follow these steps.

1. *Agree on the problem.* Even if the employee brings the problem to you as opposed to your intervening, you need to agree on the nature of the problem. You may have your own definition of it and how it may have developed. Although you may assume that the employee agrees with you, that may not be true.

A good way to approach the definition of a problem is to describe how it manifests itself. Use observed behavior: "She is at least 20 minutes late two or three times a week." Performance records provide objective data: "That unit has increased its output 18 percent in three months and there has been no change of personnel." There are other kinds of documentation: "XYZ Company has 35 percent of the market, and we can't get above 20 percent." Or, "Our training budget has been cut, and I still need to run three people through the program; I have enough funding for not even two." Or, "I can't get the task force organized, because Jed Lewis in Accounting is balking at letting us have one of his people, and we really have to have a financial person on the team."

Don't rush to a solution. Nor is it necessarily a good idea to insist, as some managers do, that employees come to you with a solution as well as a problem. For one thing, you may discourage them from letting you know that some problems exist (for which they can't come up with a solution). For another, they may define the problem in a way that facilitates a solution that is not always appropriate. In other words, they may alter the definition of the problem to fit a solution.

2. *Define the various options.* The problem that you have agreed on obviously needs to be corrected. But what kind of situation would you prefer to see in its stead? Asking the question in this way may open up new possibilities that otherwise would not have

been considered. After all, the result of correcting a problem may simply be to return a situation to its previous condition. Thinking of alternatives is one way to be innovative in dealing with the problem.

3. *Set goals and subgoals that will help you to know when you are making progress.* You need some standards and measurements. Progress can be measured in a behavior change (better telephone technique that results in fewer complaints from callers), more units of output (15 percent more per day), new competence (the ability to sell a new product or program for the first time). Remember that since goals are set in a time frame, establish schedules as well.

4. *Have a Plan B.* Just in case the option you selected does not work out and may have to be modified or scrapped, retain one or more of the other original options that you considered.

5. *Determine your role.* Should you provide authority, training, or reassignment? If the problem is one in which your subordinate is experiencing difficulties in managing another, get your subordinate's agreement as to what part you should play.

As the manager, you may have to step in if your subordinate's efforts to solve the problem prove faulty. The situation may be too risky for you to sit back and wait for the subordinate to correct the situation.

In your consideration of your role, you want to provide as much of a learning experience for the subordinate as possible. The subordinate should also be able to feel a sense of having prevailed and of achievement. If you get involved in too many aspects of the situation, you may be depriving your subordinate of both learning and achievement.

6. *Set up a program of review.* Once you've determined a plan of action, you have to review it from time to time to make sure it is working. It's best to establish a schedule of review at the time of the coaching session so that no one forgets what should be done, and the subordinate doesn't think you're meddling or getting nervous.

7. *Give feedback.* If the plan isn't followed because, in your view, the subordinate isn't carrying out the decision to which both of you agreed, then you should let him know about it before he makes a major mistake or experiences frustration. It's just as im-

portant to let him know that he is doing well. Otherwise there may be no learning and no satisfaction of achievement.

Short-term coaching isn't always limited to problems. A subordinate manager may come to you with a plan, such as introducing job rotation into the department or asking you to help him or her to judge the candidates for a promotion. In such a case, your coaching can help the subordinate to take full advantage of the opportunities before him or her. Certainly many of the above described steps can be altered to fit planning or decision-making coaching. Your role, as in problem-centered interviews, is to help your subordinates to define both the situation and the options, to evaluate the options, and in some cases to set goals.

THE NEED TO COACH FOR GROWTH

As a manager, you have a responsibility to your subordinates to help them to increase their effectiveness over time, and to help them advance in their knowledge, skills, and experience. Managing their growth and development is important to you: You develop resources that are important to you now or in the future. They are there, waiting to be developed.

Growth is, as has been pointed out, an important factor in motivation. It is essential to most employees that they have a sense that they are developing on the job.

It makes good sense that employees look to you for guidance in their development. You know them. You have worked with them. You have seen what they can do, and you've drawn conclusions about what they might be able to do.

You know the organization and perhaps the industry or field. You can identify the trends: What will be happening to create opportunity? What will be required for people to be effective? In the organization you can speculate on what strategies are being considered and will be adopted. You know far better than your subordinates where the career paths are. You have perspectives that your employees don't have as a result of your experience, position, and knowledge of the organization.

Finally, your employees trust you. You have spent a long time building a working relationship of trust and respect between you and the people who work for you. What you say can be relied on. The advice you give can be accepted.

It is the long-term coaching, for growth, that managers have to remind themselves to do. You are probably no exception. There is no fire demanding immediate attention. For example how would you answer the following questions?

		Yes	No
1.	During every substantial contact I have had with my subordinates, I tried to provide them with some sort of stretching experience and learning opportunity.	____	____
2.	I have in mind one or two experiences or assignments for each subordinate that could contribute to his or her growth and development.	____	____
3.	I have provided one or two of such developmental experiences for each subordinate during the past six months.	____	____
4.	I have a regular schedule for discussing with subordinates skills and talents that can be developed for the future.	____	____
5.	I try conscientiously to stick with that schedule.	____	____
6.	I have some mutually agreed upon plan of action for the growth and development of each of my subordinates, either on the present job or for some future responsibilities.	____	____

Few managers would affirmatively answer all the questions and pass the test. Probably it is because *growth* and *development* carry a long-term meaning. They point to the future. Meanwhile here is today with all of its problems and pressures.

Yet, tomorrow will bring a different set of problems and pressures. Nothing stays the same. Your organization, your industry, business climate, the economy, and politics will change. New demands will be made on your people. To some extent, the needs for certain skills, knowledge, experience, and talent will change. Managers who are content to simply maintain their operations are operating regressively. In today's fast-changing world there is no such thing as standing still.

It used to be said that training is a function of management. So severe are today's needs to keep pace with changing environments, and so serious is the problem of obsolescence of skills, that it might well be claimed that management is a function of training. If you accept that the manager's highest priority is to keep an effectively functioning work force, then you can accept the reversal of terms. Managing indeed these days is a function of training, and of continually upgrading the effectiveness of your people.

COACHING INFORMALLY

You have to be alert to the timeliness of assigning stretching experiences. You might be overlooking such opportunities each day. For example, Phyllis is supervisor of customer service, which involves much telephone contact with customers. One of her newer employees, Mark, has shown exceptional aptitude for dealing with customers. One day Phyllis calls Mark into her office to tell him how pleased she is with the work he has done since the end of his training period.

Phyllis: You really have taken to this kind of work. I just wanted you to know how pleased I am.

Mark: Thank you. I really like talking with customers on the phone. And I'm doing a lot of it. But you know, Phyllis, it occurred to me that it would be more satisfying to talk with the same customers.

Phyllis: You mean, instead of an available processor taking whatever call is coming in?

Mark: Yes, and what I'm saying is that the job, at least I think, would be more interesting if each of us had our bloc of customers. That way we could get to know them better.

Phyllis: That's very interesting. What kinds of advantages do you think that kind of system would have over what we're doing now?

Mark: Well, for one thing it would make the job a little more personal. Right now we pick up the phone and take any call from anyone in the country. It would be a lot more fun to be able to say, "Hi, Mr. Johnson. Good to talk to you again." Then I punch his account up on the computer and say, "Did you get your shipment last week okay?" That sort of thing.

Phyllis: I see what you mean. It sounds very interesting. Let me ask you this: Suppose Mr. Johnson called while you were tied up. How would he feel about waiting?

Mark: I thought about that. One thing the operator could say is, "Mark's on the phone. May I have him call you right back as soon as he's off?"

Phyllis: That might work. On the other hand, Mr. Johnson might say, "I can't wait. I want to get this order in the works. I have to get out of here for an appointment."

Mark: Hm. Well, here's another approach we might try. If Mr. Johnson doesn't want to wait, we let him talk to another processor, whoever's available. Then later I call him back on the WATS line and say, "Sorry I wasn't available, Mr. Johnson. I just called to make sure everything was handled the way you want it. By the way, I noticed that you've been ordering in biweekly lots the last couple of times. You know, there's a way you could take advantage of a five percent discount if you placed two orders at once. The volume would qualify."

Phyllis: This is all fascinating. I think we need to know more about it, to see how it might work, before we can make a decision. Would you, in your spare time, be willing to sketch it out on paper, how you think we could get it to work? And while you're at it, make two lists—one to spell out the advantages over the present system, the other to cover possible disadvantages.

Mark consents, probably enthusiastically. For Phyllis, the manager, this is a potentially rewarding session. What started out as a routine session on positive reinforcement became a possible stretching experience for Mark. But Phyllis has uncovered and reinforced a talent in Mark. Mark not only likes what he is doing, but he thinks it can be done in a way that is more interesting for both processors and customers. It could also be more profitable for the company if customers feel more loyalty because of the personal contact. Mark is thinking not only as a processor but as a salesman, and even possibly a manager.

Phyllis has already made the step to the next coaching session: Mark has agreed to draw up a proposal. Undoubtedly Phyllis will have to help him in shaping it. Incidentally, she is also guiding Mark to analyze the pros and cons of such a change. If the pros are strong enough, if the plan seems workable, Phyllis might suggest a test. That would provide another opportunity for her to learn more about Mark's potential. She might ask him to draw up suggestions for training processors in the new system, for working with the data processing people to develop the necessary programming.

The important point illustrated by the exchange between Phyllis and Mark is that coaching is a continuing process. Each opportunity provides you with data with which you can plan future coaching.

GATHERING DATA

Effective coaching involves gathering data that can be analyzed and matched with future needs and opportunities. In the case of Phyllis and Mark, the data came from *observed behavior*. As manager you might note that one of your subordinates was given a rush job to complete. Instead of protesting—as he might have had sufficient justification to do—he organized it in sections, then obtained the cooperation of a co-worker and his secretary, and asked his supervisor for the temporary services of an employee in that supervisor's section. The work was completed without the need to declare a state of emergency. You could reasonably conclude that the employee had organizing ability, probably a good sense of time management (the work was done on time), and probable managerial talent, as well as negotiating skill. That type of information should be noted.

The record of performance is another source of useful data. Analyze how well the employee has been able to work in the past. If you have access to the performance appraisals or personnel records, you can put together a good profile of the person's demonstrated strengths and abilities. For example, you find that 18 months ago an employee stepped into another's operation when the latter employee became ill, and not only kept the department going but actually increased productivity by 20 percent in the three months he was in charge. He achieved the increase through reorganizing the department. What does that accomplishment suggest?

Training and education should be entered in your records. What academic credentials does the person have? What on-the-job training has he or she completed? Has the employee been taking courses at night?

When preparing to coach, you'll find the *reports* of others to be helpful. Of course, the information has to be checked out, preferably with the employee. You hear that during a recent field trip, while making a sales call with a company field representative, an employee managed to salvage a ticklish situation in which the customer lost his temper over alleged service and delivery problems. The salesman was flustered and unable to calm the angry customer. The employee stepped in, took notes, soothed the emotional customer, and straightened the problem out. That kind of behavior is useful in many functions and at many levels.

The *employee* is , of course, one of the best sources of information that can form the base of the coaching interview. You may find it helpful to refer back to Chapter 5 on personal goals to refresh your memory as to the kinds of questions you can ask. Prior to the interview, you may want to review the results of previous questioning.

LOOKING TO THE FUTURE

In preparation for the coaching session, consider the following steps:

1. *Anticipate the departmental work that lies ahead.* Ask yourself how closely your employees' demonstrated abilities match the work they will have to do in the next year or so. For example, will

you be changing the nature of the responsibilities? Will you be taking on a new project? Will new skills and knowledge be required given the nature of the mission of your department?

2.   *Specify the principal work assignments the employee will undertake in the next 6 to 12 months.*   Given the overall mission of the department, what will be the significance for each employee? Will there be substantial changes in duties and responsibilities for a particular employee? How well qualified is the employee to take over these new functions? What opportunities for growth and development lie in the changes? How best can the employee take advantage of them?

3.   *What future events will offer challenges and opportunities for the employee?*   For example, the following may be advantageous or disadvantageous for the employee:

☐ *Organizational Changes.* What departments or divisions are to be phased out or merged? What new managerial or professional positions are being contemplated?

☐ *Staffing Changes.* What internal expansions or cutbacks are being considered?

☐ *Budget Changes.* What monies are being included for the first time or are being increased or reduced? There might be a greater allowance, for instance, for management development or tuition refund.

☐ *New Facilities.* The construction of a plant or a branch or laboratory might offer significant opportunities for advancement.

☐ *New Projects or Plans.* The launching of a new product line elsewhere in the corporation could open doors for particular employees.

You may not always be able to be specific about the developments because of the confidentiality attached to the changes, but you can at least give some advice as to how the employee can best prepare, as to what skills and knowledge would be useful.

4.   *What can you do to prepare the employee to do a better job or take on more or different responsibility?*   As you review the anticipated work

assignments and new developments, list what resources you have to offer an employee. Can you contribute directly? Can you identify sources of help? Can you make organizational changes to put an employee in a better traffic pattern to take over a different responsibility? Can you set up contacts and leads?

There is, of course, the potential for conflict in you when you coach consistently and effectively. You may perform the coaching function so well that you develop the employee right out of your department. Some managers may rationalize their failure to coach by using this explanation: They don't want to encourage good employees to leave.

The fact is that employees who outgrow the responsibilities you set before them will either experience demotivation after a time or leave without being "encouraged." Capable people often find themselves in an overlearning situation after about two or three years at most. By that time they have mastered 80 percent or more of the work. Much of the challenge and opportunity to grow are gone. The quality of their work will eventually decline. If you try to hold on to them or hold them down, you'll be stuck with performance that is less than what you've been used to—or should settle for. Better to help the person to make progress and to risk losing the employee sooner or later than to take the chance that you'll get only mediocre performance from him or her.

A certain amount of turnover has to be expected, therefore. When that turnover largely involves good people who are moving on to bigger and better responsibilities elsewhere in the organization, the phenomenon has to be labeled healthy for the organization. And it's healthy for you, too. You become known in the organization as the producer of highly motivated, highly qualified people to staff the hierarchy. You will be seen as an organizationally minded manager, not just the baron of your little bit of turf. As your "alumni" spread throughout the organization, your reputation will grow.

THE COACHING INTERVIEW

Michael Halbard has been in sales for eight years. His regional manager, Tim Fix, is visiting Mike's territory on one of his periodic swings through the region. In Tim's mind, Mike, whose record as a field producer has been above average, has the potential to go further in the company, if he wants to. As part of his managerial responsibility, Tim schedules a coaching session with Mike at his hotel.

Tim: I thought it would be better if we met here for our talk, rather than in your office at home. This way, we could have some uninterrupted time. As I told you yesterday, I thought both of us ought to look at what's ahead for the next couple of years, maybe even further.

Observed Performance

Yesterday I gave you some specific feedback after the calls we made. So today I'd like to make some general comments about what I saw. I think what impressed me so much about the five calls we made is your ability to adapt very fast to different personalities. Three of those prospects were radically different from one another, yet you adjusted your selling style to suit them.

Mike: That's the fun of being a salesman. It's a challenge to me, when I meet someone new, to see how long it takes me to get on that person's wavelength.

Tim: It takes a lot of sensitivity to do that.

Mike: You have to train yourself. You know this: Everything about the company, the prospect's office, the man himself—or the woman, since I'm beginning to see a lot more women managers these days—is a clue. You look around, you keep your ears open, there's always something to tell you what kind of a person you're dealing with.

Tim: No magic formula, is there?

Mike: It's training. Like that one call we made yesterday on Hamilton. Well, you see how he treated his secretary—very brusque, even a little bit rude. I figured he'd be that way with us. So I prepared myself. I wasn't going to let his rudeness throw me off. Also I gathered that he wasn't going to let me sit there for a couple of minutes to make small talk while I warmed him up.

Tim: I noticed that you went right into your presentation, but that you asked him a lot of questions as you went along.

Mike: Right. That was my way of warming him up without being obvious. And I got an awful lot of information out of him.

Training and Education

Tim: You majored in psychology, didn't you? That must help quite a bit.

Mike: I suppose so. I mean, it gave me some of the basics, and trained me to an extent. But I still read books on psychology. In fact, that's my favorite leisure time reading.

Tim: Ever thought of getting your master's in psychology?

Mike: I like what I'm doing. I don't want to be a psychologist. I just want to think like one.

Tim: What other interests do you have that you find helpful?

Mike: Well, I've been taking a course one night a week on computers. In fact, I want to buy a personal computer.

Record of Performance

Tim: That's very interesting. I think that's a smart thing to do. Let's take a look at your performance for the last year or so. We've already talked about your meeting quotas. I think you've met them every year.

Mike: Right.

Tim: But in the last 12 months, you've exceeded your new business quotas by about one-quarter. That's quite a jump. Want to talk about what you're doing differently now?

Mike: I have you to thank for that. I've always been a bit of a coward when it came to going after the really big companies. You kept pushing me. I remember you telling me once, "Hey, you'll never make the big money until you sell the giants." I found that out. So I started to work the biggies. It takes a lot of time, you know that, but I finally cracked one. And that gave me the confidence to go after another. It's all beginning to pay off.

Tim: A lot of our people still have trouble with the big companies. If I asked you to talk about your success at the next regional meeting, could you tell what you do?

Mike: Sure. I developed a system. You know, it takes a lot of work just to find out who's responsible for what in a big company. Then you have to uncover the people who have a say in the sale even though they don't sign. Yeah, I could talk about it.

Reports

Tim: Great. I have a note here to remind me that I was talking to Phil Summers, the sales promotion manager in the home office. He tells me that you've had a couple of phone conversations with him about some of the promo stuff, that you gave him a lot of feedback that was very interesting.

Mike: Tim, you and I can talk freely, I think. I have to tell you that I'm not always so impressed with some of the stuff coming out of the home office. For example, a couple of Phil's releases were pretty technical. I had no problem understanding them, but a lot of people I talk to might be turned off. In other words, the message was, "Look how great we are," instead of, "Hey, look what great things we can do for you." So I called Phil and made some suggestions.

Tim: I agree with you on the stuff not always being customer-oriented. But what struck me was that Phil didn't seem to be defensive about your calling. You must have been pretty diplomatic.

Mike: (Laughing) I'm a salesman.

The Employee

Tim: What about you? What are some of the skills you have that you're proudest of?

Mike: One thing you pointed out. I'm very proud of the way I can relate to people. It makes selling a great deal of fun, because every new call is an adventure for me. How long will it take me to get to know this person, to be able to sell? But I think another thing that I like about the way I work is how I've overcome a lot of my fears in selling, especially to the big customers. I've developed a system. I use preheat letters. I have stuff sent out directly from the home office to certain people in the company I'm prospecting. And I keep extensive records—everyone I've talked to, names of others that have been mentioned to me, every contact and the date of that contact. In fact, I've been working on a draft of some procedures to follow when you're calling on a big account. Maybe you'd like to see it. It could possibly help some of the other salespeople.

Tim Fix has concluded the data gathering stage with respect to abilities and preferences. He has confirmed that Mike Halbard has worked hard to develop some impressive interpersonal skills with prospects and customers. But Mike has also demonstrated that he knows how to use those interpersonal skills with co-workers, as evidenced by his dealings with the sales promotion manager in the home office. Not only has Mike developed a system for breaking into the large accounts, but he has on his initiative started to put together a draft of what could be used as the basis for training of other salespeople in successful methods of prospecting. This could suggest to Tim that Mike has some aptitude for management or training.

The second part of the interview is concerned with how Tim and Mike can use the information gathered in the first half.

Tim: Let me talk a bit about what's in the future. As far as the region is concerned, you may already know that Cliff Wilkinson will be retiring at the end of the year. That means, of course, that I'll have a district open. I don't know how you feel about stepping into a management role, but I'd like to know. I also want you to understand that I'll be talking with others about this promotion as well. So I tell you that to make clear that I'm not making a decision right now about who'll succeed Cliff. I just want to know who is available.

Mike: Would I have to move?

Tim: No. The district is not that far away. But you might spend quite a few nights in a motel. Of course, that's true of any field manager's job. There's a fair amount of travel.

But there's something else you need to be told about. Home office has decided to integrate the Kelmore Company with us. You know, we acquired them last year. They've been kept separate, but now the decision has been made to merge us. They have their own sales force, and for the time being, their people will do their own thing, and we'll do ours, although I think that won't be forever. The priority, as I understand it, is to set up an overall sales management team, then combine the field people. There's going to be a lot of weeding out. If everyone is selling everything, we won't need all the people who are in the two companies now. I'm not telling you this because I'm worried about you. Your record is great and, if you maintain it, you have nothing to worry about. In fact, there could be an opportunity for you. A lot of training will take place, in both groups. How do you feel about sales training? Do you have an interest?

Mike: I've been doing some thinking about it. As I told you, I've been working on a set of recommendations for breaking into big accounts. I think I'd be more interested in training than I would managing.

Tim: How strongly would you be interested in moving into training?

Mike: Very. I'd already decided that I didn't want to stay in the trenches indefinitely. I think training would be the right move for me.

Tim: Okay. We're talking about a development that will take place in the next 12 to 18 months. Do you want to start discussing it?

Tim: Definitely.

Tim has covered the future-oriented points listed starting on page 301 (and on the Long-term Coaching Interview Form at the end of this chapter). Now it is his responsibility to start preparing Mike to take on training responsibilities. First, he advises his subordinate that ultimately the change in jobs will require relocating to the home office. He explains the company's policy on relocation expenses. He also admonishes Mike to keep up local production, that any severe drop-off in new business could cause the home office to look elsewhere for a trainer. Tim also explains that even though many of the expenses of moving will be taken care of by the company, there are always costs that are not quite reimbursed. And there are emotional problems in the family that must be anticipated and dealt with.

Mike listens carefully and reaffirms his interest in being considered for the training position.

Tim: Here's the next step. I'll tell Jerry Tale, the director of training, that you are interested in talking about joining his staff. Meanwhile, in the next couple of days, you should write Jerry a letter telling him why you want to be considered. Use your selling skills just as you would on a prospect. Probably what will happen is that they'll want you to take on a training assignment in my region just to see how you work out. When that happens, you and I will work together to get you ready.

SHAPING THE INFORMATION

In the coaching session between Tim and Mike, the manager enjoyed certain advantages that many others do not. First, the data he was working with pointed to very clear talents and career possibilities. Second, he was talking with a subordinate who had already thought about what he might do in the years to come and, third, the subordinate, Mike, was very articulate about his abilities and his preferences. Very often, in fact, discouragingly so, you will find yourself coaching an employee who is not clear about his or her goals. You will have to help the subordinate to shape the information available into growth options. It helps to have as much data on hand as possible.

It also helps to have a lot of time available for the coaching session. You may want to encourage the employee to free associate in response to a question such as, "What do you see yourself doing in three to five years?"

A CAUTIONARY NOTE

However well-meaning your questions are, you have to consider the possibility that they may seem threatening to the subordinate. You'll be fortunate indeed if you can conduct an effective coaching session initially with a new employee. There must be time for a sufficient trust to develop. Subordinates must see that you are really concerned with their growth and development. They must be assured through your behavior that you won't ridicule them should they happen to reveal ambitions that are deep and heretofore unrevealed. You must also demonstrate that you are secure enough even to hear ambitions that involve replacing or bypassing you.

Once you uncover a potential skill or interest, work to find out whether there is ambition enough to develop it. You may have to spur the ambition by describing the various situations in which the skill or knowledge can be applied usefully. Once you've established that there is an interest in developing it, then look into what can be done to develop it. Is it even feasible to do so, given organizational constraints? Should you suggest training, a program of education, reading, consultation with experts, a stretching pilot assignment?

Don't commit yourself to a course of action without first making sure that the employee is serious about it, too. It may be too easy for the employee to assume that what you want are pleasing answers instead of workable data and commitment.

In coaching, whether you start with general areas of strength, or with specific questions designed to elicit information on accomplishments or on observed or reported behavior, be sure that the session ends on a definite note: what is to be done, how, in what time period, etc.

CONTINUING COACHING

Coaching is a key step in building an effective team. But it can't be done offhandedly or haphazardly. Be sure you follow these recommendations to have a coaching system that pays off for you and the organization.

Schedule Periodic Coaching Sessions

If you don't, you risk letting your firefighting activity crowd the obligation out. You should certainly plan at least one coaching session with each employee during the year, perhaps two, especially in the case of your highly performing employees whom you consider to be on the fast track. Give the employees plenty of opportunity to discuss their interests, strengths, and ambitions so that you can build on what is already there.

Set Up a Data Bank

Take notes during the interview or immediately after it. Otherwise, you'll forget some of what was discussed. Very often, a scrap of conversation or a bit of information gleaned indirectly will alert you to a quality you never knew an employee had.

Present Specific Guidelines

"Growth and development" is in itself an amorphous phrase, and this may be another reason why managers have difficulty in coming to grips with it. Giving shape to a growth and development program is a job that requires managerial imagination—and precision. Discussions with the subordinate should point to specific developmental experiences such as further training or education, a field trip, servicing a key account, temporary duty in another department, a new assignment, and reading. These suggestions should become part of your notes.

Update Your Information

Follow up on your suggestions to see that progress has been made. You may well discover that the employee has come a significant way in developing a new skill or sharpening an old one since your last coaching session. Check on the validity of old data. What the employee said last year—for example, expressing no interest in going into management—may no longer be true.

One result of your conscientious coaching, you hope, will be to encourage subordinates to do their own assignments, to study the opportunities, to gauge their own talents in terms of the organization's needs, and to develop a growth mentality that will discourage obsolescence.

But there can be another result of your extensive coaching of especially important employees. The coaching can be perceived as a reward for good performance and for the continuing actualization of potential skills. The employee says, "The boss is willing to take the time, because I am worth it."

LONG-TERM COACHING INTERVIEW FORM

(To prepare for the interview, please refer to the Employee Personal Data Form in Chapter 4.)

Name of employee: _____

Date of interview: _____

Date of previous coaching interview: _____

1. What departmental responsibilities in the next 12 months could the employee's abilities be applied to?

    _____

    _____

    _____

    _____

2. Specify the principal work assignments the employee will undertake in the next six to 12 months:

    a. _____

    b. _____

    c. _____

    d. _____

    e. _____

3. What events such as organizational changes, staffing changes, budget changes, new facilities, projects, or plans might provide advantages or disadvantages for the employee? Please describe. _____

    _____

    _____

    _____

    _____

    _____

4. What opportunities for the employee's growth and development lie in the answers to the above three questions?

    _____

    _____

    _____

    _____

    _____

5. What specific guidance or action plans are you offering the employee as a result of the information you have entered in question 4?

    a. _____

    b. _____

    c. _____

    d. _____

    e. _____

    f. _____

6. What resources such as training, education, and specific coaching are you recommending or making available to the employee?

    _____

    _____

    _____

    _____

    _____

7. What actions or reorganization will you undertake to help the employee to prepare more effectively for new responsibilities? _____

    _____

    _____

    _____

8. What new developmental information gleaned from observation, records, and from the interview updates your knowledge of this person, his or her aspirations, growth and development areas? _____

    _____

    _____

9. Date of review of progress: _____

10. Date of next coaching: _____

REVIEW OF COACHING

	Yes	No	Not Sure
1. Short-term coaching usually involves helping a subordinate work through a problem or a plan.	___	___	___
2. The first step of a short-term coaching interview is to agree on the problem or what is to be discussed.	___	___	___
3. When employees come to you with problems, it is usually a good idea to insist that they come with a solution for the problem.	___	___	___
4. In an effective coaching session, you try to generate as many options as possible before trying to settle on a solution.	___	___	___
5. Long-term coaching is for the employee's growth and development.	___	___	___
6. It is probably true that most managers do not provide growth and development coaching on a regular basis.	___	___	___
7. You are usually the best person to provide long-term coaching for your employees because you know them better than anyone else.	___	___	___
8. During every substantial discussion or collaboration with a subordinate, you should try to provide some learning opportunity.	___	___	___

		Yes	No	Not Sure
9.	The manager's highest priority is to build and maintain an effectively functioning work group.	____	____	____
10.	Long-term coaching should always be conducted in a formal interview.	____	____	____
11.	You obtain data useful for coaching for growth from observed behavior, the employee's record of performance, the reports of others, and from the employee.	____	____	____
12.	An ironic consequence of your success in coaching is that you may develop employees right out of your department.	____	____	____
13.	In order for you to have an effective coaching session with an employee, you must demonstrate to the person your real interest in their growth and development.	____	____	____
14.	Long-term coaching is a continuing obligation.	____	____	____
15.	Long-term coaching can be seen as a reward for good performance.	____	____	____

Answers to Review

1. Yes
2. Yes
3. No. Otherwise you may discourage them from bringing problems for which they have no solution.
4. Yes
5. Yes
6. Yes
7. Yes
8. Yes
9. Yes
10. No. You can coach informally as well.
11. Yes
12. Yes
13. Yes
14. Yes
15. Yes

13

COUNSELING FOR CHANGE

A salesperson fails to make the required number of calls on prospects week after week. An engineer makes repeated mistakes in specifications. A supervisor creates conflicts that make it difficult to work with other supervisors.

You want a change of behavior. As manager, you want the calls made, the specifications accurate, the cooperation extended. It is time for a counseling session. Employees with performance problems should receive counseling when the need becomes apparent: When performance drops, standards are not met, and goals are not achieved. Of course, anyone can have an off week. You don't rush to counsel a subordinate because there's a slight or temporary deviation from the norm you have established. But when it becomes apparent that the performance problem may persist and that, if it does, the subordinate's productivity (and possibly that of others) will suffer significantly, something has to be done—and quickly. That something is counseling.

Counseling is usually a moderate to high stress situation for both manager and subordinate. That's why some managers delay the counseling as long as they can. But when necessary counseling is delayed, that delay often results in more stress. One manager discovered the truth of this when she decided that she could no longer hold off talking to a bright, talented young subordinate who was falling seriously short of agreed-upon objectives. She had delayed, hoping that the problem would correct itself, and that she could avoid getting into an embarrassing discussion. When she opened the subject with the employee, he said, "I've been wondering when you were going to talk to me about it." He had been expecting, even, as it turned out, wanting the interview. He knew he was in trouble, but he didn't know how to ask for help.

APPROACHING COUNSELING POSITIVELY

That situation illustrates an important point: No one wants to be ineffective. There may be a difference in the way the manager and the subordinate define effective. But it is hard to believe that an employee wishes to be incompetent or inadequate except in infrequent cases such as when an employee rebels against a manager and decides on a policy of noncooperation. Most people can and will change if it makes sense to them. They want to grow and to become more effective. Just because they don't ask for help doesn't indicate that they don't want it.

Thus, it is especially important that during counseling the manager approach the employee with the "you're OK" message, a parallel to saying, love the sinner but hate the sin. You don't usually have to deal with sin, but the message is similar: "I accept you but not some of the things you do." The principle being discussed here is that people will usually respond to positive expectations. The manager approaches counseling with the attitude, "I want you to be effective, and I know you want to be effective. Let's work together to see how we can achieve that." It is necessary that you believe others want to grow just as you want to grow and want them to.

When managers approach counseling negatively or pessimistically, when they reveal even the slightest trace that they doubt whether this will work, but are simply going through the motions, they risk a self-fulfilling prophecy. Employees pick up the negative hints and may agree: "What's the use?"

The question frequently arises whether performance appraisal time is a good occasion for counseling. There are two reasons why it may not be the appropriate time. First, the problem should have become apparent before the evaluation, and it should have been dealt with. But in the event that the performance appraisal is the first time the true seriousness of the problem has become clear, keep this second point in mind: Combining the performance evaluation session with counseling the subordinate on a problem can be cumbersome. A lot of territory has to be covered and much time consumed. Not only could the prolonged interview create an overload for the subordinate, it could serve you poorly by blunting the impact of your key points. It's possible that you will be trying to get across too many messages at once. The high stress related to counseling may get in the way of a satisfactory performance appraisal discussion.

Many management experts maintain that a performance appraisal should not contain any surprises for manager or subordinate. If the performance problem has been there, it should have been dealt with as quickly as possible.

The verdict is: Counsel when the need for counseling becomes apparent and appraise when it is due.

COUNSELING AS AN INVESTMENT

When you counsel an employee on a performance problem, you are investing time and effort to improve the effectiveness of an employee, thereby raising the overall effectiveness of the work group. The focus is on the questions, "How can we help you raise the level of your performance?" and "How can you and we get what we all want from your efforts?" The emphasis is on making the employee a valuable, productive member of the department. Every day that counseling is indicated and is delayed means less chance to enjoy dividends from your investment in that employee.

When an employee is failing or turning in unsatisfactory performance, you have an obligation to take every possible step to help. There are several reasons why it is preferable to counsel than to give up and look for a replacement, aside from the possibility that the employee will file charges of discrimination against you. Here are a few of those reasons:

- [ ] *The Cost of Replacement.* The more valuable the job, the more it will cost to find someone else to do it.

- [ ] *The Employee Is Already a Partial Asset.* He or she knows the organization, the rules and regulations, how things are done in general. Even though the employee may not be doing the desired level of work, the chances are that he or she knows much about the job that a new employee would have to learn. In addition there is the usual breaking-in period before the new recruit would be effective.

- [ ] *Reassurance for Your Other Subordinates.* Others in your department would like to feel that if they got into trouble you would expend every reasonable effort to help. It does not comfort employees to see others who are floundering simply discarded.

- [ ] *Your Reputation.* Turnover and failure of employees does not look good for you. When you help employees who perform unsatisfactorily or in a mediocre fashion to become productive and meet the standards for your work group, you are heroic.

- [ ] *Your Obligation to the Employee.* You need to be sure that you have in fact done everything reasonable to assist the failing employee. You don't want to overlook the possibility that by deed or omission you have contributed to the employee's problem. Counseling helps you to complete the following checklist of frequent reasons for failure and thereby prove that you have been as effective with the employee as you know how or might be expected to be.

Employees who fail often:

- [ ] Don't know what they are supposed to do.
- [ ] Don't know how to do it.
- [ ] Don't know why they should perform a task, job, or assignment.

☐ Face obstacles beyond their control.

☐ Don't think that what they've been instructed to do will work.

☐ Think their way of doing it is better.

☐ Are not achieving their personal objectives in the type of work assigned or in their working environment.

☐ Don't have the required abilities.

☐ Are personally and temperamentally unsuited to the work.

☐ Don't have sufficient time to do it.

☐ Are working on wrong-priority items.

☐ Think they are performing it in the absence of feedback.

☐ Are receiving poor supervision.

☐ Have personal problems that are distracting them or interfering in some way with work performance.

Actually the above checklist can sometimes help you in analyzing performance problems prior to counseling. From your observation and knowledge of the individual, and from the history of your interrelationship, you may be able to arrive at the appropriate recommendations for performance improvement without going through the counseling process. However, if you are not sure about any of the above contributing factors, counseling may be indicated.

COUNSELING AND STRESS

Chances are that both you and the employee will experience stress during the interview. Your stress will actually precede the session. The better documented you are and the more confident you feel in what needs to be done, the less stress you may have.

The greater your esteem and concern for the subordinate, the greater will be your stress. You may not wish to verbalize it during the session, but don't attempt to ignore it. It is a moderate to high stress situation. One reaction to your stress may be anger at the employee for having created the need for counseling. It's understandable for you to have such a reaction, but you should not attempt to counsel if you are angry. Postpone the session for an hour or so. Take a walk around the block. Find some way to get your emotions under control. You cannot be as effective as you would like if you are caught up in anger or resentment.

Adding to your stress sometimes may be the fear that as part of the employee's negative reaction to the counseling you may be counterattacked. If the employee feels attacked, he or she lashes out at you to get you off the offensive. Be prepared for a negative reaction. You'll probably get one. In fact, you are very likely to get one. People being counseled usually react negatively before they become positive and agreeable to working with you on the problem. It's a natural phenomenon of people who are under stress. You can empathize with it. If you expect it, and you should, you are less likely to be thrown by it. In most cases all you have to do is to sit it out. You'll need patience for this part of the interview and many reminders that the employee is acting in a fairly normal way.

Some managers try to reduce the stress by taking steps to control the employee's reaction. One way is to dictate to the employee what may and may not be said. For example, the employee complains about having friction with another employee in the department. The manager responds with, "Let's not get into that," or "The reasons don't interest me." Or when the employee reacts emotionally, the manager warns, "I think you should get a grip on yourself." A primary disadvantage of controlling employees' reactions is that you may prevent them from giving you the information you need. And if you don't let the resentment come out now, it will surface later in a less recognizable form. Better to unbottle it now.

In short, just as you must accept the employee's feelings, even if you don't necessarily agree that they are justified, you must take care not to deny your own. Often, simply admitting to yourself that you are upset, under stress, perhaps even angry is enough to help you get yourself in control sufficiently to be effective.

THE COUNSELING SEQUENCE

1. *State the problem.* "We agreed that you would produce $50,000 in new business by July. Here it is the first of September, and you are still 10 percent short of the goal you were supposed to

have reached two months ago." Or, "When I last talked with you about your lateness, you agreed that you would be here every morning no later than 9 o'clock. Yet, since last month when we talked, you have been more than fifteen minutes late on six mornings." Your preparation is very useful. The subordinate accepted a goal, a standard, a project, and he or she hasn't fulfilled the agreement.

In stating the problem, stick to describing behavior and performance. Stay away from attitudes and other intangibles that can't be measured. Don't make judgments about motivation or attitudes. For example, don't say (no matter how much you may be exasperated), "I accepted your word because I thought you were a person of good faith. But now I have to wonder." That will only lead to more exasperation. Aside from being offensively judgmental, the tone is accusatory. Someone charged with the crime of deception, in this case, will rush to the defense. You want to solve a problem, not run a courtroom or debating society.

To avoid an accusatory tone, you may wish to state your perception or understanding and check it out with the subordinate: "As I understand it, you and I agreed that you would have the restructuring of the department finished by November 1st. Is that your understanding?"

Don't, however, run the risk of filtering out the more serious messages by being diplomatic. The true message might be, "Your work is clearly unacceptable. It cannot continue this way." But what comes out is, "I know—and you do, too—that you're capable of far better work than you're doing, and I don't think I'd be fair to either of us if I didn't try to help you improve. "When a manager is anxious not to offend, he or she can conceal the seriousness of the problem in the verbiage.

2. *Get agreement on the deficiency.* Don't proceed beyond this point without an agreement that you both have something to talk about. Documentation can be very important here. The record showing the deficiencies or failures can usually establish the reason for the counseling and form the basis of the employee's agreement that his or her behavior has been inadequate or inappropriate.

If you slide over this step, you may find yourself locked in a futile debate. If the subordinate doesn't agree with the way you have defined the problem, invite him or her to help you find more acceptable words: "Okay, maybe I've misunderstood. Tell me how you see the situation."

Most employees will agree that you have something to discuss, especially when the record is clear and there have been prior discussions on the same subject with agreements made that have not been kept. Occasionally, however, you may get the response that the employee just doesn't understand what the fuss is about. For example, the employee who comes to work late when everyone else observes the rules and is there on time says, "I just don't regard being in here at the stroke of nine all that important. It's what I do while I'm here that's essential." You may have to explain why the issue is one of priority with you. In the final analysis it may come down to, "This is what I expect of the people who report to me. It may not be that important to you, but it is to me. If you want to continue to work here, you will be expected to observe the rules."

The employee may not be happy with your explanation, but he or she has to accept that you feel strongly about it.

3. *Listen.* Accept the probability that the subordinate has a story to tell. Let it be told without being interrupted by your rebuttal. And allow time to air an emotional reaction to what you've just said. Keep in mind that the negative reaction is normal.

You don't have to agree with anything that is said. If you sit it out, you're not necessarily endorsing the reasons, excuses, emotions, or any other negative response. You are, however, treating the person with respect and dignity. You are indicating to the employee under stress that you understand the stressful feelings. If you can't accept the person and the feelings, your chances of arriving at a solution that is acceptable to you both are extremely slim.

In counseling, two types of listening are required. There are things that are said, and there are things that are not said. The employee may not volunteer all the necessary information. For example, a salesman who is not making enough calls on prospects complains that he has to spend too much time servicing his customers. What does he mean by that? Is he selling so carelessly that he has to soothe disgruntled customers? Is he inventing reasons to make service calls on customers rather than sales calls on prospects? Or is there a breakdown in the quality of the product that should be looked into?

Sometimes subordinates will assure you that they have accepted the counseling, that everything will be fine, that changes will be made. They smile yet seem to fight to keep their hands from trembling. At such times you may want to take more time to be sure that everything is in fact being said.

If the employee does not seem forthcoming with the information you would find helpful, you may wish to apply nondirective interviewing techniques. You encourage the employee to talk without leading him or her. Silence is a principal component of the technique. Silence creates tension, and people act to break that tension by talking. If you don't talk, the employee most likely will. You can then offer encouragement to continue by saying from time to time, "I see," "Yes, I understand," and "Would you elaborate on that?"

Look at the employee. Nod to show that you are listening. Occasionally, refer to something that the employee has said to show that you have been paying attention: "So you feel the necessity to get the supervisor's okay on routine requisitions sometimes results in delay—and doing without what you need at critical times?"

Listen carefully, because counseling is a learning opportunity for you. You could be getting feedback on conditions in the department about which you are not aware, on your effectiveness as a manager, on the clarity of your communications, etc. Counseling often provides you with insights into how employees see their well-being, how they feel about what they are or are not doing, whether they believe they have a chance to achieve their personal goals through committing themselves to yours. If you don't learn something about the employee, the operation, the climate, the working conditions, then it is possible the counseling has not been a complete success.

4. *Consider the extenuating circumstances.* The employee's explanation of the problem may not be rationalization. Consider the possibilities below for starters:

☐ *Change in situation.* Working conditions may have altered since the objectives or standards were set. The location of the workplace, the people involved, the flow of the work, all may have contributed to the problem. You may want to corroborate the employee's version but, unless you are certain the excuse is flimsy, don't dismiss it without checking.

☐ *Insufficient knowledge or skill.* Neither you nor the subordinate may have known at the outset what was really required to do the job. You may now decide that the choice of this person was wrong or that training, help, or equipment can be provided to get the job done.

☐ *Work load.* Look for a change in work load that may have resulted in a disproportionate accountability. The salesperson who is asked to undertake a regional market research project, or to cover temporarily a portion of another territory, while maintaining his or her primary responsibility, may have a justification for a performance deficiency.

☐ *Conflict with co-workers.* This may occur within your department or in another with which your subordinates must cooperate. It's possible that your subordinate may be partly responsible for the conflict, but the conflict has become a factor that interferes with getting the work done. It has to be dealt with in the counseling process. You may not be able to eliminate the conflict entirely, but you may be able to help the subordinate to reduce his or her contribution to it.

☐ *Personal problems.* Be ready to offer assistance by referring the subordinate to proper help. But while listening to the account of a personal problem, don't allow yourself to be diverted from your objective: to correct performance. You can be compassionate, but the work has to be done.

5.   *Be prepared to refer elsewhere if necessary.*   You are probably ill-equipped to do certain kinds of counseling. Problems involving emotional instability, drug or alcohol abuse, family conflicts, and the like are usually beyond the ability of the manager to handle. You may find yourself in the middle of such a problem while dealing legitimately with a performance deficiency. When you recognize that an employee's on-the-job behavior is influenced by such a personal factor, don't try to play Dutch uncle or advisor. You have a right to insist that the employee seek help in order to improve work performance, but you can't provide that help. An

employee who is wrestling with a severe personal problem may try to enlist your aid, either from desperation or in an attempt to win sympathy. Be prepared to refer the employee elsewhere for professional help.

However, it is not usually a good idea to refer the person to a professional who treats you or whom you consult. That's tying the employee and the problem a bit too close to you. If you don't have an Employee Assistance Program, or Personnel can't help, then you just have to recommend that the employee seek the appropriate help and put distance between you and the problem. You must, however, make it clear that you expect the performance to improve.

6. *Find a desirable alternative.* This is, after all, what the counseling is all about. You've gotten agreement that the performance is deficient or the behavior is not appropriate. You might say, "All right, we both agree this is not the way we want it. What can we do about it? What would make you more effective?" Asking what alternative the employee would adopt rather than why he or she has been doing it this way keeps the idea of change positive. To dwell on why the person has been doing it or not doing it emphasizes the negative. It's wrong, you would be saying, stop doing it. It's more appealing to say, in effect, "If you're not behaving the way you want to or think you ought to, spell out some new behavior that we can evaluate and agree on in terms of the results we both want."

You are thus emphasizing the future and a partnership. At this point you might be tempted to say what you think would be a solution. The employee may argue the point. You are in danger of getting into a debate over a solution which the employee doesn't want to accept. For example, you say to a salesperson who is not making enough new sales calls, "I don't want you to make a single service call until you have made five new calls." That may be a solution—for you. That is perhaps the way you would do it. But the salesperson will give you 10 reasons why that isn't the way to get the job done. Rather than getting into an argument, ask her how she would accomplish what you want. It's quite all right for you to say, "I want you to make at least 10 new sales calls per week. Tell me how you think you can service your customers and yet satisfy new business needs. Remember, 10 calls on prospects a week."

When you operate in the assertive–responsive mode, you encourage the employee to tell you how she thinks the job could be done within the context of that person's style and mode of operation. Furthermore, since it is the employee's solution, at least in part, she has ownership. She has invested effort in coming up with the solution. Now she will more enthusiastically work to carry out her solution.

7. *Get agreement on the alternative.* The employee has joined with you to develop a solution to the deficiency. Now repeat it to the employee and say, "This is what we've agreed on, is that right?" Don't assume agreement *and* understanding. The employee could be agreeing with you without necessarily understanding what is to be done. He or she may be nodding so as not to offend you.

8. *Design an action plan.* Now it is time to be specific about the performance improvement plan. The action plan concerns not only *what* is to be done but *how, when,* and by *whom.* It's possible that you will have to take certain actions, or provide resources, to help the employee in carrying out the solution. Or others might be involved in the behavior change. The important thing is that both of you know exactly what is to happen in order to improve the employee's performance. So, before concluding the session, be sure you design an action plan that spells out what is to be done, how it is to be measured, the schedule of review, and the deadline date—when it is all supposed to be accomplished. (See the Performance Improvement Plan on page 333.)

9. *Get the employee's perception of what has taken place.* Again, you want to be sure there is complete understanding. So you may want to ask the employee to summarize the discussion of the solution. When the employee has satisfied you that he or she understands what has happened as you understand it, the session is over.

10. *Follow through.* Counseling is not a one-time event, such as on-the-spot criticism. If the problem is serious enough to require counseling, then it calls for follow-up. Whatever the action plan calls for, monitor it to see that it takes place. If you don't complete your obligation to see that change takes place, then the word will get around that you are not really serious. You will undermine your credibility.

When the desired change takes place and you are satisfied, reinforce it. Don't adopt the attitude that the new behavior should have been adopted without the counseling and that you don't have to express your appreciation. Perhaps you don't have to, but it will probably mean a great deal to the employee if you do. You also increase the chances that the new behavior or way of performing will become permanent.

Of course, if the desired change does not occur, then further discussion between you and the employee is called for. You may have to adjust the action plan. Try another way, extend the time-table, and apply more resources.

These steps are summarized in this flowchart of The Counseling Sequence.

THE COUNSELING SEQUENCE

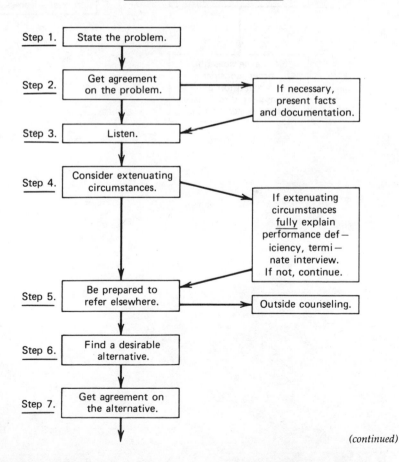

(continued)

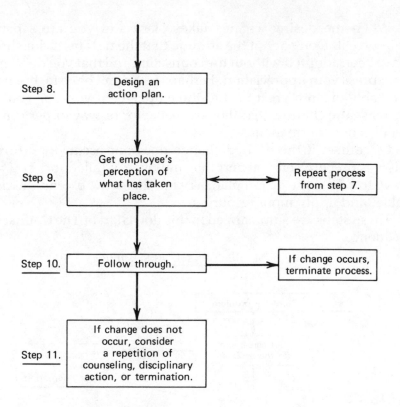

PERFORMANCE IMPROVEMENT PLAN

Name of employee: _____

Date of counseling: _____

Other persons present, if any: _____

_____ _____

Previous dates on which problem was discussed with employee.

Critical feedback session: _____

_____

_____

Feedback in appraisal: _____

_____

_____

Previous counseling on the
same problem: _____

_____

_____

1. Statement of the problem: _____

_____

_____

_____

_____

_____

2. Employee understands the problem as stated and agrees that
   it is a deficiency to be discussed.   Yes   No

   If no, list the documentation and other supporting evidence
   presented. _____

   _____

   _____

3. I listened fully to employee's explanation.   Yes   No

4. I considered extenuating circumstances that contributed to the
   problem. List the factors. _____

   _____

   _____

   _____

What actions will be taken to change the circumstances? Describe. _____

_____

_____

_____

_____

Who will take the action? _____
By when will the action be taken? _____

5. Should the employee be referred elsewhere for assistance—counseling?   Yes   No
To whom was the employee referred? _____

_____

_____

6. I enlisted the employee's aid in finding an alternative or a solution.   Yes   No
Describe the solution. _____

_____

_____

_____

_____

7. The employee agreed to the solution as described above.
          Yes   No

8. Here is the action plan agreed to.
What is to be done? _____

_____

_____

_____

By whom? _____

Steps to be taken to complete action plan (if necessary):

_____

_____

_____

Target date(s) for completion (by step if necessary):

9. Follow-through actions:
   Dates of review: _____

   Action recommended if change does not occur:

   _____   _____
   (Manager's signature)   (Employee's signature)

SCHEDULING THE COUNSELING INTERVIEW

The best part of the day to counsel is first thing in the morning. One reason to get an early start is that you have plenty of time. Counseling must never be rushed. If you have to take an hour or even two, you've got the time to do so. You won't be cut off by lunch or quitting time. But an even more important benefit of counseling in the morning is that it gives you the rest of the day to work with the employee on a natural basis. If you interact with the employee as you would during any normal work day, you convey the message that you accept the person even if you object to some aspect of that person's behavior. In all probability the counseled employee may feel a bit punished, and your acting as you would normally removes the punitive aspect from the counseling. The employee may wonder whether he or she will be in some way ostracized, and you show that you have no intention of setting the subordinate apart. In the event that the employee has further thoughts about the counseling and wants to discuss them with you or seeks clarification, you are available.

If you schedule the session near the lunch hour, you create an undesirable time pressure. You'll also spoil lunch for the employee. Chances are also that the employee will want to unburden some emotions over lunch with co-workers. Feelings of tension or anger will be translated into a hostile earful for some of your other subordinates. Why risk spreading the misery? If you counsel early in the morning, some of the negative feelings should have drained off by noon.

The next preferred time for scheduling the interview is early in the afternoon. At least you have the rest of the day to interact with the employee. It is not recommended that you have the session late in the afternoon, after which you send the employee home to fret all night or during the weekend. The employee will probably seek out friends or family, all sympathetic ears to the feelings poured out. Any residual resentment or anxiety will simply be magnified, since listeners will be taking the employee's side.

It is not useful to give the employee advance notice of the session. If you suggest that the two of you get together "first thing in the morning (or after lunch) to have a little talk," you guarantee having to face a thoroughly anxious and defensive employee across the desk.

Conduct the session in a private place where you can talk uninterrupted. Taking phone calls or receiving visitors, even for only a minute, can disrupt the flow of the interview and create even more tension in the subordinate.

Avoid having a third person present if you can. You are in a power position, which, in the employee's mind, puts him or her at a disadvantage. Having another person in the room intensifies that disadvantage. The employee has the feeling, no doubt, that "They are ganging up on me."

PREPARING FOR THE INTERVIEW

Counseling is never an impromptu activity. And it is seldom a surprise to the employee. You have probably already given feedback to the employee that his or her performance is not up to your standards. You may even have given a negative performance evaluation. By the time you reach the stage at which counseling is called for, you should have some objective evidence of the problem. For example, a salesperson fails to make a sufficient number of calls on prospects. A supervisor has unusually high turnover in his or her department. A production worker maintains an unacceptably high rate of rejects. A clerical worker fails to work the required number of hours during the day or has a high rate of absenteeism that cannot be medically documented.

Objective evidence is necessary if you are to avoid the interminable arguing of the Yes-you-did-No-I-didn't variety. And, considering today's antidiscrimination laws, you can't afford not to have documentation in case you have to terminate a subordinate for poor performance.

In your preparation concentrate on the critical issue to be resolved. If there is more than one deficient area, decide which one has priority. It's not impossible to counsel an employee in more than one area of deficiency, but it may be difficult for the person to try to change behaviors on a broad front. You might prefer to focus on one problem at a time rather than to try to effect a large change all at once.

Determine what kind of performance you want as a result of the session. This helps you keep the interview on track. You should always anticipate that the employee will try to divert your attention from the problem through excuses, explanations, or rationalizations. If you know where you want to wind up at the end of the session, you are better prepared against diversions.

Do not prepare a so-called laundry list of problems and complaints. Some managers, fearing that the employee will not be convinced of the seriousness of one problem, make up a list of several other problems for which the employee has been responsible in the hope that they can score with at least one, or that the combined weight of all problems will compel the employee to change his or her ways. To the employee you will seem to be conducting a vendetta or a grudge session. The result of a managers bringing a laundry list to the session is more often a resentful employee than a change in behavior.

COUNSELING THE ALCOHOLIC EMPLOYEE

He may be quite obvious about the drinking. There may be frequent absences, especially on Friday or Monday. She may come to work with alcohol on her breath or return frequently from a long liquid lunch. But those are easy-to-spot symptoms. Many problem drinkers go to great lengths to hide the disease. Eventually, though, the work pace becomes chaotic and uneven, the moods unpredictable—tense and jittery now, outgoing and affable later. When errors or lapses are pointed out, the employee may turn hostile and defensive. Finally, after the quantity and quality of the work have sunk, you step in.

Don't Play the Friend

Your well-intentioned and friendly advice probably won't have any effect, except to make the employee try to hide the drinking more expertly.

Have Your Facts on Hand

You should have abundant evidence of the drinker's poor performance. Be specific. Arrange your data so that the pattern of behavior is unmistakable. You will make it clear that this is a problem from which the employee cannot just walk away.

You also need to give specific information on the steps the drinker can take to get help. If your organization has no employee assistance program for the treatment of alcoholism, you will have to obtain information about local treatment centers, community programs, nearby chapters of Alcoholics Anonymous, and similar organizations.

Be Firm But Positive

The organization wants to keep a valued employee. The employee wants to keep a job. In talking to the employee, you must state firmly that (1) a problem exists, (2) it is recognized, (3) it is affecting job performance, (4) it cannot continue to do so, and (5) treatment is available and is mandated. Do not lecture, moralize, or argue. Let the facts of the employee's performance speak for themselves. You want to get this one message across: If the employee continues on the present course, he or she will be out of work.

Don't Label

Don't call the employee an alcoholic. There are widely varying definitions of that term. There's no point in getting sidetracked by an argument over whether the employee is or is not alcoholic. The performance, or lack of it, is the focus of the discussion.

Give the Employee a Reasonable Amount of Time

The path back is not an overnight trip. You may want to give the drinker some time to think things through. The two of you may want to discuss the matter again. But there must be a definite time period within which the employee must either get help or get out.

Even after help has been obtained, there may be a lapse. You may choose to be understanding up to a point, so long as work is not seriously affected. But even while you are understanding, you must be firm: The problem must be corrected. After a relapse, you may have to say, "If I have any evidence that you are drinking or under the influence of alcohol at work, I'll terminate you on the spot." That final step may do the job where all previous attempts have failed. But if it doesn't, follow through on your threat. You owe yourself, the organization, and your other subordinates that much.

THE DRUG USER

Many of the preceding recommendations are useful when you counsel an employee who abuses drugs on the job. Here are some other considerations.

Don't Counsel the Addict on Your Own

He or she needs professional help. However well-intentioned you are, you cannot give her the kind of help required. As with the alcoholic, you have to refer the person elsewhere. Your personnel or medical department ought to be able to help you.

Insist That the Person Get Help

Especially if you catch the person in the act of taking drugs, put the employee on notice: Get help or get out.

Don't Spy on the Addict

You can't go around constantly trying to find evidence of addiction or of drugs on the premises. It's hard enough for a person to try to kick a drug habit and hang on to dignity without having someone looking over his or her shoulder every day. You have to invest a certain amount of trust and confidence in your decision to keep the employee on the job. However, that decision is based on the employee's willingness to seek professional help.

Consider a Change in Job Assignment

Many people turn to drugs—alcohol included—as an escape. This might be true of your drug user. Perhaps the employee finds the job demands too heavy, the atmosphere too competitive, and the deadlines too taxing. If the employee is making an honest attempt at rehabilitation, then you may wish to realign job responsibilities, thus retaining some of the employee's talents but not stretching them beyond the point of endurance.

THE EMPLOYEE WITH PERSONAL PROBLEMS

An employee's performance may be adversely affected by problems outside the office—for example, marital, parental, and financial problems. There are at least two reasons why you should not encourage the employee to divulge details of those personal problems in counseling. First, you could be drawn into the middle of the problem. If the employee is having marital difficulties, he or she might want to confide in you subsequently as changes in the situation occur. Second, the employee might later resent having you know intimate details. That resentment or embarrassment could hamper you in your efforts to work effectively with the troubled subordinate. You are well-advised to stick with manifestations of performance problems that may result from personal factors. Below are some suggestions you might follow.

Express Understanding

Certainly you can understand how personal pressures can affect the work. But your understanding doesn't require you to encourage divulging those pressures.

Be Firm About Improvement

Your understanding, even sympathy, should not get in the way of pointing to the performance deficiency and saying that you want an improvement.

Discourage the Employee from Getting Too Personal

When the intimate details start to roll out, you may want to say to the employee, "You really don't have to tell me this. In fact, you ought to think about it. I wouldn't want you to tell me anything that later you might wish you hadn't."

Listen to the Personal Details But Don't Discuss

If the employee shows signs that he or she needs to discuss the personal pressures, if you feel that you cannot gracefully stop the revelation, then listen but don't comment. After the employee finishes, advise the person to get other help. You are not a doctor, clergyman, or psychologist.

Based on the seriousness of the problem, you may want to consider temporarily lightening the work load, making changes in assignment or hours, or suggesting that the employee take time off. But whatever your course of action, don't lose sight of your objective: Improvement of performance.

HOW TO FIRE

You've criticized the employee's performance. You've probably given a negative performance evaluation. You've gone through the counseling procedure. None of it was sufficient to induce or to help the employee to change behavior or to correct deficient performance. Perhaps you applied disciplinary measures, and they didn't work either. Now you have the options of letting the problem continue or of terminating. While many managers, especially those dealing with civil service employees, may throw up their hands because of the pain and complications of the firing procedure, other managers will reflect on the complications of permitting the "failure" to continue on the job.

First, you will have lost any credibility with the problem employee. If you do not apply sanctions, you will lose power over the person who has been seriously deficient for so long. Second, you create tension in yourself. Your self-image and feeling of authority will erode. A loss of face for you will hurt you; it is bound to affect your dealings with others. Third, the "forgiven" prodigal employee may become a model for one or more others in your department. They reason that if nothing happened to the chastised and threatened employee, nothing will happen to them. Frankly, some employees need sanctions, the threat of discipline, and rules and regulations to stay in line (in most organizations, they are a distinct but unfortunately conspicuous minority). In an environment where anything seems to be tolerated, anything may well be what goes.

But aside from the image, the imitation by others, and your reputation and credibility is the effect that your lack of decisive action has on employees who are motivated to work well for you. They may very possibly continue to perform well for you. But their respect for you will undoubtedly diminish. The rewards you grant them will lose their luster, if only because they now feel that incompetent performance or counterproductive behavior has, in effect, also been rewarded. The "guilty" person has been permitted to keep his or her job—unjustifiably, in their eyes. When you tolerate performance that, in the opinion of your better employees, should not be tolerated, you risk alienating them.

Thus, terminating the employee who will not or cannot work according to your standards is your only option, no matter how painful or embarrassing it is. And it can be both, especially in the case of someone who seemingly has good intentions, acts in good faith, but who simply is not up to the demands of the work. Terminating such an employee heavily reinforces your motivational message: If you do good work, you will be rewarded. If you cannot or will not perform according to my standards, you will be fired.

If you cannot remove the hurt and embarrassment altogether, you can fire an employee in a professional and compassionate manner.

Come Right to the Point

There's no point in making small talk. This is an extremely tense moment for you, even if the employee does not yet sense the meaning of your talk. Don't delay with preambles, and don't preface the firing statement with a history that explains what has brought the two of you to this point. Say it. For example, "There's no easy way for me to put this. I have to ask for your resignation (or, I have to terminate you). We can talk about this as much as you wish. But you should understand that the decision is not reversible." It is very important that you gain the other's acceptance that your action is irreversible. Otherwise you may find yourself subjected to agonizing arguments to get you to change your mind.

Give Reasons

The more documented and objective your reasons are the better, especially in these days of restrictive legislation. Even if there were not the possibility of charges of discrimination, documentation ultimately makes it easier (though probably never easy) for the employee to accept termination. For example, "Your performance has been below par for the past year. You agreed to improve your productivity. You actually slipped further. I put you on probation for the past quarter, warning you that termination was the next step." Or, "Your absentee record exceeds the limit of tolerance. You were warned that if you could not justify it with medical evidence, you would be discharged."

The more your explanation is based on fact and record, the safer you are. However, don't give a long explanation. The employee may be in shock and may not be able to hear you. Say what you have to say and little more.

Chances are that you truly feel sorry that it had to come to this. It's all right to say it. But keep the focus of the blame where it belongs: on the employee. To make such statements as, "It's just not working out," or "I really never thought you were comfortable here," or, "I think you're suited for a different kind of atmosphere," is to blur the issue. The employee didn't do the job. The fault lay with him or her. At least, the deficiency was in the person.

To try to suggest that it lay elsewhere may cheat the employee, who needs to learn a lesson for the future. The employee failed to meet performance standards, and he or she must be encouraged to think about why. Termination is painful, but that doesn't mean it cannot and should not be a growth experience.

Be Prepared to Listen

After you've explained why, resist the temptation to give a speech that will amplify your reasoning and justify your action. That won't make the news easier to take, and the employee probably isn't listening. This is your time to listen. The employee needs time to absorb the shock. Let the employee know that you are prepared to discuss what led up to the decision to terminate and that you will answer all the questions you can. This is no time to be in a hurry. Be patient. You will probably have to sit there while the employee talks defensively, even angrily. But this rambling time is necessary for the employee.

If the talk turns nasty and personally abusive, you have a right to protect yourself from insult by saying something such as, "I know you have strong feelings about this, but I don't think you want to say things now that you'll regret having said later." If that kind of statement doesn't shut the abuse off, then add, "As I said, I'm willing to talk this out with you, but I'd like us to get together later after you have thought about this for a time." Then get up and open the door.

Have Help and Counsel Ready

After the employee has calmed down, be prepared with help. Will an office and a phone be available for the employee's use? What are the severance benefits? How long will the employee be covered by the group insurance plan? Is he or she eligible for the pension plan? How will the departure be announced?

You may want to arrange an immediate session with a specialist in the personnel department who can answer all the employee's questions. Some managers believe it is good at this point to keep the employee busy working on practical issues surrounding leaving.

Don't underestimate your ability to help. Make yourself available for any follow-up conversations, any lingering questions. Above all, don't treat the terminated employee as a pariah. The person is hurting. He or she certainly has not ceased to exist as a human being in your eyes.

Is there a time to fire that is more suitable than another? Termination notice should probably be given early in the day and during the workweek in order to give employees time to absorb the shock, to express their feelings, to ask questions, and to busy themselves with practical steps to take for the future. The practice of firing people on Friday afternoons may make managers feel better because they don't have to see the employees. But it does more than wreck the employees' weekend. An employee should not have the feeling that he or she has been tossed out into the street; he or she needs time to talk with others (probably co-workers, rather than with the family immediately), and to plan what to do next. By the time the weekend arrives, the employee should be well into a transition period rather than still in a numb state.

No matter how justified the firing is, it will be painful for you in most cases. You can console yourself with the knowledge that you are giving the person an opportunity to start over somewhere else, where he or she will do better. Even more important for you, you have the knowledge that your employees who have worked hard and well for you will appreciate that you take decisive action when performance is good—and when it is not.

HITS AND MISSES IN COUNSELING

Following are three counseling interviews. You are asked to read and think through each one. If you believe the manager's style of counseling is successful, give the reasons why you think so. If you have criticisms, record those in the space provided. Then compare your analyses with the author's at the end of each of the three sessions.

Counseling Session I

Manager: Come in, John. I appreciate your taking time out from your Monday morning. I know how rushed things can be in your department. Sit down. I thought we might have a chat about how things are going. It's been some time since you and I got together.

Subordinate: Things are going fine, I guess.

Manager: Are you having any problems?

Subordinate: Well, you know that things are never perfect. Why, is something wrong?

Manager: I thought maybe you could tell me.

Subordinate: Tell you what?

Manager: Whether you think you have any problems.

Subordinate: I told you. Nothing's perfect, but things seem to be going fairly smoothly.

Manager: I agree. They seem to be.

Subordinate: Are you saying they're not? I don't know what you're getting at.

Manager: I walked through your department yesterday afternoon after the break. I'll bet half of your people weren't at their desks. There was a lot of milling around. It had to be a good 10 minutes after the break had ended.

Subordinate: Yeah?

Manager: People are supposed to be at their desks when the break ends. After all, those are the rules. I talked with you about it before.

Subordinate: When? I don't remember.

Manager: Yes, you do. It must have been a month or maybe a month and a half ago. I said then that we couldn't allow people to decide on their own when breaks were over.

Subordinate: Oh, that was a long time ago. And I explained that I don't come down hard on my people. They do the work. As long as they do the work, I'm not bugging them to sit down the split second the break is over.

Manager: This wasn't the split second. This was a good 10 minutes.

Subordinate: All right, 10 minutes. Look, have you had any problem with our output? We've increased productivity in that department by something like 20 percent in the past six months.

Manager: That's true, but...

Subordinate: But what?

Manager: There's no discipline. You can't run a department like that.

Subordinate: Not even a department that produces better than it ever did, in fact, probably better than the others?

Manager: That's not the point. The point is that we have rules, and those rules should be followed. What if everyone else decided to ignore the rules, why there'd be chaos.

Subordinate: But there isn't chaos.

Manager: That's because other managers are observing the rules. But your people are providing the wrong example to the employees in those other departments. We just can't have it.

Subordinate: So what are you saying? In spite of the good work my people do, I've got to tell them when the break bell sounds, they've got to be at their desks?

Manager: That's what I'm saying. I'm afraid I shall have to insist on it. This is, after all, your second warning. I can't risk having a third such conversation.

Subordinate: All right. I'll tell them what you've said.

Manager: Good. I'm glad you're being so cooperative.

How would you analyze the above counseling session? Did you spot any mistakes the manager made? Would you have done it differently? What do you predict will be the outcome of the session? Write your analysis here: _____

_____

_____

_____

_____

_____

_____

Author's Analysis: The manager in Counseling Session I initially risked arousing the resentment of the subordinate manager by describing their get-together as a chat, a word that suggests casualness. In fact, the reason for the meeting was quite serious in the manager's mind. Then he took a minute or so to let the subordinate manager know that he did not think things in the manager's department were going well, allowing time for the subordinate to feel the first sign of tension as he began to suspect there was a serious reason for the session (although he had no way to know what it was).

The statement of the problem was clear and adequate. At that point, the manager would have been well-advised to let the subordinate respond, to explain why the employees were late in getting back to their desks. Instead of listening, he plunged right ahead to muddy the stream with his statement that he had talked with the supervisor about it before. Apparently the supervisor had thought the previous conversation was concluded in a satisfactory manner with his explanation as to why he didn't "come down hard" on his people.

The supervisor, who has been doing a good job, is not a partner in this transaction. He has been told to comply, and he leaves the office promising to tell his people what the big boss has said. He is thanked for being cooperative, but it is very doubtful that he is acting in the spirit of cooperation. Probably the rules will be obeyed for a time. But what will happen to the motivation of the supervisor and the employees is not even open to question.

Counseling Session II

Manager: I've asked you to come in this morning, Ronnie, because there is a serious problem I feel I have to discuss with you. In fact, I've discussed it with you before—last month and the month before. I have two memos in the file recounting those talks. It's about your lateness in making telephone reports after you have inspected apartments.

Subordinate: I'm still having the same problems I had then. Some of the phones on the street don't work. They've been vandalized. I could spend half the day just walking down the street to find one that works.

Manager: I don't think you understand how serious the problem is.

Subordinate: I know how serious it is. You want to know whether the apartment is ready so you can send in a new work team.

Manager: That's right. And sometimes we don't get reports from you until late in the afternoon, and then it's too late to get in touch with the contractor to get workmen there. You must realize that a delay of one or two days even, spread around all the apartments we own, can mean the loss of a lot of rent.

Subordinate: You don't have to tell me that.

Manager: They why are you still so late with your telephone reports?

Subordinate: I told you. Sometimes I can't find a telephone on the street that works.

Manager: Why don't you use tenants' phones in the building?

Subordinate: Some of those people aren't there during the day. And those who are are scared to let me in. After all, they don't know who I am.

Manager: I think you could find someone in. In fact, you're going to have to do it. We need those reports as soon as you complete the inspection.

Subordinate: You know that I'm going to have to cut the inspections I make if I stop everything to look all over a building for a phone.

Manager: That's an exaggeration.

Subordinate: No, it isn't.

Manager: Ronnie, I have to make it clear: I want those phone reports on time.

Subordinate: Even if it means that I stop doing everything to find a phone? I can't bunch the inspections any more?

Manager: That's right.

What is your analysis of the session? Is the manager effective? Your views: _____

_____

_____

_____

_____

_____

_____

_____

Author's Analysis: The manager documented her case and made a clear statement of the problem. But will she be successful? She already failed twice before. There is little guarantee that she will get the change of behavior she wants this time. She may get a behavior change, but she will probably pay a tremendous price for it. Ronnie has hinted that, instead of bunching her inspections, she will follow orders to find a telephone, however long it takes her, before she resumes her inspecting.

The manager does much of the talking. She would be better advised to find a way to involve her subordinate. Ronnie is a capable employee who is not following orders. The manager should first have asked Ronnie to help her find a solution. The manager herself spelled out the alternative behavior desired without getting agreement from Ronnie. It's safe to predict that Ronnie will now operate "by the book," and neither manager nor subordinate will achieve satisfaction from this exchange.

Counseling Session III

Manager: Come in, Bob. Shut the door, would you? Oh, would you like some coffee?

Subordinate: No, thanks.

Manager: How's the family? That boy of yours must be getting up there, huh?

Subordinate: He's thirteen now.

Manager: Well, they grow up too fast. Right? Listen, Bob, I asked you to come by because I want to talk to you about something that's been bothering me for a few days. Last Friday I walked through the store. I was in your department I'll bet three times and you were nowhere to be seen.

Subordinate: I was there on Friday.

Manager: Well, you may have been there. In fact you were. I saw you in the morning. But where were you that afternoon?

Subordinate: I remember. I wasn't feeling too good. I went outside to get some air.

Manager: You know the policy. If you're going to be out of your department for more than a few minutes, you should let me know. We went over this several months back.

Subordinate: Look, it was just for a short time. One day? You're getting all uptight about that?

Manager: Bob, I'm concerned about how you run your department, and you can't run it if you are not there. Your people need a manager on the spot.

Subordinate: Don't worry. Listen, my people get a lot more help from me than they do from some of the other managers.

Manager: What do you mean?

Subordinate: Take Lois Newcombe. Her people don't have such a great deal. You ought to hear them complain.

Manager: About what?

Subordinate: How she plays favorites. And she's always prowling around to catch someone making a mistake.

Manager: What's Lois got to do with what you and I are talking about?

Subordinate: I'm just telling you. My people get supervision, and it's fair.

Manager: I'm sure they get good supervision, but not when you're away. I'm talking about your being off the floor. When we talked about it before, it was a real problem with you. I don't want us to get in that bind again.

Subordinate: Look, I'm under a lot of pressure. Sometimes my stomach gets all knotted up.

Manager: Pressure here at the store?

Subordinate: No, it's some problems I'm having at home.

Manager: What kind of problems?

Subordinate: With Jo, my wife. I think she's going through menopause.

Manager: Doesn't she have a doctor?

Subordinate: Yeah, but she gets a little crazy at times.

Manager: Maybe you'd better talk to somebody about it. Maybe she'd better.

Subordinate: Who?

Manager: You're the best judge of that—the doctor, your minister, someone who's qualified to help. But I need you, and your people need you.

Subordinate: I don't know. Sometimes it gets to me. I have to get away for a few minutes.

Manager: Tell you what, Bob. I can't help you with your personal problems. But while you're getting things straightened out, I'll help all I can. But in return, you'll have to promise me you'll get some counseling.

Subordinate: Okay, sounds fair.

Manager: So we have an agreement. What's your understanding of it?

Subordinate: That if I feel I have to get away, I'll tell you before I go. That way you can fill in.

How would you evaluate this manager's effectiveness in conducting the session with Bob? What do you think he might have done differently? What mistakes do you think he made? Your comments: _____

_____

_____

_____

_____

_____

_____

Author's Analysis: It may seem to be the compassionate thing to do to try to relax someone you're about to call on the carpet. But the employee's reaction to what the manager in the above example tried—asked whether Bob wanted coffee and asked about his family—may be quite different from what the manager assumes. First, the attempts to relax by making small talk in a counseling session may actually increase tension as the employee sits there wondering what is about to happen. The employee might even develop resentment if he or she suspects that the manager is deliberately trying to "disarm" him before letting him have it.

It was a mistake for the manager to let Bob get him off the track with his gossip about Lois Newcombe. Newcombe had little or nothing to do with the problem the manager wanted to discuss: Bob's absences from the floor. The second that Bob tried the diversionary tactic about Newcombe, the manager should have replied, "We're not talking about Lois Newcombe. We're talking about your being off the floor." It's quite common for employees to reduce the pain of the counseling session by distracting the manager's attention, sidetracking the manager by bringing up an unrelated issue. That's very human. But it doesn't serve the manager's purpose.

Bob again tried to get the manager off the track by talking about his problems with his wife. But those were not really any of the manager's business. If you know an employee well and feel comfortable talking about personal issues, you may be willing to let the employee talk about nonwork-related matters. But you should try to avoid doing so in a counseling session. Acknowledge them: "I'm sorry to hear that you're having problems. Perhaps you can talk with a qualified professional about them. Meanwhile you and I have a problem here that we must talk about." You can be firm and gentle at the same time.

The solution that was agreed on was offered by the manager. It was definitely a solution that Bob was unlikely to turn down, since it worked in his favor (unless he preferred to sneak off the floor). In effect, the solution had the consequence of the manager's buying Bob's problem—and becoming a victim of it. It might have been in fact the best solution, but it probably would have been better to let Bob have a say in what corrective action he thought he should take.

It's typical in many counseling sessions for the manager to jump too fast to propose a solution that may not be as reasonable or fair as if both parties had come up with an answer which they jointly agreed on.

A COUNSELING SCENARIO

Ted writes regularly for a monthly magazine published for sales-people. He has been a member of the editorial staff for nearly 20 years. Recently the managing editor for whom Ted worked for many years left the staff and was replaced by Peter, a man younger than Ted in years and experience. Peter has not been happy with Ted's work in the nearly six months since he took over as managing editor, and one morning, early in the week, he called Ted into his office for a counseling session.

Peter: Close the door, will you, Ted? I want us to have a private discussion about some aspects of your work that are troubling me.

Ted: Oh?

Peter: I'll be upfront with you, Ted. Your work is just not acceptable.

Ted: How come I've managed to be here for 20 years if my work is not what it should be?

Peter: Ted, I'm not going to talk about the past 20 years. I'm going to talk about the past six months.

Ted: In other words, what went on before you took over doesn't count.

Peter: I don't say that. But I was not managing editor then, and now I am. And your work is not up to my standards.

Ted: I was writing this stuff before you were out of college. It's a little tough for me to have you come in here and tell me I'm not up to snuff, especially since I worked for Terry for years and he never had a complaint.

Peter: Okay, look, let's get one thing very clear: I respect the working relationship you had with Terry. But Terry is gone, and I'm the one you have to deal with. Terry may very well have liked the inspirational kind of articles you do. But my emphasis in the magazine is on more how-to, hard stuff. I like articles that say to the salesperson: Here's the problem, here's how to solve it.

Ted: There's more to selling than that. Everyone likes some stimulation.

Peter: I'm not arguing whether people want the inspirational copy. I'm just laying out for you what kinds of articles I want for our magazine.

Ted: Peter, you've been on my back for several months. I've been writing one way, and suddenly you want me to do something else.

Peter: I haven't been riding you, but I have made it clear that I want you to change. There's nothing sudden about this. Think back to when I took over. I gave a little speech in which I told everyone the new directions I wanted us to take. I followed that up with a memo. You had the same notice everyone else had. Since then, you've gotten a lot of flak from all of us in the editorial meetings because you keep submitting the same kind of stuff you did before.

Ted: I don't worry about that. I'm used to people giving my stuff a lot of flak. I write what I think is important and, if they don't see that, then there's not much I can do.

Peter: We have rejected seven out of your last 12 pieces. That can't go on.

Ted: I still say it's the judgment of one person against another.

Peter: All right, let's put it on that basis: It's my judgment against yours. I'm the managing editor. I want certain kinds of copy. You don't give me what I want. In fact, more than half the time you don't give me what I ask for. You were told what I expected. You've gotten feedback from your colleagues. Now you've having a session with me.

How would you evaluate Peter's effectiveness thus far in dealing with Ted?

Author's Analysis: Ted's reaction is predictably negative, and Peter has tolerated it. It took Peter awhile to state the problem in terms that Ted could not argue against: I'm the boss; I want a certain standard followed; you haven't been following it. Other than being somewhat slow in getting the problem stated, Peter is doing well, with one minor exception. In the beginning, he said, "I'll be upfront with you." There is always the implication in such a remark that the person has not previously been upfront. Watch such seemingly innocent words such as "frankly" or "honestly."

Peter: Would you agree with me that you and I have a problem?

Ted: I don't agree with you about your editorial specifications.

Peter: That's not the issue here. Let me state it again. I'm the managing editor, and I have the right to set the standards. I have, plainly, and you're not meeting them. There's a problem, right?

Ted: Right. You're the boss.

Peter: If that's the bottom line, that's true. Now, we've agreed on the problem, what can be done to resolve it?

Ted: Write harder copy.

Peter: That's a start. Can you do it?

Ted: Sure I can; after all, I go back a long time. When Terry came, I taught him the business. Terry really hadn't a background in selling, and I showed him how to put the magazine together. He was a writer, not a salesman. It was very difficult to get guidelines out of Terry, you know. You pretty much had to figure out for yourself what he wanted and give it to him. He was a good man. He could be exasperating and vague. It was hard for him to make a decision. But he's helped me. He really has been good to me.

Peter: I realize that you and Terry had a good relationship.

Ted: It was more than that. For the past couple of years. . .I haven't talked with anyone about this. Terry knew, he was the only one. But my wife and I, well, things haven't been smooth. She's had some problems. Anyway, Terry was very patient. Look, Peter, I know my work hasn't been the greatest, but I've been carrying a heavy load. My wife has had to be institutionalized a couple of times, and it's been a bad experience.

Peter: Is she under professional care?

Ted: Yes, but the problem isn't taken care of.

Peter: Ted, I can't help you with your personal problems. I'm glad your wife is getting professional care. And I can appreciate the load you've been working under. First of all, the change from Terry to me, and then your wife. But I have to go back to my question: What can we do to get harder copy from you? I'm ready to help in any way I can.

Author's Analysis: Peter has shown that he is ready to listen to Ted. But he is unwavering in what he wants: a change in the kind of copy the Ted writes. He doesn't permit himself to be thrown off his course, although he shows some compassion.

Ted: I can do it. I told you that. I just hope you can have some patience with me. When things are bad with my wife, I find it hard to work.

Peter: Ted, I can't give you professional help. But I think you ought to look into it for yourself. You know we have an employee assistance program. Why don't you get in touch with Personnel and see whether you can arrange an appointment.

Ted: Maybe I should.

Peter: Good. Now, let's get to a plan of action. First of all, we are in agreement about what has to be done.

Ted: I know what you want; I'll just have to try to give it to you.

Peter: Not try, Ted. I want you to do it. Look, let me express the seriousness of this. You've had six months in which to change. You haven't. I'm giving you three months more.

Ted: What do you mean by that? Are you going to fire me?

Peter: I'll have to consider it.

Ted: You mean you're going to put me on probation? What kind of a person are you? After 20 years, after the work I've done here. And you come along and say, "I'm going to fire you." I'm really shocked that you would even think in those terms. I know you don't like some of the stuff I'm doing now, but I can still outproduce anyone on this staff. I don't understand you. You don't have to lean on me like this. You just tell me what you want. I'm enough of a professional to give it to you. You don't have to threaten me.

Peter: Yes, I am putting you on probation. And I'll tell you what kind of person I am. I am in charge of a magazine that has fallen in circulation for each of the past three years. It's my job to turn it around. I need you and everyone else on the staff to help me. Ted, I'm not forgetting what you've done for this company in the past. That's one reason why I'm taking this time with you now. I want you to work with me. But I'm also telling you that, if for any reason you can't, I'll have to replace you.

Ted: Do you want me to quit now?

Peter: No. I want us to put together an action plan.

Author's Analysis: It is usual during a counseling session for the person being counseled to become emotional. It is not a comfortable situation. Peter has remained firm but understanding. He let Ted get the emotions out on the table. He didn't try to shut him off. But when the older employee had finished, Peter reiterated that the older man would have to change his behavior. Peter also handled the other emotional issue competently, the one dealing with Ted and his wife. He declined to get any further into the case than to assure himself that Ted's wife was receiving professional care. He suggested that Ted avail himself of the employee assistance program, then moved on. A manager should always be prepared to refer an employee elsewhere if serious personal problems arise during the session.

Ted: I'll just change the way I write.

Peter: That's trial and error. You don't want to get into a story session and get shot down. How can we make sure that you and

I agree on what you've written—before you submit it to the story session?

Ted: I'll let you see the article first.

Peter: That's one way. That could still mean that you've written a piece you may have to write over.

Ted: Do you want me to discuss with you in advance any story ideas I have?

Peter: If we did that, I'd have a chance to show you more precisely what I want. And we'd both be satisfied that you were going in the right direction before you wrote the story.

Ted: Boy, it's tough after all these years to have to discuss story ideas in advance. It's as if you can't trust me.

Peter: Look at it this way, Ted. You eliminate the risk that way. Here's what we can do. For the first few times, you bring your story ideas to me. When it's pretty obvious that you and I agree on what you're doing, then we'll stop the practice. From that point, you're on your own with the story conference. How does that sound?

Ted: We can try it.

Peter: Okay, that's our action plan. Now just to be sure that you and I are in agreement, tell me the action plan as you understand it.

Ted: For the time being, I'll bring to you every story idea so that we can discuss it in advance. When you feel sure that I'm doing what you want me to do, then we'll stop discussing stories in advance. And I'll get my feedback in the story sessions.

Author's Analysis: Peter hasn't trusted his own sense of communication to ensure that Ted has heard what has been agreed to. He has asked Ted to describe his perceptions and understanding of what has gone on between the two men. Earlier he very wisely involved Ted in the solution-finding process, which not only increased the chance of understanding in Ted but also his sense of ownership: The solution was in part suggested by Ted. He therefore would have more commitment to it than had it been proposed by Peter.

Of course, the follow-up has been built into the counseling. It will occur in two ways: first in private sessions with Peter and, later, in the general story conferences.

Peter has demonstrated that in a good counseling session, you must:

☐ *Be Prepared.* Obtain as much documentation as possible. There was really no way for Ted to dispute the negative feedback he had received. He had had ample warning. He did not agree with the standards, but he did not disagree with Peter's prerogative to set them.

☐ *Show Firmness.* He gave Ted space in which to move, to protest, but in the end he impressed on the subordinate that he knew what he wanted and was determined to have it—if Ted remained there.

☐ *Be Patient.* The counseled employee, you'll remember, will usually have negative feelings about being counseled. That's natural. You must be prepared to let the employee work through those feelings. To insist upon suppressing them is to risk having to face the buried resentment, perhaps even hostility, of the employee at a later date.

☐ *Be Empathetic.* It's important to be able to understand what your subordinate is going through. Being empathetic, however, is far different from being sympathetic. Peter appreciated that Ted was feeling abused as an old-timer, and he tried to treat the older employee with dignity. But he never felt that, had he been in Ted's shoes, he would have resisted standards, as Ted did.

Counseling is often a painful experience for both manager and subordinate, as has been pointed out. No wonder some managers delay it as long as possible. But counseling that is delayed creates more problems. Not only does the undesirable behavior continue, but it is reinforced in the employee's mind. It then becomes harder to show the employee why he or she must change it.

REVIEW OF COUNSELING FOR CHANGE

	Yes	No	Not Sure
1. Counseling is needed when a performance problem threatens to seriously disrupt the employee's productivity or that of co-workers.	____	____	____
2. Counseling that is delayed can create tension and stress in both you and the subordinate.	____	____	____
3. Employees who sense that they are not competent or productive usually welcome counseling.	____	____	____
4. It's important to approach counseling with the attitude that the employee is not "on trial" but his or her performance is.	____	____	____
5. You are more effective in counseling when you have a positive attitude that you will get the employee to agree to improve performance.	____	____	____
6. Performance appraisal time is usually the best time for counseling.	____	____	____
7. Counseling is generally cost-effective because salvaging an employee is cheaper than recruiting a replacement.	____	____	____
8. When an employee is failing or turning in unsatisfactory performance, you have an obligation to take every reasonable step to help that employee.	____	____	____

9. When you counsel an employee, you reassure others who want to

	Yes	No	Not Sure

believe that you would help them in a performance problem. ___ ___ ___

10. Employees who fail often should be gotten rid of quickly or else they will demotivate and demoralize others. ___ ___ ___

11. Employees who perform deficiently may not know what they are supposed to do or how to do it. ___ ___ ___

12. The more documentation or evidence of performance problems you have the less stress you'll probably feel when counseling. ___ ___ ___

13. You should never counsel when you are feeling angry at the employee. ___ ___ ___

14. The employee will probably show negative feelings at being counseled, but all you have to do is say, "Don't get emotional." ___ ___ ___

15. The healthy employee does not have negative reactions to the counseling and should be able to accept your counsel. ___ ___ ___

16. If you can identify employee attitudes that you believe contribute to poor performance, identify them. The identification will be helpful in the interview. ___ ___ ___

17. In order to get the employee to accept your counsel, you should do everything possible to avoid offending the person. ___ ___ ___

	Yes	No	Not Sure
18. It's helpful for you to listen to the employee's reactions or explanations, even though you don't have to agree with everything the person says.	___	___	___
19. When the employee does not volunteer the information that you need, be patient and nondirective in your approach.	___	___	___
20. If you don't learn something about the employee, the operation, and working conditions in the counseling interview, it is possible that the counseling has not been a complete success.	___	___	___
21. There may be extenuating circumstances to explain at least part of the employee's performance deficiency, and you should pledge yourself to take quick, effective action to remove such barriers.	___	___	___
22. When an employee's performance deficiency is caused by personal problems, you should try to understand what the problems are before you try to counsel.	___	___	___
23. When you are in the assertive– responsive mode, you encourage the employee to come up with a solution he or she feels responsible to carry out.	___	___	___
24. When you agree on a solution, you can regard the counseling as successful.	___	___	___

	Yes	No	Not Sure
25. When the desired change takes place, you should reinforce it.	____	____	____
26. The best time for counseling is late in the day, so that the employee has plenty of time to think about it at home that evening.	____	____	____
27. Another good time to schedule counseling is just before lunch. This gives the employee time to get away from the office before resuming work.	____	____	____
28. It's a good idea to recruit your manager for the session so as to impress the employee with your seriousness.	____	____	____
29. When more than one performance problem is involved, it is generally a good idea to pick the one that has the higher priority.	____	____	____
30. If you do not impress the employee with one problem, have a back-up list of others just in case.	____	____	____
31. If you have to fire an employee, it's best to do it early in the day and week.	____	____	____
32. When you fire, be ready to offer whatever help and counsel you can—or that the organization can.	____	____	____
33. When the deficiency or problem that brought about the termination is the employee's, don't try to assign blame elsewhere.	____	____	____
34. If you do not terminate an employee who will not or cannot work accord-			

	Yes	No	Not Sure
ing to your standards, you risk demotivating others who do.	____	____	____
35. Compassion is an acceptable emotion for you to have in a counseling session so long as it does not prevent you from taking appropriate actions.	____	____	____
36. Generally, empathy is more desirable for the counselor than sympathy.	____	____	____
37. Patience is an essential characteristic of an effective counselor.	____	____	____

Answers to Review

1. Yes
2. Yes
3. Yes
4. Yes
5. Yes
6. Not sure. Counsel only if the seriousness of the problem becomes apparent at that time. Otherwise, schedule the counseling when the problem becomes clear. Don't wait for appraisal time. Appraisals should have as few surprises for the employee as possible.
7. Yes
8. Yes
9. Yes
10. Yes
11. Yes
12. Yes
13. Yes
14. No. Expect a negative reaction, and let it be expressed.
15. Not sure. Most people will have initial negative reactions, but some may not.
16. No. Forget attitudes; stick to behavior.
17. No. Even if you risk offending the employee in order to counsel effectively, you must counsel in the most effective way possible.
18. Yes
19. Yes
20. Yes
21. Not sure. It may be more proper to enlist the employee's aid in doing so, as in the case of personal problems.
22. Not sure. You may not want to get deeply involved in the

details of a personal problem. And you probably aren't qualified to deal with them anyway.

23. Yes

24. Not sure. You should also check to make sure the employee understands the agreement.

25. Yes

26. No

27. No

28. No. No one else should be present unless absolutely necessary.

29. Yes

30. No

31. Yes

32. Yes

33. Yes

34. Yes

35. Yes

36. Yes

37. Yes

14

GIVING CRITICISM

Criticism of employees' performance is vital to the success of your management of their motivation. People need to know how they are doing on the job. Uncertainty usually creates tension. The salesperson whose ratio of orders to sales calls is lower than it should be, the clerical worker whose work is studded with errors, the supervisor who misses deadlines, and the factory worker whose reject rate is higher than the departmental average, all have a sense that they are not working as well as they should.

They may not seek criticism. Being criticized usually brings with it some pain and embarrassment. But if criticism is offered in good faith, if the need for it is made clear, they will often accept it even if they don't exactly welcome it. Most people want to be effective at what they do. They have no wish to bumble and to waste time and energy on inadequate results. If, for whatever reason, they feel that they are prevented from accomplishing their work, they are likely to be frustrated, even demotivated. When they are not confident that they are performing correctly, they often become anxious, and those feelings may add a further impediment to effectiveness.

Criticism from their managers can help those employees to understand and correct their failings, to achieve the results that they want to realize from their efforts, to develop confidence that they are indeed doing the right things—and doing them well. Both the confidence and the achievement provide a powerful boost to their motivation.

One key to the efficacy of the negative feedback that you supply in the case of less-than-satisfactory performance lies in the assumptions you make. For example, assume that the employee:

- [ ] Doesn't know what to do or how to do it.
- [ ] Doesn't understand the seriousness of doing the job right.
- [ ] Wants to do the task in an acceptable manner.

The assumption that you should *avoid* in many such cases of inadequate effort or quality is that the employee knows what is expected of him or her. As a result of the feedback session, you may have to explain the work assignment more clearly or in greater detail. Or you may find that the subordinate understands what is to be done but may lack the necessary knowledge and skills to accomplish it. In such a case, you may have to be prepared to do some coaching or to provide training.

Giving criticism is an excellent opportunity for you to broadcast and reaffirm your standards of performance, especially when the problem is one of flouting your authority, bypassing organizational rules, and shortcutting procedures. Unquestionably other employees observe the employee who often comes in late, is absent without convincing reasons, makes it difficult for others to work with him or her, or uses unsanctioned, even risky, methods to get things done. By taking prompt action with the employee who is out of line, you demonstrate to everyone—your subordinates, your boss, and other managers—that you are alert and in control.

You make sure that the undesirable behavior doesn't take root and create more serious counseling needs later. Perhaps even more important, you underscore the truth that what is valued in the operation is adherence to your standards and to those of the organization.

Finally, criticism sessions provide you with a chance to learn more about your department and your management. You may find that some people could benefit from more training, that there are factors and people in the work group (or outside of it) impeding the efficiency of subordinates, and that you are not as careful and helpful in assigning work as you think.

Yet all the above benefits of criticizing can't be gained without some pain. The manager in giving negative feedback runs the risk of inflicting hurt, causing embarrassment, and arousing anger and resentment. Any criticism session is potentially a stressful moment for both manager and subordinate. Some managers try to reduce that stress by softening the impact of the feedback, such as in the so-called "sandwich technique." The criticism is a filler between slices of praise. For example, the following manager observed that one of his employees has recently developed the habit of taking extended lunch hours, coming back to the office 15 and 30 minutes late. He tells himself that he doesn't want to make a "big deal" out of the matter; he doesn't want to put the employee on the spot. He just wants to call attention to what has been happening. Here is how he conducts the feedback interview:

> Ed, got a minute? Come into my office. You know, you and I haven't had a chat for a long time. Well, I guess that's the penalty you pay for being such a good worker. The squeaky wheel gets all the attention, right? I'm overdue in telling you how much I appreciate your being so conscientious. That's why I thought I'd mention something to you. I've noticed lately that you've been extending your lunch hour, which is unlike you. It isn't that I worry about your getting your work done. It's that some of the other people might look at one of the best people I have and figure they can do the same. I thought I'd better caution you. You know, a word to the wise, and all that. And that's all it takes with you—a word.

You know, of course, that good old Ed is getting some criticism. But it may take him a while to realize what has happened to him. First he was praised, then there was that little almost unimportant item about the long hours at lunch, then he was praised again. No doubt Ed left the interview with mixed feelings, which later probably turned to anger. In the sandwich technique, the criticism is diluted by the praise, and the praise is contaminated by the criticism. Instead of avoiding pain, this manager postponed it and perhaps amplified it.

MAKING CRITICISM COUNT

While there is no easy and completely painless way to criticize a subordinate's performance, there are steps you can take to create the proper conditions for getting the employee to understand and accept what you have to say.

1. *Describe the undesired behavior that you've observed.* And stick to behavior. Don't get into attitudes. To say, "You have a poor attitude toward work," may mean many things and is certainly arguable, from the employee's viewpoint. But when you point out that the employee has been more than a quarter-of-an-hour late to work four mornings this week you are being clear and not disputable. Talk about behavior that you (not others, except for behavior that is documented by the person's supervisor) have observed—being absent, making errors, turning out work that has to be scrapped or done over, being rude to customers, missing deadlines, creating conflicts with other employees, etc. You cannot get into the other's mind to determine attitudes or motivations.

Be specific about the behavior. For example, the employee may have been rude to a customer, but what seems rude to one person may not be to another. So you might say, "I heard you tell her that she was being a pest. I realize that she was asking a lot of questions, but she didn't deserve that kind of label."

2. *Criticize as quickly as possible after the event.* You can be more precise in describing what you find objectionable, and the employee can be clearer in remembering what he or she did—or failed

to do. Also, if you catch the mistake or other undesired behavior immediately, there is less chance that the employee will have time to repeat it. If the employee is aware that he or she made a mistake or failed in some way, the person will feel tense until you've dealt with it. You certainly don't want the possible hurtful comments of others who have witnessed the behavior to reach the employee first.

3. *Get the employee's agreement that a problem exists.* Don't go any further until you are sure that the employee understands what you find objectionable. There's little that is more distressing than to give lengthy feedback only to have the other person shrug and suggest that you're making much of little. For example, tell her that calling customers "pests" is hardly consistent with the way things are done in your organization. She will probably, albeit reluctantly, agree. If she doesn't, make it clear for all time that it is not consistent. The point is not up for debate.

4. *Listen, indeed invite, the employee's analysis of the situation.* Whatever you have observed, bear in mind that the employee may have seen the situation differently. The employee missed an important deadline, but there was another person, or procedure, that caused or at least contributed to the delay. You can expect an employee who is on the spot to be defensive, maybe even antagonistic. But it helps to let the employee sound off a bit, make explanations, and even rationalize, if you are to win acceptance of your ideas for improvement. It's possible that you will learn something about your department you didn't know, such as the person who contributed to the missed deadline. However, don't let yourself be sidetracked by lengthy excuses and explanations. If you feel in danger of that, go on to the next step.

5. *Emphasize that you want improvement.* Much time in criticism sessions is wasted looking for the *why* behind offensive or deficient behavior. Once you've agreed that the problem exists—the disparity between what is and what should be—get the employee's help in looking for solutions. If the employee seems absorbed in explanations and rationalizations, continue to come back to what you want. "Yes, I understand that your car is old, that you cannot afford a new one, that it keeps breaking down, but I want you here on time, every morning. How do we accomplish that?"

Agree on what is to be done, by whom, how, and in what time frame. You may want to ask the employee to repeat back to you what the two of you have agreed on just to be sure that the employee has heard what you've heard. Let your subordinate know that this agreement is a contract that you expect him or her to fulfill. (See the accompanying Record of Criticism Interview.) Also be sure that the employee knows there will be a follow-up session if the solution is not applied or does not work. The important message to give at this time is, "I know you want to be effective, and I want to help you to be. That's why we've had this talk."

An emphasis on future effectiveness and on solutions does not necessarily preclude defining causes of problems. It may be necessary to eliminate certain causes and contributing factors before a solution can be found. But often, a search for causes can be translated into "Who is to blame for this mess?" It is usually more constructive, therefore, to look for alternative solutions first, then, if it seems constructive, work backward to correct those factors that may stand in the way of the solution.

RECORD OF CRITICISM INTERVIEW

Name of employee: _____

Department: _____

Problem or event: _____

_____

Date observed: _____ Date of interview: _____

Date of previous interviews, same subject: _____

Change agreed to: _____

Results of change: _____

Resources (if necessary) to be supplied: _____

Date for change to be accomplished: _____

Type of follow-up or monitoring: _____

Further action if necessary: _____

_____

CRITICIZING IN PRIVATE

Most criticism should be delivered in private, if only because your primary objective is to gain a change of behavior, not to humiliate a person, not to reduce his or her standing with co-workers. Most public criticism is seen as punitive. Is it ever constructive? Possibly, as in the case of a problem to which everyone ought to be alerted. One employee regularly "misplaces" his safety glasses, exposing his eyes to possible damage. You don't want him to be a role model for other employees who, following his example, occasionally work without their glasses. You've discussed it with him privately. Finally you criticize the erring employee in front of others, thereby letting them know that they might get the same embarrassing treatment if they neglect to take precautions.

Another use of public criticism that could bear fruit is taking the consistently poor performer to task. One of the secretaries, for example, disappears into the women's room several times a day for long stretches of time. Her work piles up. She is not around to answer her phone or to respond to questions. Other secretaries have to step into the vacuum. You've warned her repeatedly to no avail. The fact that she flouts your authority is well known. You wait near her desk, and when she returns from one of her frequent trips, you say something such as, "I've been trying to talk with you for the past 10 minutes, but you were nowhere to be found. This is the fourth time this morning that I couldn't find you. I think you'd better come into my office so that we can talk about this."

The rest of the criticism can be delivered in private. The message, however, has gotten around. You've shown that you mean business, and you've also given some of the other employees satisfaction. They've undoubtedly resented that she has gotten away with her malingering.

In general, however, you will want to observe the familiar rule: Love the sinner, hate the sin. You want to rid yourself of the sin. You don't want to destroy the subordinate in the process. Despite the momentary embarrassment or resentment over the criticism, you want that employee to continue to work with you and others with comfort and respect. You want a change of behavior, not an angry, sullen subordinate. You want an employee to look at your criticism as a helping step. On the other side of the temporary pain, there is greater effectiveness. Through your feedback you are showing the employee how to get better results more often from his or her work.

The following reminders can help you to gain greater and faster acceptance from an employee for your criticism:

☐ *DO Be Private with Your Criticism.* It's unlikely the employee will hear much of what you are saying if he or she is concerned about what others think.

☐ *DON'T Be Punitive.* Your language and your tone should not convey the message that you are "out to get" the employee for what he or she did or did not do.

☐ *DO Be Positive.* The purpose of your criticism is to help the employee work more effectively and happily in the future.

☐ *DON'T Be Personal.* You are questioning an aspect of the employee's behavior, not his or her value or worth.

The longer Checklist for Criticism Interview at the end of the chapter can help you to evaluate the effectiveness of your criticism interview.

MIXING POSITIVE WITH NEGATIVE

Ideally, praise and criticism should be separate. As you saw in the oft-used sandwich technique, the praise dilutes the criticism, even hides it for a time. The important negative message loses a lot of its impact. When the criticism finally sinks in, the praise doesn't mean much to the person who sat on the other side of your desk.

Yet there are times when the whole message has to be delivered at once—the bad with the good. It may be important for your subordinate to get the total picture of the project in which he or she is involved. Or perhaps this is the only chance you have to talk with this person for a time. Maybe the subordinate has to take some remedial action for a project that has developed some soft spots. Or you've scheduled a progress report, and the employee is expecting to get detailed feedback.

At such times, it may be difficult or unrealistic for you to resolve to stay only with the good or the bad. The following recommendations will help you to convey both positive and negative feedback without harming the impact of either:

1. *Start with the negative.*   Many managers believe that they should be positive at the beginning of a session, to "relax" the subordinate, or to "soften" him or her up. But that technique smacks of manipulation and resembles the "sandwich" described earlier. Furthermore, if the employee even remotely suspects that there will be criticism, he or she will find it hard to concentrate on what is being said as preamble.

It is better to announce that you are concerned first with the negative. You might say, "I have some positive feedback for you later, but let's get the criticism out of the way." Cover what is wrong without mixing in any praise.

2. *Get agreement on the points of your criticism.*   You may both be tempted to get through the minuses to the more pleasant pluses, but there's no point in giving criticism unless the person on the receiving end agrees with your negative observations. You have to make sure of that agreement before you can be confident that corrective action will in fact be taken.

3. *Agree on remedial action, if required.*   What will be the solutions or alternatives devised? Agreement is one thing; a firm action plan is another.

4. *Keep positives and negatives in proportion.*   You may understandably want to exaggerate some of the good features of the subordinate's work to ease the pain of the negatives you've just unloaded. At the same time you want to be sure that the other person hears everything you say. So keep the positive message in proportion to the negative. If the major part of the feedback is negative, then you might want to say, "There are some good things I want to say. They aren't major, but they're encouraging. The most important things for you to take away from this discussion are the action plans to correct the problems."

If the positives far outweigh the negatives, you might say, "I wanted to cover the negative points. There aren't that many, but they are important. Now that we have taken care of them, I want to tell you how very impressed I am on the whole."

5.   *Don't return to a discussion of the negative.*   You have already established an understanding of what is wrong and what should be done about it. Leave it. You don't want to take the pleasure out of the praise.

WHEN POSITIVES ARE MAJOR, NEGATIVES MINOR

But there are exceptions to the above advice. One of your subordinates has finished an important task and has done it well *for the most part*. But you found slight fault with some actions or decisions. You want her to learn from this successful experience. Next time, you reason, the job can be done even more skillfully. You must therefore give some minor negative feedback, but you don't want to take away from the sense of genuine accomplishment that she feels. Because of that sense of accomplishment, you may encounter some resistance on her part to accepting anything negative.

The answer is to encourage the subordinate to render a critique of the job.

1.   Ask for her own assessment of the work. For example. "How do you feel about your handling of the project, say, on a scale of 1 to 100?" You'll probably get a high rating.

2.   Ask her to describe the successful steps. Reviewing what she did right can be a useful learning experience.

3.   Encourage her to talk about what went wrong. "Tell me what you think accounts for your not reaching 100." Listen while the other person tells you about relatively minor deficiencies.

4.   Add your analysis. First, though, ask whether she is agreeable to your adding your comments. Probably the subordinate will agree. Reinforce the positive points, in addition to the negatives that she has mentioned. If you have some additional points, positive and negative, go over them briefly.

5.   Ask for a plan of improvement. "If the situation comes up on a similar project or job in the future, how would you handle it, knowing what you know now?"

It is true that the above approach puts the positive before the negative. But since the emphasis is overwhelmingly positive and the first part of the critique is handled by the subordinate, there will be little or no resistance to the negative feedback. In addition, the criticism has been put in the proper proportion. It is almost as if you were saying, "You were excellent this time. How can you be perfect next time?"

CRITICIZING THE RESISTANT EMPLOYEE

From time to time you will encounter employees who are very defensive and resistant when being criticized. They are thin-skinned. Your problem is that their defensiveness often blocks their hearing what you want them to hear. Such an employee presents you with a special challenge. The following recommendations have been developed to help you with the resistant employee.

Get Right to the Point

With another employee, you might believe that some history could be useful. For example, "A few years ago we had a rash of Workers' Compensation claims because of the way some of the warehouse-men were lifting boxes. As a result we developed specific procedures . . . " However, with an unusually sensitive person, eliminate the preliminaries and describe the behavior that you want to criticize. If you indulge in any prefacing, you just give him or her time to start getting tense and resistant.

Don't try to relax with small talk. Small talk, of course, is out of place in criticism sessions anyway, but you might be tempted to use it to get the employee in a more positive, accepting frame of mind. Don't. Chances are the employee will "smell" the criticism coming. Delay will raise his or her anxiety level.

Keep Your Remarks Brief

This is good advice generally when you are giving negative feedback but, in the case of the thin-skinned person, the longer you talk (granted that you're feeling a bit tense yourself), the greater the chance that you'll repeat yourself, and the greater the possibility that the person will blow out of proportion the deficiency that you are talking about. And this kind of person does that easily, without your help.

Be Firm About the Objective

Again, this is advice for any kind of criticizing session, but with the thin-skinned person, you may have to get tough. Defensive people usually produce clouds of words in their anxiety. You have to cut in periodically and remind him or her of what you want. "Yes, I can see that you are having trouble with Elaine, but the issue is this: I want all files back in their proper place within an hour of when you receive them." Don't try to be subtle or terribly "reasonable." Avoid being argumentative. For example, if you get a long, self-justifying explanation of why such-and-such isn't done, and if you don't see a close connection to the issue, you may say, "I don't see what this has to do with what we're talking about right now." That may trigger another long response or defense. Stick to the simple formula: "Let's not lose sight of what we're talking about. I want. . . . "

Accept the Employee's Feelings

This is especially important advice in dealing with a highly defensive person, and you may have to be more explicit about your acceptance than you are when criticizing another employee. You might say, "Mary, no one likes to be criticized. I know how you feel. I'm not trying to put you down. My job is to see that everyone works effectively. When you don't complete assignments on time, you aren't working effectively. I want you to get work done on time."

Be Constructive When Possible

With some employees, you can simply agree on what has to be done. But you may have to take more care with the sensitive employee and explain how what you want may be accomplished. Even in your explanation you'll probably have to employ much tact: "You might find it helpful to do what I do, which is to break the job down into segments. Each segment has a time period for completion. With a schedule you'll know if you're behind."

Wait Out the Emotions

If the employee's reaction is very emotional, even tearful, just fall silent and wait until the moment passes. You won't accomplish much by trying to shut the emotions off or denying the employee his or her feelings. No doubt they are very real. You don't have to reinforce them either. When they seem to subside, resume the interview.

Of course, you should follow the recommendations for a criticism session as summarized here.

FLOW OF THE CRITICISM INTERVIEW

LEARN FROM YOUR CRITICISM

Criticism is obviously a learning experience for the person receiving the feedback. But it should be for the criticizer as well. If you do not see criticism as a chance for you to learn, you could be missing much. For example, you could lose the opportunity to uncover some organizational problems you didn't know existed, problems that interfere with the motivation of more than the one employee. It is true that you don't want to be sidetracked during a criticism interview, but it is equally true that you don't want to ignore related problems that cry out for attention. Your employee might not have been able to do the job properly because, as you discover, another employee who was supposed to supply necessary data or help has begun to drink on the job.

You might even discover that you are part of the problem. The employee may say, "Yes, I agree the job was not done right. But every time I made some progress, you interrupted me with a rush project that had to be done yesterday."

Criticism is an investment. If the work is to be done as you want it to be done, you have to insist that behavior that gets in the way be corrected—and the sooner, the better.

Criticism is really considerate. The employee wants to do the work as it should be done. Your feedback, even though it is negative, is necessary and welcome because it guides the employee to better results.

CHECKLIST FOR CRITICISM INTERVIEW

		Yes	No
1.	I criticized as soon as possible after the event or behavior.	___	___
2.	The interview was in private.	___	___
3.	I stuck to describing the deficient behavior.	___	___
4.	I described behavior specifically.	___	___
5.	The behavior I discussed was observed by me (except for a supervisor's documented report).	___	___
6.	I avoided discussing attitudes.	___	___
7.	I avoided discussing previous, unrelated behaviors that were a problem.	___	___
8.	I avoided interviewing while angry.	___	___
9.	I did not repeat hearsay.	___	___
10.	I did not mix positive with negative feedback.	___	___
11.	I took time to make sure that the employee understood and agreed on the problem.	___	___
12.	I listened carefully to the employee's analysis of the problem.	___	___
13.	When discussion strayed, I reminded the employee of the change desired.	___	___
14.	I enlisted the employee's aid in looking for an alternative or solution.	___	___
15.	If the problem was beyond the control of the employee, I made a note to develop an action plan for improving conditions.	___	___
16.	I emphasized the consequences of continuing the undesired behavior.	___	___

	Yes	No
17. I accepted the employee's feelings.	——	——
18. The employee and I agreed on an action plan for improvement.	——	——
19. I made sure that the employee understood what was to be done.	——	——
20. We agreed on a time frame for accomplishment of the change and what follow up would be done.	——	——
21. I looked for something I could learn from the discussion.	——	——

15

GETTING—AND MAINTAINING—THE BEHAVIOR YOU WANT

Reward the behavior you want; don't reward the behavior you don't want. The employees' behavior that you reward is very likely to be the behavior they repeat. In that sense, you have a great deal of power. You have rewards, and some of those rewards are very important to employees. What you reward is what you can expect to see more of. Thus, when you grant rewards, be sure that you are encouraging the behavior you want.

As a manager, your first concern should be the performance of the people who report to you. Logically, that is what you encourage— good performance. But surprisingly, that is often not the basis on which rewards are given. Chances are you can see instances in your own organization of the following values (other than performance) that prompt rewards.

Not Making Waves

Some organizations value tranquility over anything else. People who agitate for changes that they believe are beneficial often receive the label of troublemaker. Their ideas threaten the way things have been done traditionally, they seem to criticize past judgments, or they infringe upon someone's power and status. In their enthusiasm for change and progress, they often step on people's toes, creating conflict. While in some organizations, conflict is an indicator that good things are happening, in others it is not to be tolerated. People who bring conflict about and create dissent are lepers. If they press too hard or make too much noise, they may be given assignments or relocated out of the mainstream. Management stops listening to them.

Other employees view the humiliation or the neutralization of the would-be innovator and conclude that it doesn't pay to make waves. They are absolutely correct. Around here, they say, you keep a low profile, stay out of trouble, and do what you have to do. People who become ambitious and work to excel are bound to threaten someone. Better not to do it. Placidity and mediocrity abound.

Guilt

People who have been passed over for promotion, or who have only a couple of years to go before their pension is available, or who have become obsolete, sometimes get rewarded primarily out of guilt. It's a strange phenomenon. Employees outlive their usefulness to the organization, or perhaps never had much value in the first place. Management should have taken corrective action, but didn't. Management feels guilty about its inaction, its failure to establish the proper working relationship with the employee. Partly as a result of the guilt (knowing that it has not been fair to the organization or to the employee) management continues to find rewards for the inadequate employee.

Guilt rewards can become bizarre. One manager was kept in a managerial position long after it became clear to executives that he was simply not competent. Actually he was considered so incompetent—by his employees, other managers, his boss—that people felt sorry for him. Executives also felt guilty that they had done nothing to right the situation. It was easier, apparently, for them to give big raises each year. Finally, biting the bullet, they told this inadequate manager to go home, wait out the year until he could draw his pension, and collect complete salary and full benefits for that year.

The message for others: It doesn't matter whether you do a good job or not, you'll get a nice piece of the cake.

Loyalty

In almost every organization, there are the old faithfuls. They are company people, loyal, reliable, and steady. They probably have low absentee records. It's wonderful to be able to recognize such steadfastness, such loyalty, but only if the performance matches. To reward those characteristics when the performance has not also been admirable is to let everyone know that all you have to do around here is to stick it out. You put in your time. That's what counts.

Halo Effect

In the case of the halo effect, the employee receives a reward for an attractive skill or characteristic that causes the manager to overlook deficiencies in other aspects of the employee's performance. Some employees package themselves well, are unusually articulate, are positive and assertive. They sell themselves well. Unfortunately they can't perform beyond the initial merchandising of themselves. But the packaging keeps them going, wins them rewards, because their bosses are impressed.

In another case, a manager was immensely impressed by a subordinate's intelligence. In fact, the employee was erudite. He was a so-so performer but an admired conversationalist. The manager overlooked the performance, and gave high marks to the intelligence.

Friendship

The boss feels temperamentally or intellectually closer to some subordinates than others. In one department, the manager regularly had lunch with three employees with whom he had close rapport. To other employees it seemed as if the choice assignments and the bigger rewards went to these three. They weren't incompetent, but in the eyes of their co-workers they were no more competent than others. The message: Get close to the boss; that's what counts when the rewards are passed out.

Potential

Recognition is given not for what employees do but for what the manager thinks they are capable of doing—someday. The manager may justify such rewards as encouragement. He or she may say something such as, "I know that Ellen isn't working quite up to expectations, but I know she has great ability, and I want to encourage her." Meanwhile other employees are performing well and feeling somewhat aggrieved over Ellen's special place.

Politics

The employee has a friend or a relative in a high place in the organization. Or a mentor. The employee's manager hopes to build a reservoir of goodwill with the highly placed person by bestowing rewards conspicuously on the employee. Performance may have nothing to do with it.

There are other bases for nonperformance rewards. Sex is a somewhat obvious one, still to be observed in spite of the feminist movement and the antidiscrimination laws. Another is intimidation. The manager is somewhat fearful of the employee.

Many rewards that are given for reasons other than the quantity and quality of the employee's work are rooted in goodwill and good intentions. For the most part, they may seem quite innocent. Certainly in the case of guilt, compassion, or friendship, the act of giving nonperformance rewards is very human. But if you do it, accept the consequences of the reinforcement you are extending. Perhaps the greatest risk you take is creating misunderstanding, both in the person reinforced and those who see the reinforcement.

Other employees who are committed to working according to your standards and who share your desire to achieve organizational goals will probably experience demotivation when they see their less involved, less conscientious co-workers receiving the same rewards and treatment as they. Thus, when management does not clearly reward the behavior they want, when they unwittingly encourage performance that isn't up to desired standards, they risk getting more of the poor or mediocre performance, not only from employees who have always worked below par but from people who have been good workers but who are now demotivated by what they regard as injustice.

KEEPING PRIORITIES CLEAR

Recognize exactly what you want to reward, and be sure that employees recognize it also. If everyone in your department receives merit increases that are substantially equal, then you risk conveying the message that it doesn't matter how well you work here, you'll still share in the benefits. In one company, all employees received a bonus in the first week of December. The percentage of salary on which the bonus was based was the same for everyone. It was never clearly explained to those employees why they received the bonus. What the company hoped to achieve by granting the bonus is a mystery. It made the employees feel good for a few days. But it probably had a negligible effect on motivation.

Remember that when everything is rewarded, nothing is. If you treat everyone equally, or try to, you may undermine your own effectiveness. If you strive to be "fair" about giving out the interesting work, if you distribute responsibility impartially, if you grant rewards equally to all employees, then you may be encouraging behavior you don't want. People who habitually straggle in late, who are absent a great deal, who are careless about quality or deadlines, will probably continue their counterproductive habits because they feel rewarded for doing so.

Clearly, your best managerial policy is to reward for the performance that meets or exceeds your standards.

One of the best rewards you have to give is praise. But as was pointed out in an earlier chapter, many managers don't know how to use praise to best effect. The next section gives some recommendations to apply to your praising.

HOW TO PRAISE

If you want the benefits of praising your employees, if you want them to feel good about what they've done, and if you want them to repeat the behavior that you've recognized, then you must follow some rules.

1. *Be consistent.* When praiseworthy performance occurs, don't miss the chance to praise it. Soon people will understand that not only do you want good work but that you will reward it. This doesn't mean that every day you come to the office or plant and say to your high performers, "You're doing a great job. Keep it up." That, for a number of reasons, won't be effective. But you must make sure that people who perform according to your standards understand that you appreciate what they do. Occasionally you may want to pull an employee aside for special attention. Periodically you'll want to make sure that good performers are reminded that you are still appreciative. The point is that you don't have to tell good performers each day that they are good. You do have to reinforce them intermittently. When someone really excels on a task or assignment, don't be inhibited. Furthermore, when an employee is trying new behavior that looks successful, applying new skills or knowledge, give praise often.

Just make sure there is not one high performer in your department who is uncertain about your appreciation.

2. *Be honest.* Praise what is deserved. Earlier in the chapter the point was made that managers often praise characteristics

other than those of performance, such as amiability and loyalty. But keep your message clear. If it is good performance you want, then that is what you praise. But praise only when the performance truly merits it.

3. *Be proportionate.* Praise doesn't cost anything, but it shouldn't be carelessly expended. Watch out for situations such as the following when you might be tempted to praise excessively and out of proportion:

☐ You feel compassion for someone who has been having a rough time personally, and through your praise you want the person to know you care.

☐ One of your employees has performed consistently low, and suddenly shows promise of doing much better. You shower praise on the employee because you feel good about your success with that person as a manager and because you want to give encouragement.

☐ An employee you like very much has performed in an exemplary manner, and you feel much warmth toward that person. You praise extravagantly, knowing that you are biased.

When you praise out of proportion to the performance, you risk losing your credibility not only with the other employees who witness it but with the praised employee, who must know he or she doesn't deserve the excess.

4. *Be specific.* Managers sometimes say such things as, "You're doing a great job," or "Keep up the good work." Such comments may be better than no recognition at all, but they don't have much impact. The trouble is that they don't define what aspects of an employee's performance you like. For example, you might tell a salesman, "Charlie, you're tough, and I like that. You really hang in there. Three times the prospect tried to terminate the interview, and each time you came back with another close."

To the subordinate who has written a clear, concise report, you may say, "You don't know how much I appreciated the way you made your point clearly and quickly. I didn't have to read several pages and wonder what it was all about."

The more specific you are about what you want and like, the greater the likelihood that it will be repeated. Also the subordinate will feel complimented that you were so observant. Finally, being specific prevents you from falling into the sameness trap: Your feedback doesn't always sound alike.

5. *Emphasize behavior.*   Referring back to the example of Charlie the salesman, the manager might have said simply, "I like your toughness." That could be a personality trait. And it could be manifested in any number of ways, not all of them good.

If you wish to praise someone's personality, translate the attitude or trait or characteristic into behavior. To illustrate, saying "You're popular with your co-workers" doesn't encourage repetition of important behavior. But try instead, "The people who work with you tell me that you try to accommodate their requests whenever you can. And when you can't, you always give a full explanation. They tell me they like that about you." The subordinate knows what behavior has made her popular and what to continue to do.

6. *Praise soon after the event.*   What is true in negative feedback is especially true in positive reinforcement. What the employee has done that is praiseworthy is still fresh in his or her mind shortly after. Recognizing the performance immediately offers greater insurance that the behavior will be repeated in the form you wish. Also, immediacy underlines the value you put on the specific performance. "Susan, I couldn't help hearing you on the phone with that customer. Apparently he was furious. I like the way you calmly kept coming back to his practice of paying late and how that has caused his problems. Very good way to handle that kind of person."

Delayed recognition of praiseworthy performance sometimes conveys a by-the-way quality. The praise loses impact. There is the unfortunate suggestion that the behavior wasn't worth mentioning at the time.

PUBLIC VS. PRIVATE PRAISE

How public should you be with your praise? After all, you want others in your work group to know that you will recognize good performance. At the same time, you don't want anyone to feel discriminated against. For example, one manager put out a memo citing several employees for meeting standards consistently. They were pleased, but one employee was outraged. She reminded the manager that she had been disadvantaged by having to work under certain constraints that the others had not had to work under. There was some merit to her case, although the manager felt she was rationalizing a bit. But her feelings and perceptions were what counted. She was demotivated. The manager admitted that she should have tried to anticipate the reaction of the hurt employee.

Good advice: Anticipate how not only the recipients of public praise but also those who are not so recognized will respond.

Really outstanding performance by an individual can usually be recognized publicly, especially if the performance has been exceptional for a long time. "Mary Beth has led the unit in sales each year for the past five years." That is certainly not an accident. Mary Beth is consistently doing something right, and that should be noted.

When to go public with praise is not always easy to define. For you, the manager, there are advantages in public recognition of subordinates that will in turn reflect favorably on you. But always ask yourself these questions:

☐ *Is the performance you praise something that others in the department can also achieve?* If the performance is due largely to a talent not shared by others, you are probably best advised to keep your praise private, directed solely to the talented performer.

☐ *Have others in the work group been working under constraints or restrictions that have reduced their chances of duplicating the exceptional performance you want to praise?* They may feel disadvantaged when you praise someone who is free of the restraints they have had to put up with. Consider the possible demotivating effects of your public praise.

The above recommendations for praising and the considerations for rewarding in public or in private apply generally to giving any kind of reward.

CHANGING EMPLOYEE BEHAVIOR

One of your employees is bright but disappointing in meetings. He becomes defensive, doesn't listen, and interrupts others.

A saleswoman gets very flustered during the closing process. She gives an excellent presentation, has great credibility, but her nervousness at the time she asks for the order undermines much of the good work she has done.

Both of these people are capable and motivated. Their behaviors need some adjusting. They want to be more effective, and with some behavior change they can be. Most people are agreeable to changing their ways of doing things and interacting with others when it makes sense to them and will bring rewards.

You are in a position to help your valuable employees to alter their behavior so that they can achieve more satisfaction. Techniques of behavior modification are relatively easy. *Behavior modification* is a term, however, that carries much negative connotation. People tend to confuse modification with brainwashing or manipulation. Actually behavior modification is an open, honest process. Each person, in your case you and the subordinate, agree to the change and know exactly what is going on during the change. There is nothing covert, deceitful, or undignified.

Here are some techniques you can use to help your employees to make changes in their behavior that will result in greater effectiveness.

Choose the Right Time To Talk About the Ineffective Behavior

Sometimes when an employee has gone through a rough, frustrating experience as a result of the present behavior, he or she is ready to talk about how to make a change. For example, an employee who works poorly in meetings has had a particularly bad time trying to communicate with and influence his colleagues. He feels somewhat "beaten up" as a consequence. He is probably more receptive to your suggestions that you help him to learn other behaviors that would make him more influential and acceptable.

Your saleswoman has had a run of interviews with no orders. She is probably open to the idea of discussing how she could achieve better results through changing behavior.

However, even when the subordinate doesn't see the need for a change, the manager may be able to do a bit of persuading: "I have to tell you that as a result of the way you talked with that employee, a grievance has been filed. It's going to cost us a lot of time and money."

Some managers prefer to discuss behavioral objectives during periodic coaching sessions to avoid the implication of blaming the employee for a serious deficiency or mistake. The message is clearly, "I want to do what I can to help you to be more effective all the way." The occasion and the message are less threatening. Then both manager and subordinate explore ways to more effective behavior and set behavioral objectives along with other goals.

Getting an Agreement

On occasion you might have coached an employee on a behavior change that made sense to you, then wondered why it didn't take hold. Chances are the employee didn't find that the change made sense. If the behavior modification is to be successful, the employee must see it as important and feasible. For example, you have the following conversation with your talkative subordinate about his meetings behavior:

You: The point I'm making is that you have a lot to contribute— if people will listen to you. But when you start to talk, I notice that people around the table look bored or tuned out. It's almost as if they are saying, "Oh, there he goes again." They slump and they fidget and they yawn.

He: I know I blab a lot. But sometimes I can't believe the stuff I hear around that table.

You: I understand what you're saying. But, you know, you might hear things a bit differently if you spent more time listening before answering or defending yourself. All I'm suggesting is that a slight change in your behavior might cause people to sit up and really take notice of the fine things you have to say.

He: You might be right.

Your subordinate is willing to give it a try.

Focus on Behavior

Attitudes are hard to deal with. You probably wouldn't have gotten far with your subordinate had you said, "I think you ought to be less defensive." Instead, you can make a concrete behavioral proposal: "In a meeting, if someone asks you for clarification, answer, by all means. But if someone seems to differ with your opinion, I suggest you sit there for 15 seconds without saying a word." What could happen in those 15 seconds is that someone else might answer the criticism or challenge the difference of opinion. Or the subordinate might find that, through waiting and listening, the other person was not really taking issue. In general his practice had been to jump in quickly with a defense on the assumption that if the co-worker did not immediately seem to agree, that must mean that he or she disagreed.

Recognizing the Change

The best feedback comes from success in trying the new behavior. It might not come at the first attempt or, if it does, it might not be recognized as success by the employee. That's why your reinforcement is so necessary. It answers the question in the subordinate's mind, "Am I really doing it the way we agreed?"

To maintain behavior, occasional reinforcement by you is necessary. From time to time you select some especially good performance at meetings by your subordinate to comment on. You don't have to say much. Just recognize that he has continued to sharpen his skills and that his contributions in meetings are important. That's usually enough to maintain the new behavior. For example, you say, "When you do such a good job I'm sure you can see how much your contributions mean. It must give you a great sense of satisfaction." You've enhanced his internal reward and added an external reward.

PUT MORE SYSTEM INTO YOUR REWARDS

Here's an exercise to help you determine how effective you are in giving rewards and recognizing good performance.

1. Make a list of your subordinates.

2. After each name list the person's performance characteristics that contribute to getting the work done for the accomplishment of your objectives.

3. Ask yourself these questions: How recently have you recognized that performance? How regularly have you rewarded the behavior you want?

4. Review the quick reference checklist of rewards on page 171. Of how many of them have you availed yourself?

What you will probably find is that you are not regularly and predictably recognizing the good work that people do. Furthermore, don't be surprised if you discover that you are not reinforcing with more than a fraction of the rewards available to you.

Keep in mind that increasing the value of the work requires continuing effort. But the payoff in productivity is well worth it.

But what happens when employees come to you asking for rewards, such as a raise or more money, when you can't give them?

TURNING DOWN A REQUEST FOR A RAISE

One of the most delicate issues a manager must face is having to deny a raise to a good performer. You don't want to demotivate the subordinate—or at least you'd like to confine the damage as much as possible. A simple "no" may sound harsh and uncaring. On the other hand, you don't want to talk too much. Otherwise you may seem to say things that aren't necessarily true. Thus, for the sake of showing concern and for preserving your credibility, you must choose your words with great care. Here are some recommendations that can guide you.

Respond Simply and Directly

Express yourself along the lines of "I'd like to, but I can't. There just isn't the money." The employee may try to get you to talk more, perhaps may try to encourage you to promise something for the future. You may want to hold out hope. But unless you have definite indications that you'll have the money in the near future, restrain yourself from making what seem to be promises or assurances. They will muddle your message and may weaken your credibility with your employee.

Maintain Your Credibility with the Subordinate

It may seem harmless to say, "When next month's sales figures are in, we can take another look at the situation," or, "The boss may be in a better mood if we are able to renegotiate the Tate contract." But unless you are certain the picture will change, don't seem to hold out hope. Such replies merely keep the pay issue alive when you would be better off putting an end to it. If you hold out hopes for the future and then have to turn the employee down a second time, you may be tagged as evasive and untrustworthy.

Explain as Much as Is Necessary

Offer an explanation, but be wary of sounding apologetic. Mention the facts behind your inability to give the raise. Make it clear that it is the facts that you regret. It is best to avoid a statement such as, "I'd like to give you the raise, but my boss won't let me." Even if the statement is true, you come across as passing the buck. Saying "I have been told that all salary increases are frozen for the next quarter. I wish I had the power to make an exception, but I don't" is factual, sympathetic, and firm.

Expect Your Explanation To Be Accepted

There is no reason to prepare yourself for a big argument. A subordinate who asks for a raise will often be content to show dissatisfaction with the current salary. If you agree that the subordinate truly deserves a raise, you may want to say so. You probably don't have to say any more than that (and you probably shouldn't). Having made the point and received your assurance that a raise is justified, the subordinate may drop the subject for now.

Avoid the Comparative Trap

If the employee is greatly disturbed over not getting an increase, he or she may want to argue that so-and-so doesn't do nearly the work he does yet gets more money, etc. There is no rational way you are going to win points by joining in and trying to rebut the comparison argument. If you believe he deserves a raise, say, "I don't think how much Art makes has anything to do with the merits of your request. I agree with you that you deserve a raise. But I can't give it to you at this time."

Let the Subordinate Go Over Your Head If Necessary

If the subordinate is not satisfied with your response, let him speak to your boss. He will feel better having given it a good if unsuccessful try. So don't discourage a request to speak to the executive you report to even if you're sure that it will prove to be a futile action.

What about the employee who requests a raise but who, in your opinion, doesn't deserve more money? In such a case, your expressed regret is that the employee does not perform to your satisfaction. And you do not need to apologize for your decision.

DENYING A PROMOTION

It's an awkward moment when a good employee shows up in your office, asking you to promote him or her to a position for which the employee simply is not qualified. There's no question about good work. It's just that it would be inappropriate to consider this person for the greater responsibility.

Some managers would assure the employee that they were considering him or her, even though they were not. But that approach instills unrealistic expectations in the employee. When those expectations are disappointed, the person is bound to feel resentment and suffer demotivation.

The best answer is the truth. Still, the person is a good performer and you'd like to deliver the bad news as gently as possible. Here are some possible steps to take.

Find Out Why the Employee Wants the Job

You don't have to give an answer immediately. Obviously there are reasons why the employee is interested in this job. Encourage the person to talk about them.

Listen

This is a learning opportunity for you. If you want to know what motivates this employee and where he or she wants to go in the next year or two, there is no better chance than now.

Look for Another Option for the Employee

It's possible that the employee is not overwhelmingly set on going into management but rather that he or she would like some kind of change, a new opportunity or challenge.

Level with the Employee

"Look, Jim, that particular job isn't for you, at least at the moment. For one thing, that job calls for a lot of sensitivity in dealing with people, especially those in Bowen's department. Now my observation of you is that you're a very good worker, in fact one of the best, but you like things done your way. That's okay, when you're working alone. But since you wouldn't have any authority over Bowen's people, you'd have to have a lot of tolerance for other people's ways of doing things. And it takes a while to develop that tolerance and patience."

If Jim's enthusiasm for the promotion doesn't waver, continue with something such as, "But it's plain to me that you're ambitious. You want more challenge. I think that's what we ought to be talking about and how to get you ready for something bigger."

Develop a Coaching Plan

One possible reason this employee doesn't see that he is unsuitable is that you have not done an effective job of coaching with him. This employee's unrealistic ambition indicates the area in which you haven't done proper coaching. Right now start developing a plan of growth and action. How can this employee become more skilled in other areas of interest? What goals would be realistic? How can they be achieved? This is your chance to supply the coaching that has been deficient or absent.

REVIEW OF GETTING—AND MAINTAINING—
THE BEHAVIOR YOU WANT

		Yes	No	Not Sure
1.	The employees' behavior that you reward is very likely the behavior they repeat.	___	___	___
2.	When rewarding, your first concern is to reinforce good performance.	___	___	___
3.	Managers confuse employees when they reward not only performance but nonperformance factors such as loyalty, compliance, and friendship.	___	___	___
4.	Good performers may become demotivated by the manager's rewarding on a nonperformance basis.	___	___	___
5.	If you want full value from rewards for good performance, make sure that all employees know exactly what you reward.	___	___	___
6.	If you try to treat everyone equally in giving rewards, you may create demotivation in better performers.	___	___	___
7.	Praise is one of the most effective rewards you have at your disposal.	___	___	___
8.	It is never possible to praise too much.	___	___	___
9.	The more specific you are in praising, the more effective you'll be.	___	___	___

	Yes	No	Not Sure
10. While it is not good to criticize someone's personality, it is all right to praise a personality trait.	——	——	——
11. You should generally criticize in private but praise in public.	——	——	——
12. The reason why people resist behavior modification is that it is manipulative.	——	——	——
13. If people join with you in trying to change their behavior, they must see that change as important and feasible.	——	——	——
14. Behavior change isn't permanent until you change the attitude as well.	——	——	——
15. A good thing to remember is that when everything is rewarded, nothing is.	——	——	——

Answers to Review

1. Yes
2. Yes
3. Yes
4. Yes
5. Yes
6. Yes
7. Yes
8. No. Extravagant praise cheapens its value.
9. Yes
10. Not sure. Generally it's best to translate the trait into some behavior that manifests it.
11. Not sure. There are some circumstances in which even other good performers may be affected adversely by praise of a colleague in public.
12. No. There's no evidence that people resist behavior modification, since it is a public and mutual effort.
13. Yes
14. Not sure. You have no idea whether the attitude is changed. Concentrate on the behavioral change and be content with that.
15. Yes

16

MOTIVATIONAL TECHNIQUES FOR HIGH PERFORMERS

If you are typical, you have some employees who perform diligently for you. They commit themselves to your standards and goals and cooperate with you and their co-workers to turn out a high quantity and quality of production. You have others who have demonstrated not only the potential to do an outstanding job but are working actively and obviously to transform that potential into reality. Then you may have still other employees who have established a record of success but who, for some reason, have slipped in their performance. They are all high performers, now, in the past, and in the future, and they need your attention.

Also, if you are typical, you are probably not giving them the special attention they need and deserve. There are at least two very human and very unfortunate reasons for this. First, the squeaky wheel does need help. You have some people whose work is below standards, who are not effective in achieving departmental goals, and whose behavior is not appropriate. Therefore, you have to intervene, correct, counsel, and guide them. If you don't, the record of the whole work group will suffer.

The second reason why you may not be giving your high performers the attention they deserve is that, in the pressure of time, faced with mounting pressures of deadlines and quotas, you have forgotten. If someone makes a mistake, your alarm system goes off and you give corrective attention. But if people don't make mistakes, if they work smoothly without making a fuss, you may tend to take them for granted. Perhaps you say to yourself, "Well, they are achievers. They get their greatest rewards internally." You may be right that they have strong internal reward systems, but if you think that they do not need your recognition as much as those who get more of your attention, then you could be making a very expensive mistake.

For one thing, people whose good work goes unrecognized for a long time either become demotivated or go elsewhere to get what they want. Therefore, if you neglect them, you may eventually find that you don't have them. In addition, if you improve the performance of high producers, the dividend you reap will be proportionately greater than what you get from efforts to raise the productivity of lesser performers. To be more specific, if you can raise productivity in the better worker by five percent, you may get more than if you doubled the productivity of a less effective employee, because you start with a higher base. The salesperson who turns in $200,000 and whose performance goes up five percent will bring in $210,000. The person who does $100,000 in sales probably needs twice as much of your time and effort to achieve the same increase. In fact, the lesser performer will require more of your effort than you have to give to the higher producer since the former probably has less developed skill.

But when you work with an actual or potential high performer, recognize his or her accomplishment, and help that person to increase motivation and effectiveness, you not only achieve worthwhile results in the person you work with but also in your whole department. This occurs because you advertise a very important message: When you perform well here, you will get attention, help, and recognition. You won't have to endure the attitude of, "What's the use? Around here, you do a good job, and no one notices." Quite the contrary, you say through your actions, "You do better, you receive more."

Clearly, then, your high performers need your help and attention. The work you do with them to improve their effectiveness and intensify their motivation can pay handsomely for you.

IDENTIFYING YOUR KEY PEOPLE

Part of your responsibility is to know who are the cornerstones of your work group. That may sound easy to do, but bias may get in your way. You have closer rapport with some people and may therefore tend to exaggerate their importance to the department. Other employees possess certain qualities that you especially admire and, as a consequence, you may overlook some serious deficiencies. In contrast, you may dislike other employees, and that dislike may cause you to overlook good performance characteristics. You need to look beyond the bias that you and everyone else are prone to exhibit.

Make a list of all the people who report to you. About each person, ask yourself the following questions:

- ☐ *Uniqueness.* What can this person do that no one else can do?
- ☐ *Superiority.* What does this person do better than anyone else? It can be useful to record high-level skills even if they are not necessarily unique in your department. Then ask yourself, "Who performs regularly in a superior fashion?"
- ☐ *Indispensability.* What would happen if this person stopped doing the job? Perhaps other people could fill the gap. Then again, although the work would get done, perhaps others wouldn't do it as well.
- ☐ *Interdependence.* What other employees' work depends on this person? Think about quantity as well as quality of work. If someone else were to take over and do less work or work

of lesser quality, how would that affect the performance of other employees? If a serious inconvenience would result, this person would have special value.

These are some of the people to whom you must pay special attention. Ask yourself the following questions with respect to your key performers:

1. Do I regularly convey to them my expectations that they continue to perform in the outstanding way they have performed?

2. Do I, when necessary, give them both positive *and* negative feedback that will help them to sharpen their skills and to achieve even higher standards?

3. Do I, when it is deserved, recognize and reward good performance from key people so that they and others know that in my department such performance is always rewarded despite my personal relationships and attitudes toward the people doing the work?

HELPING YOUR STAR SHINE MORE

As part of the special attention you give to exceptional performers in your work group, make sure you include the recommendations given below.

Set High Standards for Them

Good performers welcome them. But they must also know what they are. Don't assume that people who work well for you know what those standards are. High standards, incidentally, provide high satisfaction when they are met. So, as with the high jumper, move the rod up a bit each time your goals and standards of performance are met.

Provide Independence

You don't need to supervise the star performer closely. In fact, you might contribute to demotivation if you do. But you can be a resource. You are there if the employee needs the special help you can provide. But don't let go of the reins altogether. That may be interpreted as an "I don't care" attitude. Your exceptional performer doesn't want you to stop being boss. He or she just wants more control over what is done and how.

Give Feedback

You may feel that the star performer knows that she is doing a good job. Perhaps. But don't trust the possibility. She needs to hear it from you. When the outstanding subordinate does it wrong or not well, she needs to hear that, too. Nothing demotivates faster than the feeling of an employee that, "I'm floundering, and the boss doesn't seem to care."

Show Pride in Your Subordinate's Success

Your caring manner adds impact to your praise. For example, the employee has written a project report. You read it, stick your head in the door of the person's office, and say that it is first rate. But your praise and esteem gain value if you take five minutes to sit down, go over the report, and talk about what you especially like about it, what you think is outstanding.

When you talk about your exceptional performer to others outside the department, let him or her know about it. Make a point of saying, "I had lunch today with Rick Blake, and I told him about that terrific overhaul you did with the inventory reporting system."

Reward Periodically

True, the star gets much satisfaction from his or her internal reward system. Factors such as self-esteem, achievement, and progress in one's skills area mean a great deal. But find ways of recognizing the achievement such as praise, perquisites, and special privileges. You may want to review the various kinds of rewards described in Chapter 6.

As you read through the above items, your reaction may be that you should take many of these steps with any person who performs well. That's true, but some of them are for the person who performs exceptionally over a period of time.

MANAGING PEOPLE WHO DON'T LIKE BEING MANAGED

In many respects ideal subordinates are capable, experienced, reliable, and agreeable. They take great pride in their work, especially since they do it in their own way. That can be a problem to you. You may like a task to be done one way, and they insist on doing it another. Some persistent people may simply be an annoyance. Other people, however, who persist in going it alone can interfere with productivity, with the work of those who depend on them, and with meeting deadlines. You need to find ways of managing people who don't like to be managed without demotivating them. Here are some suggestions.

Discuss Assignments in Detail

Rather than telling such an employee flatly what to do and how to do it, alert the person to the results you want. Let the employee suggest to you how he or she will achieve them. If the employee proposes procedures you cannot approve, explain your objections. Then ask the subordinate to work out an alternate way. Allowing the employee to participate in deciding how the work is to be done gives him or her the freedom to choose what is enjoyed most. This choice is a powerful motivator. At the same time you can make sure that the employee's course of action meets with your approval.

Emphasize the Big Picture

Very often such employees do things in their own way because they reason that it doesn't matter how they do things, as long as they do the job, and do it well. They act only on their own interests and those demanded by the specific work at hand. In doing so, they lose sight of the big picture. One way for you to cope with this myopia is to try to convince them that their work is not done in isolation. Show them how their failure to obey orders or follow conventional means causes trouble for others.

Respect Their Needs

Chances are the people who disregard directions are motivated by pride in themselves and in their own work. This is especially true of some people in highly routine, monotonous jobs, where it is difficult for them to establish any real sense of identity. Because of the need for self-expression, they may complicate something basically simple just to personalize their efforts.

If this seems to be true of some of your subordinates, give them outlets through which they can express and utilize their individuality. There are occasions on which you can give the independent employee the freedom to develop both tasks and means. Make sure, though, that you establish clear distinctions between the tasks in which the employee has a relatively free rein and those in which he or she does not.

Reinforce the Behavior You Want

If you want an employee to follow orders when he has had a tendency not to do so, you must reward him when he does as you wish. This kind of positive action is usually more effective than the negative action of berating him when he does not do what you asked him to do.

INTEGRATING THE HIGH POTENTIAL EMPLOYEE

You have hired a promising employee with a good track record elsewhere. Understandably, you are pleased that you were able to bring her on board. But because this new employee, no matter how promising she may be, has not performed for you and with the members of your work group, you must be careful how you introduce the new person. Too much praise may in fact create the risk of demotivation. In the entrant, your high expectations create pressure that could result in anxiety. And you probably have unwittingly fallen into that trap because you are trying to convince the people in the department that you would not have gone outside except for someone unusual. You could turn them off by your praise of the new person, which they regard as excessive. You seem thereby to discount the value of the work they have done for you.

Therefore you must walk a very fine line between explaining why you went outside the company and how you found this extraordinary person without causing motivational damage to the new employee or to the steady members of your work group.

Follow these suggestions:

☐ *Emphasize the Newcomer's Record in Terms of the Qualifications to Join Your Team.* You might announce that you "looked long and hard for a person who could measure up to this department. I'm convinced that Jan's record shows she can do it."

☐ *Talk About What Your Group Can Do for Her.* "Jan brings some unusual experience and qualifications. However, she hasn't been handling the kinds of challenges you've been meeting here. I know you'll give her everything you can in the way of cooperation."

☐ *Touch on What Jan Brings to the Group.* "We have a work group second to none. There were a few credentials that Jan has in the way of training and experience that we don't have in our group. It would have taken us perhaps a year to get these credentials. Since Jan has them already, it made sense to bring her on board and make use of them now."

☐ *Give Credit Close to Home.* "We attract good people because of our reputation. When you have a first class team, you are able to bring in a first class person like Jan."

HELPING YOUR SENIOR EMPLOYEES STAY VALUABLE

He was an outstanding producer for much of the time he worked with you. She was loyal and very committed. They were valued employees during their prime. But now they seem to have retired on the job. Hardworking employees, as they grow older, can sometimes seem to coast their way through the final years to retirement. And there's no reason why you should simply abandon these once-valued assets.

Faced with senior employees, many managers make certain assumptions:

☐ "The older employee doesn't want to take risks. The primary concern of the preretiree is to hold on to the job until pension time."

☐ "Since senior employees recognize that they have been passed over for advancement, they really have no incentive to put out extra effort."

☐ "Change represents a threat to older people. Why should they disturb themselves and take risks?"

☐ "Reduced effort is how they see their reward for having put in hard work and shown loyalty for all those years."

Any or all of these attitudes may have been adopted by the person whose performance has become increasingly disappointing. You as manager can reinforce these attitudes by being indifferent to them. Or you may inadvertently create the impression that you expect such attitudes among senior employees, and you may wind up getting just what you expect. In either case, of course, you are helping to create a liability that you can ill afford. It is not a matter of only one senior employee but your entire work force: They will probably come to resent the extra burdens they must assume to make up for their colleague's declining performance.

The older employee represents a valuable resource: He or she possesses experience, knowledge of the operation, and seasoned judgment. Perhaps you can't always stoke up the old enthusiasm, but there are ways you can help the oldster to be useful still and to want to work effectively for you. Here are several ideas.

Consider Expanding Responsibility

This traditional method of restimulating an employee's motivation has much in its favor. Perhaps the senior employee's job has become old hat. (You might well have encouraged the coasting by deciding not to change the employee's responsibility.) What additional duties can you give older subordinates? How can you enlarge their responsibilities? Don't be afraid to dangle a new challenge or adventure in front of them. You might be surprised to find them enthusiastic about accepting it.

Change the Job Completely

Maybe the senior person wants a complete change. In one company a manager wanted to create an important new position of assistant to him. But he did not have anyone in the younger group quite willing to step into it. He asked an older employee to take it on for two years while he could groom someone else for it. The older man was delighted, and assisted in training a younger employee to fill his shoes.

Offered a choice between staying in the old, comfortable routine for two or three years until retirement or experiencing new and exciting responsibilities, the senior employee may well choose to be shaken up for a short time, and to go out in glory.

Assign the Older Employee to a Task force

There are undoubtedly persistent problems that you have wanted to tackle but have not felt that you could justify the time. Or, even though the department has been running well, there is always room for improvement and an innovation that would cut costs or time or people from a sequence or a process. There is probably no one who is better informed about the operation than your senior person. Form a task force to explore the problem or an innovation. One of your key members will be the old-timer. Peer stimulation and pressure may serve to tap resources no longer being exercised.

Provide Counseling Geared to the Future

There are emotional and practical pressures on soon-to-be-retired employees. Relieving those feelings of anxiety can only have a beneficial impact on work. Arrange for these employees to talk with someone in the personnel department or from the outside who is knowledgeable about the financial considerations of retirement, such as health plan continuance, pension, and Social Security benefits. If counseling is available, encourage the older person to meet regularly with the professional to talk over any fears and anxieties about leaving the workaday world.

Whatever the new goals you help the older employee to set, to spur him or her on to greater productivity, remember these tips. Keep them:

☐ *Practical.* Any reeducation or change should satisfy both the organization's and the individual's needs.

☐ *Specific.* Each step in the process of development should have a beginning and an end, with a time limit.

☐ *Imaginative.* Combine appeal and flexibility, so that the person doesn't feel "boxed in" or "shoved aside."

☐ *Attainable.* The goals must be attainable even though the individual may have to stretch a bit to meet them.

THE AMBITIOUS SUBORDINATE

Sometimes you can do so well in managing the motivation of people that one of them aims for your job. You are bound to have ambivalent feelings about this employee. On the one hand, this person points to your success as a manager. On the other hand, you can't overlook the fact that his or her ambition is directed at your job and you.

By following certain recommendations you may be able to utilize the resources of this able employee without fearing unduly for your own security and without demotivating him or her.

Have Ambitions Yourself

If you have a path already marked out for yourself, then you will feel less threatened. If you want to go further in the organization, one mark in your favor is a good record of success in developing the resources of subordinates. The fact that you are being crowded is evidence in your favor. Don't tie yourself to one path. There are too many variables that could spoil your plans. Have an alternative route of progression. One thing is certain: You will have less apprehension about your would-be successor if you have a career strategy of your own.

Feed the Subordinate's Ambition in a Practical Way

Don't discourage the employee. Take advantage of her ambition to expand your job. You can gain more time to solve problems and to innovate if you give her assignments that you might otherwise feel obliged to do yourself. Help her direct energy into constructive channels. This will assure the employee that she is being given every opportunity to move ahead while you benefit from her talent. In short, the subordinate gets to do more of the kind of work she wants to do, you get to do more of what you want to do, and the greater glory accrues to you.

Be Open About the Chances

Unless you know for certain of a specific opening and when it will be available, confine your encouragement to the generalities. There's no point in building false hopes which, when shown to be just that, will cause the subordinate to resent and distrust you (and others, too, if they are looking on). If the organization cannot offer the subordinate the upward mobility he or she wants, face the fact that you will lose the subordinate in time. But in the interim, you will have gained from the loyalty, commitment, motivation, and productivity of an able assistant.

Here are specific recommendations to follow when you know that you cannot promote an able and ambitious subordinate.

Put the Subordinate on His or Her Own

Reduce the amount of monitoring and managing you do. Let the subordinate have greater control over his or her assignments, scheduling, methods, and the like.

Make the Employee a Project Manager

Give him or her some associative management authority on specific projects. Let the employee (under your guidance) run some part of the operation or your program; in effect, this lets him or her handle some of the administrative details you have previously kept to yourself.

Make the Ambitious Subordinate a Teacher

Use the person's proven skills and knowledge to break in new employees and to supervise their orientation and integration. Perhaps the employee can teach older subordinates new skills. In the process the able and ambitious subordinate will learn more about managing people.

Use the Subordinate as a Consultant

Use the person's experience and skills to solve problems that the organization faces. If Stanley's knowledge and experience could be useful, offer him on a temporary basis to another department. Or if the organizational structure doesn't permit that, form a task force with the help of other managers to handle interdepartmental problems with him as chairperson. Get his ideas on product planning, organization changes, and procedures. Give him some of the tough problems you've been wanting to work on but for which you probably haven't had the time.

Have Him or Her Trained

Arrange for the subordinate to be trained in an area that is valuable to you and new to him or her. Let him or her become your group's expert in some vital area of the operation. While he or she is learning a skill or acquiring credentials, there is less likelihood of the person's leaving you.

BRINGING A SUBORDINATE BACK FROM FAILURE

A subordinate who has proven capability and a fine performance record has suffered a significant failure or has made a serious error that has resulted in much expense or inconvenience. Your problem may not have ended with the mistake or failure—or with the counseling, if you conducted such. You may have to be on watch for lowered self-esteem and self-confidence on the part of the subordinate. You may have to render special help if his or her future performance is not to suffer.

Here are some optional steps you can take.

Talk Seriously About It

Talk about what happened but put it in perspective. Yes, it was a setback, but hardly a disaster. Both the employee and the organization will survive. Take the employee's fear of not surviving into consideration. Assure him or her that this failure has not put the employee in a position to be fired.

Discuss with the Subordinate

☐ *What Went Right.* If some part of his or her work that resulted in failure or the mistake was at all noteworthy, mention it. However, don't exaggerate or build up routine accomplishments into triumphs. That won't do him or her any good and could undermine your credibility.

☐ *What Wasn't the Subordinate's Fault.* It could be that other people contributed to the failure or that some factors were beyond the subordinate's control. You might say, for example, "Yes, you could have handled that differently, I suppose, but if I had been in your shoes, I probably would have done the same thing you did." Or, "That was something you couldn't have anticipated, and we should have but didn't." Take responsibility for any mistakes the organization made.

☐ *Where You Agree with the Subordinate About His or Her Mistakes.* You don't have to do much more in most cases than agree with his or her assessment of the mistakes. If the subordinate makes it clear that he or she would like more of a postmortem and if you believe that would be useful, then discuss what you see as better alternatives than the ones the employee chose.

Build Progression into the Subordinate's Tasks

The employee needs some opportunities to see himself in a favorable light. Give him a chance to do that through a wise selection of responsibilities, going from simpler to more complex. This is not to say that the person should be relieved of regular duties. But it is important that he have a crack at extra work in order to see that you are not withholding the extra, challenging assignments.

THE EXCEPTIONAL, DIFFICULT EMPLOYEE

You have a highly valuable employee who is sometimes a pain in the neck. The person is temperamental, insisting that schedules be constructed around her. She does not conform easily to conditions imposed by others. Her standards of performance are high, not because you insist on it, but because they are self-set. She may from time to time throw her weight and temper around. The person's loyalty is plainly to self and her professional field rather than to you and the organization. You feel you need this person, yet wonder how you can live with her. Should you meet the difficult person's need for special treatment?

Here are some considerations.

Insist on Continuing Special Work Performance in Exchange for Special Treatment

Don't use, or let the other person use, past accomplishment or credentials to justify special treatment. The only way you can justify it is by rewarding current productivity, as measured by quantity and quality. Also, be careful not to let the quality blind you to a dip in quantity. This, of course, cannot be an ironclad rule, since occasionally you may have the special employee working on an unusually complicated task. But for the most part insist that goals and quotas be met. Otherwise employees who are producing a greater quantity of work may become resentful.

Be Able to Show Other Employees Reasons for Your Special Treatment

Discuss the work that the exceptional subordinate is doing. Make sure that others know how the work that he or she is doing fits in with that of the entire work group. Be as matter of fact about it as possible. You don't want to emphasize too strongly that you regard the exceptional employee as superior. But you do want them to see what it is that this person does that wins the label of exceptional.

Avoid Excessive Public Praise

The highly performing employee deserves some public praise, of course. But you don't want to alienate others with less capacity who are working to give you the best they can. Always try to remember that there are others in the department whose work, though less outstanding, also is worthy of praise. If everyone believes that their good work will win recognition, then you will create less resentment among the "ordinary" people.

Don't Permit Yourself to Be Bullied

Some anger, sulking, and silence are probably to be expected from the superior subordinate. But never let this person humiliate you in front of others, make public threats, or be rude. If the person wants to have a confrontation in your office, with the door closed, you might allow it. But in public he or she must not embarrass you. Otherwise you will have a work group that will not respect you. That is a price you cannot afford, because it is bound to affect your ability to manage their motivation.

MOVING A WINNER OFF THE PLATEAU

Your high performer seems to have run out of energy, doing the job but with no evident enthusiasm. The employee's past record is very good, but the current record is only adequate. He or she has hit a plateau. You would like to move the employee off that plateau. You would like to help your former star to enjoy the work, do it with eagerness, and reach the level of productivity that he or she previously maintained.

Ask yourself questions such as the following.

Does the Employee Have Enough to Do?

This is an obvious reason for the problem and one often overlooked. Many underutilized people create busywork for themselves (which may consume a lot of energy), or simply retire on the job, doing what is absolutely necessary. They don't have enough to do, or they don't have the kind of work that really challenges them. The solution is not a make-work project. The talented employee needs a project or responsibilities that will demand attention and concentration and spur him or her onward.

Does the Subordinate Have Too Much to Do?

This other extreme can also encourage retirement on the job. The person who is truly burdened beyond capacity—and who may well be reluctant to admit it—will often, in effect, give up. Accomplishing everything the person has to do becomes impossible. So the employee fritters time away, worrying about what cannot get done no matter how much effort he or she expends. This employee needs your help to do the job correctly.

Is the Employee in the Right Slot?

The scientist saddled with administrative work may let down and dream of being back in the lab. A fine accountant may feel uncomfortable supervising the work of other accountants. A former sales manager who has now become a market planner may long for the days of traveling in the field. Their talents are not well suited for the job. People often cope with this kind of frustration by looking for on-the-job excuses to get away from the work.

Is Your Door Really Open?

A subordinate hits a snag that he cannot handle alone. If he feels free to talk about it openly with you, he can get the advice, assistance, and authority needed to get around it. But if you are unavailable, seen as unresponsive, or have shown impatience with people who come asking for help, then he may respond to an obstacle by puttering around and wasting time worrying about it.

Are You Overmanaging the Subordinate?

When a subordinate feels too closely supervised, when the person is given no freedom to make decisions that affect the work and little responsibility for what is done, he or she will become indifferent.

THE UNDERPERFORMER WHO IS OVERMANAGED

You have an employee who seems to have unrealized potential for great things, but who is not performing even well. Consider the possibility that you are overmanaging this person. People with a strong desire to achieve are often uncomfortable with close supervision and may actually do poorer work as a result. If you suspect this subordinate is not working up to potential, and if you have maintained close control (as you probably have because of the performance), you might want to try a different approach, as a test. Here are possible actions:

- [ ] *Don't* set goals for the employee.
- [ ] *Do* let the subordinate set his or her own goals.
- [ ] *Don't* try to inspire the person with pep talks.
- [ ] *Do* give the subordinate specific praise for specific accomplishments.
- [ ] *Don't* try to use money as a carrot. He or she doesn't need a carrot and may resent that you think it necessary. However, don't go to the other extreme and assume money means nothing.

☐ *Do* give the employee as much money as possible but make it a recognition of achievement not a prod to greater performance.

☐ *Don't* give advice about what you think the person ought to do and not do.

☐ *Do* give the subordinate as much specific information—for example, facts and technical assistance—as you can.

☐ *Don't* assume that the subordinate knows that he or she is doing a great job and doesn't need to hear you say it.

☐ *Do* give the person specific feedback on the work he or she does. Always praise the subordinate for a job that is obviously done well.

☐ *Don't* punish the person's errors by tightening control, unless you see a pattern of failure emerging.

☐ *Do* criticize exactly what the subordinate did wrong. Offer knowledge, understanding, and techniques that will help the person to avoid repeating the mistakes.

After a reasonable period of time, you should know whether you have a person with unrealized potential or an employee who doesn't perform well with or without your tight controls.

17

HOW TO DEAL WITH SPECIAL PRODUCTIVITY PROBLEMS

Some employees fall into behavior patterns on the job that constitute management problems for you. Some of those behaviors get in the way of the employees' own effectiveness. At other times the behaviors interfere with smooth working with others. Often the people who exhibit such irritating and counterproductive behaviors know how to do the job adequately. But you suspect that they could do much better if you could neutralize their self-imposed impediments. Usually you can do just that, without having to go through a counseling procedure. The key is to take steps on a regular basis to manage the employees' behaviors. Granted, it takes time to discourage behavior that you don't want and to encourage substitute behavior. But your option is ultimately much more expensive: to put up with barriers to better performance and eventually to counsel. Counseling in most cases proves to be very difficult for you since, by having neglected the behaviors for too long a time, you may have unknowingly reinforced them. They will have become deeply ingrained.

Most people, you will find, are less resistant to gradual attempts to get them to change their ways.

THE NEGATIVE EMPLOYEE

The negative employee is forever making such comments as, "They won't let us do that," or, "I really can't see that being successful here," or, "We tried that, and it didn't work." Every time you or one of your subordinates comes up with a possibly better way to do things, this person can be relied on to show why it won't work. He or she can kill initiative, innovation, and enthusiasm as fast as water can put out a small blaze.

Take the following steps to counteract the influence of such a negative employee.

Don't Try to Argue the Negative Person
Out of the Pessimistic Stand

When the employee says, "It won't work," don't bother to reply, "Sure, it will." You won't get anywhere. You'll just drive the negative person further into nay-saying. This is deeply rooted behavior that you probably can't change by meeting it head on.

Present a Reasonable Optimism

Talk about similar problems in the past for which you did find a solution: "Yes, it's true that when we first tried it, it didn't work. But then we redesigned it. It took us several tries, but we finally got it to work. So it wasn't a failure in the long run."

Perhaps you can't come up with an example of past success. Try saying, for example, "I'm not sure the conditions we faced then are the same as now. Let's look at what may be different today." Or, "Let's talk about this problem some more. I can't believe that we've said everything that needs to be said on the subject."

What you are signaling, of course, is that what will be rewarded most is positive thinking, not uncritical positive thinking but thinking that focuses at least as much on why you should do something as on why you should not do it.

Ask for a Worst-Case Scenario

For example, you reply, "I can see you have a lot of reservations about this change. In your opinion, what's the worst thing that could happen if we go ahead?" You may find that what the negative person regards as a calamity is a condition you might be able to live with or solve. Furthermore, by insisting that the employee give you the worst results he or she can think of, you have taken a lot of the person's bite away. Anything this subordinate can come up with subsequently has to be less severe than the "worst" consequences.

Don't Overrule the Negative Person Too Quickly

The employee is playing a devil's advocate role. Some of the points that are negative may have been overlooked by the planners involved. These points may need to be examined. In addition, the fact that they have been brought up will lead to a better evaluation of options.

Use the Lesser-of-Two-Evils Argument

The negative employee warns that if you choose A, the consequences will be bad. Develop an argument showing that if you do not choose A, the consequences will be worse.

Get a Contract

Let the negative person have the floor. Then say, "All right, I've heard your opinions. Now I want to hear from others. We'll go with the majority. If that decision is different from what you decide, will you commit yourself to the majority view?"

COPING WITH THE HOSTILE EMPLOYEE

A person who is surly and disagreeable can be disruptive in a work group. First, people don't want to have to work with such a person. Second, if the employee resists your managing, you are letting the wrong kind of model exist in your department.

Try Not to Take the Hostility Personally

He or she probably displays it with others. Even when harsh words are directed at you, they're probably not aimed at you as a person. However, you don't have to take abuse. You might respond to such words in this way: "I'm sorry you said that. I really think you'd better think that over. You have nothing to gain by offending me."

Apply Negative Selling

If you want the employee to do something and you receive resistance, be straightforward about the consequences of that resistance. You can't afford to let the employee feel privileged. And you don't want others in the department thinking that all they have to do around here to get your way is to show bad temper.

Use Praise When It Is Deserved

When the hostile person does a good job, it should be recognized. The only way you can hope to help this employee to be more effective on the job is to make doing the right things the right way rewarding for him or her.

DEALING WITH THE DEADLINE MISSER

Meeting deadlines of one sort or another is an important part of many jobs. There are some people who just can't, for one reason or another, meet them on their own. They need help if they are to do the job in the way you—and their co-workers—need to have it done. Take the following steps with the person who misses deadlines.

Make Sure the Job Is Adequately Analyzed in Advance

Many projects involve a number of tasks, each of which must be completed satisfactorily and in sequence if all of the tasks and the whole job are to be done correctly and on time. Poor deadliners often plunge into a project at an inappropriate starting point and then try to handle other stages on a haphazard basis or when the need for their completion becomes all too apparent. The result is that by deadline day the project is not yet complete.

Some people seem constitutionally unable to analyze the requirements of a job on their own and to see how much work it involves. You may find yourself having to help them when you assign them a task. It may be burdensome to do so, but the irritation and inconvenience are far less at the outset than after the deadline has passed.

Insist on a Realistic Schedule

Just as some people are unable to analyze a task in advance, they may also have problems estimating the time frame required to complete it. With them, list the steps involved and gauge the time that each step will take. It will become clear that some steps must be completed before others are started and that this must be taken into account in calculating the total time required.

Set Firm Subgoals

Out of the many tasks that must be accomplished to complete the whole project on time, a few of them are critical. If they aren't completed as planned, much other work will be held up. Thus these subgoals must be taken as seriously as the overall deadline itself. A useful technique is to help the poor scheduler to plot out the various tasks on a calendar, underlining the critical points in red. The planner then concentrates on making sure that these deadlines are met, knowing that less important aspects of the assignment can be handled at the last moment if necessary.

The employee should understand that if he or she fails to meet the deadline on a critical part of the task, you should be notified immediately. The failure to meet the deadline may be explainable and excusable, but the failure to inform you of the failure will definitely result in a poor performance evaluation.

Follow Up on Promises

When you ask an employee who has a history of procrastinating or not completing work on time for a report or a set of figures, say by Tuesday, make sure that on Tuesday you follow up. The employee may well have consented to supply what you asked for but have assigned a low priority to the job. Your follow-up underscores the priority you place on meeting deadlines.

In some cases, the deadline misser tends to go slowly on work because he or she is a perfectionist. It seems to be very difficult for such a person to let go of a task until it has met personal standards of perfection. The need to be perfect may stem from sources deep within the person, far too deep for you to influence. But you don't have to be helpless. Where possible, be more selective about the kinds of work you ask the perfectionist to do for you. Generally, the most desirable assignments for the person preoccupied with extraordinarily high standards are those that:

- ☐ *Can be Extended over a Long Period of Time.* The perfectionist cannot be rushed, so give him or her jobs that must or should be done but don't have to be completed instantly.
- ☐ *Require Detailed Work.* This kind of employee is usually great on detail work that others get impatient or careless with.
- ☐ *Don't Call for More than One Person as the Primary Doer.* Perfectionists tend not to work well with others whose standards are lower. Assign this person work that can be accomplished primarily by one person or one person working only occasionally with others.

THE CHRONIC ABSENTEE

The employee does acceptable work when she is on the job. But her absentee record has become intolerable. Although she always telephones with an excuse, you find it hard to believe the excuse that's offered. You have established to your satisfaction that she can do the job. In this case you have probably already counseled, but with no lasting results. You must take firm, perhaps decisive, action.

Keep Accurate Records

You may need them to prove that you didn't terminate or discipline the person for discriminatory reasons.

Always Have a Postabsence Interview

Don't let an absence go by without an interview. You want to know, once again, why the employee was absent. Your requiring a second explanation plants the suspicion in the employee's mind that you don't believe, or are skeptical of, the excuses offered on the telephone. Even more important, you want the interviews to convey the message that you are keeping a record.

Confront the Employee with the Records

If absenteeism does not improve, show the employee the records. Make a decision. Will you give her another chance to do something about her absenteeism? Or will you discipline or terminate? If you decide to warn and to give her another chance, let the employee know what your action will be should she not improve.

COPING WITH CARELESSNESS

A careless person is annoying, usually expensive, and possibly even dangerous. Careless behavior results in mistakes and work that has to be done over. Here are some steps to take to bring the quality of work up to par.

☐ *Explain and Insist on Standards.* It is especially important that this employee clearly understand what the standards are that he or she should meet in doing the work.

☐ *Don't Give This Employee Hazardous Work.* There's no point in endangering the employee or the employee's co-workers.

☐ *Make Sure the Employee Understands the Consequences of Carelessness.* Explain the inconveniences to fellow employees, expense, delays, errors, risk to the reputation of the department, and so on.

☐ *Maintain Pressure for Careful Work.* This person requires extra monitoring. Failure by you to keep up the pressure may be interpreted by the employee as representing an uncaring, lackadaisical attitude on your part.

☐ *Warn the Employee When He or She Lapses.* When signs of carelessness appear in the employee's work, warn the person formally. He or she needs reminders. You need documentation.

☐ *Take Extra Care in Giving Instructions.* When you tell this employee what you want done, have him repeat your instructions to make sure he understands.

THE "LAZY" EMPLOYEE

When this employee works, he or she works well. It's just that this person doesn't contribute much exertion, doesn't perform extra work, and almost never takes on more responsibility. The performance is not deficient enough to warrant termination, but it vexes you. You think the employee is capable of giving you more, and you'd like that more.

You might consider these steps.

Make Goals and Standards Specific and Clear

Let this person know what you expect—and how you expect it. Spell it out verbally, and, when necessary, in writing. Your orders and directions must be very clear, so that the employee cannot claim later you were vague.

Monitor Performance Carefully

If there are significant lapses, give feedback immediately. If goals aren't met, find out why. If you believe that the employee has no valid reason for not having met them, do not overlook the failure. If you do, your credibility will vanish. You'll lose whatever influence you have.

Never Pile on Work Suddenly

You may be tempted to load much responsibility on the employee suddenly in the belief that it will force him to change. But you will probably be frustrated and disappointed. Sudden disparities between his former work load and the new one will not help you produce convincing documentation in case you want to take disciplinary action.

Create Peer Pressure

If you've created a team concept, let him know how much he is letting his co-workers down, forcing them to work harder because he isn't pulling his share of the load. The employee may respond better to peer pressure than to your influence.

Express Your Disappointment

If the employee has talent or pride, play on them by letting the person know that he has lost your esteem by the lackluster performance.

Try More Challenging Work

It's possible that the employee is bored. Experiment occasionally with more challenging work. If he responds, you may have the key to the solution of the problem.

THE STUBBORN EMPLOYEE

The employee is very stubborn, resistant to change, and locked into one way of doing things. When you ask for a different approach, when the way you want the job done is different from the way he or she does it, you get a hard time. You want this employee to be more versatile and open to ideas and suggestions as well as to be a more smoothly functioning member of the work group.

In Introducing or Suggesting a Change, Get This Employee Involved at the Outset

Don't ask the person what should be done or expect the employee to come up with new ideas on his or her own. Sketch out the results you want and why, and suggest that the employee come up with ways to achieve them.

Listen to the Employee's Objections to Anything New

Expect them. They're going to come. You don't have to argue against them. The resistance is natural. It is a behavior that has been conditioned over years. In fact, your arguing may reinforce them.

Ask What Could Make New Ideas Work

After you've heard why they won't work, urge the employee to tell you what would have to happen to make them work. The subordinate, with your encouragement, may begin to argue with himself or herself.

Sell the Benefits of the Change

Don't sell the ideas in the abstract. Show how the employee could benefit from the new ideas or methods. Use as much of the employee's language as possible. If the preceding tactics have worked, the employee has already given you some ammunition to throw back.

Use Requests When Possible

Whenever you can phrase an order or a directive, do so. If you have good rapport with the employee, occasionally suggest that doing such and such would be a favor to you.

Be Liberal With Explanations

Tie the why in with the what as much as possible.

Suggest Experimental Behavior

Instead of saying, "Do this," describe what you want in terms of an experiment: "Let's try this and see what happens."

Draw the Line When You Have To

When you must be firm, don't hesitate. You want such-and-such done in this or that manner by a certain time. If the employee has no options, let the fact be known. If you suspect that from time to time the employee tests your resolve, you may be right. Don't be surprised, therefore, to see the stubbornness dissolve in the face of your firmness.

You have to guard against building expectations in yourself that you will automatically get resistance from this person. If you approach the employee with that expectation, you will probably broadcast it unconsciously. And you will no doubt get the resistance you expect. Although it may be difficult to do, you should try to be positive with this person. Or, as the salesperson would say, be assumptive—assume that the employee is reasonable enough to go along with you.

THE PUSHY AND INSENSITIVE EMPLOYEE

You would describe this subordinate as aggressive. She may work hard but she inhibits her own effectiveness by stepping on the toes of others. The pushy employee also turns you off, and that could affect your success in dealing with her.

Sell Behavior Change

Don't talk about organizational norms or even your own. If you want to persuade this employee to change her ways, show the person how, by doing so, she will find it easier to achieve important personal goals.

Show the Employee the Importance of Cooperation

When you give this person an assignment that involves working with others, ask how he intends to achieve results. Suggest what could go wrong in those working relationships, because, in all likelihood, he is not looking at the people problems that could get in the way. Encourage him to think about alternative behaviors and ways of getting the job done. Remember that this person's behavior toward people is determined by the perceptions of how they can help or hurt him. If you can base your suggestions on that argument, you are more likely to be persuasive.

Don't Publicly Approve or Disapprove of this Kind of Conduct

Suppose that at a meeting this employee becomes heated while opposing another employee. If you agree with his arguments, support him so long as the employee is not putting down or ridiculing the other. If you disagree with his position, say so.

People will come to you with complaints about this employee's behavior. Don't be sympathetic with them or make jokes about it. If a person's complaint warrants it, offer to bring the two of them together with you to work the problem out. You have to walk a fine line: You don't want to appear to be sanctioning his or her aggressive behavior, but you don't want to undermine the employee either. The point that you must make to other employees is that he or she is a co-worker with whom they must find a way to work—as with any other person. If you don't maintain this stance, you can expect to find complaining people in your office frequently.

Use Yourself as an Example of How This Person Offends Others

If the employee becomes aggressive toward you, point it out and express how it has affected you. You can imply that such behavior is probably not effective with other people.

THE EMPLOYEE WITH THE READY EXCUSE

There is always some external force that prevents this employee from doing a good job: family problems, car trouble, a colleague, the absence of a secretary, or the breakdown of office equipment. The excuses seem quite valid in themselves, but there are so many of them.

Such people see themselves as victims of forces that "conspire" to prevent them from doing their jobs. Since these outside forces are real and presumably beyond their control, they feel excused from having to measure up. Your failure to transform this person into a responsible employee may seem to reflect on your skills as a manager. But it is safe to assume that the psychological roots of this person's problems are deep. Only the employee can make the decision to change and to begin to assume responsibility. You can, however, provide the encouragement and the incentive. Here are some possible ways to do this.

Focus on What You Want Done

Tell the employee what behavior and performance you expect. Document each case in which your expectations were not met. But when you present your documentation to the employee, don't expect a quick agreement. Instead, you'll probably get a rehash of the excuses you've already heard. The employee might even appear offended that you are upset about the deficient performance, because in the employee's mind it was, after all, a situation beyond his or her control.

Avoid Debating the Merits of the Excuses

Just keep coming back to the performance and the objectives you want. You cannot allow the objectionable performance to continue, whatever the circumstances. Whenever the employee tries to discuss the validity of the forces that have provided excuses, accept their existence but return to your point: You want improvement regardless.

Emphasize That You Expect Successful Performance

The employee may remind you of times when he or she performed well for you. Capitalize on that fact: The employee has done it before and can do it again. You expect it.

Insist That the Employee Take Responsibility

The more specific you can be about the tasks you expect to be done and the time period for their accomplishment, the better. Lay it on the line that you will not accept good intentions, that you will hold the employee accountable for completing the work as you want it done. You'll probably have to be explicit about the seriousness of this warning.

THE SLOW EMPLOYEE

The plodding employee can try your managerial patience. It isn't necessarily a matter of intelligence. It's the way the employee has always worked. The best course of action for you is probably to find ways such as those given below to capitalize on the employee's patience and attention to detail.

Be More Patient in Your Expectations

Allow plenty of time between instructions and carrying them out. Be very detailed in describing what has to be done. Remember that this person regards details as very important. Make the assignment as clear and specific as possible.

Check the Person's Understanding of the Assignment

The employee may get bogged down thinking about the details involved. In giving a complicated or lengthy assignment, stop periodically and check for understanding. Listen carefully to the employee's comments to judge whether you should repeat or expand your instructions.

Provide Assignments That Call for Thinking, Research, and Detail

The person's work may be slow but not his mind. Chances are that he reflects before doing, is careful, and makes few mistakes. These qualities are invaluable on certain kinds of work.

Use This Employee to Train Others

The employee has patience. He might be useful in breaking a new employee in. Take advantage of his methodical style and absorption with detail.

Negotiate Tighter Deadlines

Do this gradually. Each time you give an assignment, try to get the employee's agreement to finish it a bit faster than she would normally. However, don't be surprised if the shorter deadline is not always met. Slow people tend to fuss over their work. If the deadline is accomplished, give recognition. Your reward may encourage her to want to speed up the work.

Ask the Slow Person to Sit on Committees

This employee will offset the tendency of other committee members to rush. That rush may cause some important points to be overlooked. The slower employee will decrease the pace and force the group to be more careful in its deliberations. At the same time, the slower member may be compelled to work faster than usual because of pressure from co-workers in the group.

THE THIN-SKINNED EMPLOYEE

Some people overreact to anything that sounds like criticism. It is difficult to communicate with them because you have to watch every word. They seem perpetually on the defense. They may be good workers, but when they feel offended or hurt, they may not work as well. You can hardly protect them from reality. Sometimes they must be corrected and criticized. Sometimes you may be irritated with their defensiveness and express that irritation. The result is a demoralized, possibly demotivated employee. You can't cure this condition, but you can avoid unnecessary defensiveness in the employee by taking the following steps.

Watch Any Kidding

What seems to be gentle ribbing may be translated by a sensitive subordinate into a dig or a sarcastic remark. Save the kidding for your tougher subordinates who know exactly what you are doing.

Temper Your Criticism

A little moderation of your criticism goes a long way with this person. You generally don't need to sit down hard on the employee for a transgression. Usually a gentle reminder or correction will do the job. Even then you may have to be prepared to listen patiently while the person justifies the action you are criticizing.

Make Suggestions

Say that you want the employee to switch some duties with another person in the office. That move might be interpreted as criticism of the work he or she is doing. So you might say, "I was thinking that Janet needs more experience in order expediting. You're very good at it. How would you feel if we were to let Janet do some of what you do for a while to give her a chance to learn? How could we go about it?" The more you can bring this person in as a partner, the less the threat.

Disagree Indirectly

If the thin-skinned employee offers a suggestion or a solution to a problem that you disagree with, don't say, "That won't work," or "Our budget won't allow for it." Ask the employee to tell you how he or she might work it out, given the authority. If you describe the constraints, the person might come to the conclusion that the idea is really not feasible after all.

Give Sincere, Deserved Praise

When the person has done something praiseworthy, say so and spread the word to others. Since this person is thirsty for approval, you'll often find that your praise will encourage him or her to repeat the desired behavior.

GENERAL RECOMMENDATIONS

Although recommendations for correcting performance problems will vary depending on the behavior that is involved, certain basic steps such as the following apply to correcting almost any deficiency.

Take Prompt Action

If employees are exhibiting the wrong kind of behavior, move fast to correct it before it becomes ingrained and habitual.

Be Clear About What You Want

Make sure the employee knows what you expect her to do. Convey your firm expectation that you will get what you want.

Accommodate to the Employee's Manner of Working

Do this when it doesn't impede overall performance results or violate your integrity. You can hardly expect each employee to work the same way or the way you would like him to perform. You can afford to make individual allowances so long as you get the results you want.

Look for Ways to Capitalize on the Person's Work Manner

What may in one situation or one kind of task seem to be a liability may be an asset in another. Look for opportunities to assign employees to tasks and duties that are appropriate to their style.

Praise Improvement

When employees who have demonstrated problem behaviors succeed in correcting them, recognize their achievement. It encourages them to repeat their new ways of acting.

Take Firm Action When Employees Do Not Change

Don't delay in counseling, disciplining, or terminating when employees have been warned and have not taken the warning seriously. If you don't follow through appropriately, other employees may experience demotivation and you will lose credibility.

18

TRAINING, THE KEY
TO EFFECTIVENESS

The traditional definition of a manager is one whose job is to get things done through other people. That's an inadequate statement. A manipulative manager can get things done through people for a time. But that kind of manager ignores his or her obligation to build resources for the future. (In fact, the manipulative manager may destroy them for long term.) No organization can be static and function well for any length of time. Resources that are adequate today will probably be inadequate tomorrow. If they become so, clearly the manager has not done a good job.

Those resources become inadequate because they were not developed to cope with the increasing change that characterizes our society. Change demands growth in people to meet its challenges.

And that change is not necessarily traumatic to people. People will accept change if they are brought to see the benefits of that change to them (and given the means to take advantage of it). People will accept even an unpleasant change if it seems the least unfavorable of all the options.

Without change there is no growth. And growth is natural to people. Frederick Herzberg maintains that people see growth as good. In his view, growth is a motivator. Abraham Maslow refers to self-actualization—becoming what one is capable of being—as a growth need. Most people feel the need to be stretched. If they feel that the work has any purpose or meaning at all, they would prefer to do it well rather than poorly. It is safe to say that most people feel that what they do well today, they can do better next month. In fact, they feel that next month, they will be learning to do some tasks and functions they cannot perform now. Thus, most people not only want to be effective on the job now, they want to grow in effectiveness.

The manager's job is to increase the effectiveness of subordinates and to continue to help them to sharpen their ability to carry out the manager's and organization's objectives. Many managers tend to believe that the training function should be left to the training department—or some outside agency or consultant. They believe that training and development take place in the classroom.

THE LEARNING LABORATORY

Actually the entire organization has the capability of being a laboratory for learning. After all, no organization can expect to continue to achieve its objectives in a rapidly changing world unless its employees are engaged in learning effectively, in acquiring new skills and sharpening old ones, and in applying the lessons gained from experience and analyzing that experience.

The most effective learning takes place in the working environment. It is on the job that the needs for expanding skills and knowledge are perceived, it is there that the learning is applied, and it is there that the employee's successful applications of those skills and knowledge are reinforced and become part of the employee's permanent behavior patterns.

If the organization is to adapt and benefit from change, each member of the organization should be engaged continually in some phase of improvement of effectiveness. And each manager is responsible for making sure—as only the manager can—that employees who report to him or her take advantage of all growth and learning opportunities. The manager's function, then, is to see that employees are increasingly effective in achieving organizational goals.

Furthermore, employees can be effective only if they can deal with constantly changing conditions. They must be able to analyze and diagnose each new variable and develop ways of dealing with it. All members of an organization, therefore, are in an unceasing learning situation, whether they realize it or not. As manager, you probably have more influence on how well they learn.

Training is too important to be left solely to trainers. Trainers, educators, and consultants can be valuable resources. But you are the key to employees' growth. You know your employees. You know what they need to learn: technical or administrative skills, conflict management techniques, supervisory and management methods, problem-solving and decision-making techniques, and so on. Ideally, the manager works with the professional trainer, whether a staff person or someone contracted from the outside, to design an education program that will help employees to learn what they and you need and how to perform these new skills and apply the new knowledge on the job.

Most people would probably agree that they and their organizations still are a long way from such a learning system or that they are even a long way from recognizing that their organizations can and must function in this way.

TRAINERS AND TRAINING

Much of what is called training probably does not contribute to effectiveness. Or if it does, people are not sure how much. The professional trainer is not solely to blame. In many organizations, the trainer's job is to see that certain programs are provided. Such programs are mandated by management. The trainer has little or no discretion in choosing them. Whether the content of such programs is relevant or applicable, whether it can in fact help employees to increase effectiveness, is usually beyond the educator's province to know.

In other organizations, trainers have become little more than purchasing agents. They bring in programs from the outside, which often are prepackaged for the general market. Each organization has its peculiarities and specific needs. Packaged programs may have limited value.

Quite often, training staffs are isolated from much of the operation. Consequently, sitting in corporate headquarters away from the operating divisions, they may have little knowledge of the training needs of the company.

Another factor that may inhibit the effectiveness of the trainer is the traditional perception of learning in this country. Education in and out of industry and in the lives of most people is fragmented, compartmentalized, and deductive. For most people, education has been provided in stages, in definite locales, such as classrooms, and by people designated as educators. Certain dichotomies exist in the minds of many people: for example, theory and practice, the classroom and the "real world." Much training that is delivered in the classroom is seen as theory.

Actually what goes on in the classroom may have little or no relevance to the situation or the environment in which the learner works. In the classroom the trainer may undertake a program or course of dubious value that reflects his or her values or perceptions of reality, which often are what should be rather than what is. That is, the training program concerns itself with principles that are unrealistic in view of the constraints under which the learner works. It is sometimes true that the instructor's training design may be one that he or she has been able to get management to approve, one that is safe, does not threaten the organizations' traditions or policies, and one that does not offer much practical help either. Or the program may be one that the trainer has brought or borrowed from a different organization that has a different culture.

Often trainers are well aware that their assessment of the needs of the organization is in conflict with what management wants them to deliver. Then you will hear trainers admit with candor, "I'm running programs that are interesting and well-designed, but their practical value is limited."

On the other hand, trainers often come to the training situation prepared to impart their values, what they perceive to be the needs of the learner, or what the organization's management wishes them to impart, which may not in the least meet the learner's needs.

We have just seen why training conducted by trainers in organizations is not as successful as it might be in increasing the effectiveness of the learners. At the same time, there are in many organizations highly skillful, knowledgeable training professionals who know the needs of their "clients," who design and conduct programs that are relevant to trainees, but who in these days of economic belt tightening operate with limited staffs and budgets.

In short, although training may be too important to leave to the trainers, they can be invaluable partners and resources in the training process. Their techniques in helping people to learn and your knowledge of what your people need and want to learn can make a potent combination.

EMPLOYEES' EXPECTATIONS

There are values other than those of the trainers that enter into the success or failure of the process. The employees who are to be trained come to the learning situation with their own values. They want the content of the program to be consistent with behaviors that are comfortable to them and that they believe are rewarded by the organization.

Many employees frequently come to a training situation with disappointingly low expectations that are born of experience with relatively unproductive sessions. Employees often suspect that they will encounter little resemblance between the training and work environments. When they find that little effort is made to overcome the effects of conditioning or values they have acquired in the past, they themselves do not unfreeze the behavior patterns they carried into the training. Once back in the work environment, they resume the old patterns because they believe those behaviors will bring them rewards. And they are probably correct.

HOW PEOPLE LEARN

For all of the reasons that have been described, you as manager are pivotal to the learning of your subordinates. You can't afford to leave the training and education entirely to outsiders. And you probably don't think of yourself as a trainer or educator. But you must accept the major part of the responsibility for keeping your employees in a growth environment. You need to know how adults learn. Their learning is vastly different from how children learn. Very often, the pattern in children's education is that of stuffing knowledge into them. Children are not always shown the importance of learning something. They know what they are expected to do if they are to avoid penalties. But adults need reasons. The motivation to learn is very similar to the motivation to do anything else.

A Reason for Learning

It's not enough to say, "I want you to take a course on instructional methods." You may have a reason that is valuable to you, but it may not carry much value for the employee. Another approach might be, "I've noticed that newer employees seem to ask you for help quite a bit. You have a talent for showing them what we do here—and how we do it. How would you feel about taking this workshop in instructional methods so that you could set up and conduct an orientation program for new employees?" If the employee finds that prospect a challenge, then you have an eager recruit.

The Assurances of Learning

You might have to convince the employee that he or she has the ability to learn the new skill. For example, how many times have you observed the employee display a talent for the work, however undeveloped? You might say, "You seem to have a knack for this kind of work. I'm selecting you for the training because I think you'd like to be better prepared to handle it. You show a natural ability, so you ought to have a good start on the training." Sometimes people may express some hesitation about taking on something new, until you demonstrate from what you've observed of what they know that the training won't involve something altogether new and strange to them after all.

A Chance to Apply

Employees in learning situations need opportunities in practicing. The practice completes and reinforces the learning. One of the biggest drawbacks to learning away from the work situation is that there is a time gap between the learning and the doing. During that gap, some of the learning is lost. You aren't getting value for your money if you don't arrange for a quick application and repetition of the new skill.

Feedback

"How am I doing?" is a question to which everyone wants the answer. It is just as important in the learning process as it is in any other aspect of motivation. Not only do you provide the chance for the employee to practice or to apply the new knowledge or skill, you provide guidance and support through feedback. The more positive your feedback is, the better. If you lack the expertise that the employee demonstrates or if you can't really judge how well he or she is doing, ask someone whose feedback will be relevant and valuable to reinforce or criticize the employee.

Recognition of Successful Application of the New Behavior

When the practice is successful, recognize it. Once the new knowledge is well established, reinforce it intermittently.

You should see yourself as primarily responsible for the continuing effectiveness of the people who report to you. This is an unceasing and usually varied task. The trainer is one resource working within the open, responsive system that you establish. The learning should be equated with effectiveness. It should be continuing. It should be inductive as well as deductive. It should permit the learner to take certain evidence and phenomena and from them develop principles and concepts. The learning should be situational and directly related to the learner's needs. Finally, it should be rewarded.

REVIEW OF TRAINING, THE KEY
TO EFFECTIVENESS

	Yes	No	Not Sure
1. A manager's role is to help employees not only to be effective today but to grow in the effectiveness of handling increased or different challenges tomorrow.	___	___	___
2. Without change, there is no growth.	___	___	___
3. According to Herzberg, growth is a motivator.	___	___	___
4. As manager, you are probably the best person to determine the training and development needs of your employees.	___	___	___
5. If the organization is to adapt, each member should be engaged on a continuing basis in some phase of improving effectiveness.	___	___	___
6. The training of your employees should not be left entirely to training professionals, no matter how skilled they are.	___	___	___
7. Adults generally do not learn as children do.	___	___	___
8. In training an adult, you may sometimes have to persuade the person that he or she is indeed capable of learning a new skill or knowledge.	___	___	___
9. Feedback is just as important in the learning process as it is in every other aspect of motivation.	___	___	___
10. The best learning is situational and directly related to the learner's needs.	___	___	___

453

Answers to Review

All 10 answers are Yes.

INDEX

455

Valence, 16
Vertical loading, 13, 150
Vroom, Victor, 15–18

Walters, Roy, 13

"Win-win" mentality, 28, 83, 238
Work as motivator, 10, 108, 149–153
Work and the Nature of Man, Herzberg, 10

"Yes, and" approach, 238